The CCNA Cram Sheet

This Cram Sheet contains key facts about the CCNA exam. Review this information as the last thing you do before you enter the testing center, paying special attention to those areas in which you feel that you need the most review. You can transfer any of these facts from your head onto a blank sheet of paper immediately before you begin the exam.

OSI MODEL

Layer	Name	Protocols and Devices	PDU
7	Application	FTP, Telnet, TFTP, SMTP, POP3, SNMP, DNS, NTP, HTTP, HTTPS, DHCP	Data
6	Presentation	ASCII, .jpg, .doc	Data
5	Session	RPC, SQL/Telnet (for login only)	Data
4	Transport	TCP—Connection-oriented, reliable using PAR UDP—Connectionless, unreliable, uses upper layer protocols for reliability	Segment
3	Network	IP, ICMP, RIP, IGRP, EIGRP, OSPF Routing and Path determination, logical addressing	Packet
2	Data Link	Ethernet, Frame Relay, PPP, HDLC Physical (hardware) addressing (MAC addresses)	Frame
1	Physical	Bits transmitted on media Hubs, Repeaters, Connectors	Bits

TCP AND UDP

Know the following protocols and port numbers:

TCP		UDP	
FTP	20, 21	DNS	53
Telnet	23	DHCP	67, 68
SMTP	25	TFTP	69
DNS	53	NTP	123
HTTP	80	SNMP	161
POP	110		
NNTP	119		
HTTPS	443		

TCP utilizes Positive Acknowledgment and Retransmission (PAR):

- The source device starts the timer for each segment; retransmits if acknowledgment is not received before the timer expires.
- The source device records all segments sent and expects acknowledgment of each.
- The destination device acknowledges receipt of a segment by sending an ack for the next sequence number it expects.

Be able to recognize a TCP header.

Source Port	Destination Port
Sequence Number	
Acknowledgment Number	
Misc. Flags	Window Size
Checksum	Urgent
Options	

Be able to recognize a UDP header.

Source Port	Destination Port
Length	Checksum

CDP

- Proprietary (Cisco only) Data link (Layer 2) protocol
- L3 protocol- and media-independent
- Uses L2 multicast to gather hardware and protocol information about directly connected devices.
- Enabled by default; can be disabled globally by `no cdp run`.
- To learn remote device L3 address, hardware platform and IOS version, use `show cdp neighbor detail` or `show cdp entry`

LAN TECHNOLOGY

- Ethernet physical addressing = MAC addresses.
  - 12 hexadecimal digits
  - First six digits are OUI of NIC manufacturer
- PC to switch/hub = straight-through cable.
- Hub-hub, switch-switch, PC-PC, router-router, PC-router directly (no switch/hub : use cross-over cable.
- Switches, bridges, and routers segment a network. Hubs and repeaters EXTEND a network.
- Switches increase the number of collision domains, do not segment broadcast domains. Routers, L3 switches, and VLANs segment broadcast domains.

SWITCHING

- A switch is a multiport bridge. Switches forward frames using hardware ASIC, making them faster than bridges. Dedicated bandwidth per port.
- Bridges and switches learn MACs by reading the source MAC of each frame.
- Switches operate in one of three modes:
  - Store-and-Forward: Entire frame is buffered. FCS is run (error checking).
  - Cut-Through: Only destination MAC is read, frame is forwarded.
  - Fragment-Free: First 64 bytes of frame are buffered, frame is forwarded. Cisco proprietary.
- Half-duplex: Shared collision domain and lower throughput
- Full-duplex: Point-to-point and higher throughput
- To remotely manage a switch, you need an IP address, subnet mask, and default gateway. The switch must be reachable on a port in its management VLAN.

VIRTUAL LANS (VLANS):

VLANs:

- Logically divide a switch into multiple, independent switches at L2
- Create separate broadcast domains in a switch, increasing the number of broadcast domains
- Span multiple switches using trunks
- Allow logical grouping of users by function
- Simplify adding, moving, and changing hosts in the network
- Enhance security

VLAN configuration steps:

1. The VLAN must be created.
2. The VLAN may be named.
3. The desired ports must be added to the new VLAN.
   Routing between VLANs requires a router or a Layer 3 switch.

TRUNKS

Trunks carry traffic from multiple VLANs over a single connection (cross-over cable). The VLAN ID is tagged using one of two methods:

1. ISL
2. IEEE 802.1q

A trunk can operate in one of five modes:

- Dynamic Auto
- Dynamic Desirable
- On
- Off
- Nonegotiate

VTP (VLAN TRUNKING PROTOCOL)

VTP simplifies VLAN administration. Configuration of VLANs is distributed to all switches in a VTP domain from a single server-mode switch.

The three VTP modes are as follows:

- Server
- Client
- Transparent
- Switches must be in the same VTP domain and must use the same password to exchange VTP information.
- Spanning Tree Protocol (STP IEEE 802.1d)
- L2 protocol prevents switching loops in networks with redundant switched paths.
- Root switch is the one with the lowest STP Priority; if tied, low MAC is the Root
- Root Port has the least-cost path to the Root switch
- STP path cost is determined by the sum of the costs based on bandwidth.

Spanning Tree Topology Port states:

1. Blocking: Sending no data, listening for BPDUs
2. Listening: Sending and receiving BPDUs
3. Learning: Recording MAC addresses
4. Forwarding: Normal operation

Convergence: 50 seconds (20 sec Max Age + 15 sec Fwd Delay + 15 sec Fwd Delay)

BOOT SEQUENCE FOR ROUTER/SWITCH:

1. POST—Device finds hardware and performs hardware-checking routines.
2. Locate IOS.
3. Load IOS.
4. Locate configuration (startup-config).
5. Load configuration (running-config).

CCNA Practice Questions (Exam 640-802)

Third Edition

Jeremy Cioara, CCIE No. 11727

CCNA Practice Questions (Exam 640-802), Third Edition

ISBN-13: 978-0-7897-3714-4
ISBN-10: 0-7897-3714-0

Library of Congress Cataloging-in-Publication Data

Cioara, Jeremy.
CCNA practice questions (exam 640-802) / Jeremy Cioara. -- 3rd ed.
p. cm.
ISBN 978-0-7897-3714-4 (pbk. w/CD)
1. Computer networks--Examinations--Study guides. 2. Computer networks--Examinations, questions, etc. 3. Electronic data processing personnel--Certification--Study guides. I. Title.
QA76.3.C48 2008
004.6--dc22
2008008365

Printed in the United States of America

Sixth Printing: May 2011

Trademarks

All terms mentioned in this book that are known to be trademarks or service marks have been appropriately capitalized. Que Publishing cannot attest to the accuracy of this information. Use of a term in this book should not be regarded as affecting the validity of any trademark or service mark.

Warning and Disclaimer

Every effort has been made to make this book as complete and as accurate as possible, but no warranty or fitness is implied. The information provided is on an "as is" basis. The author and the publisher shall have neither liability nor responsibility to any person or entity with respect to any loss or damages arising from the information contained in this book or from the use of the CD or programs accompanying it.

Bulk Sales

Que Publishing offers excellent discounts on this book when ordered in quantity for bulk purchases or special sales. For more information, please contact

U.S. Corporate and Government Sales
1-800-382-3419
corpsales@pearsontechgroup.com

For sales outside of the U.S., please contact:

International Sales
international@pearsoned.com

Associate Publisher
David Dusthimer

Acquisitions Editor
Brett Bartow

Senior Development Editor
Christopher Cleveland

Managing Editor
Patrick Kanouse

Project Editor
Seth Kerney

Copy Editor
Geneil Breeze

Proofreader
Kathy Ruiz

Technical Editors
Ishaq Mehr
Michael Valentine

Publishing Coordinator
Vanessa Evans

Multimedia Developer
Dan Scherf

Book Designer
Gary Adair

Page Layout
Trudy Coler

Contents at a Glance

Part I: ICND1

CHAPTER 1	Operation of Data Networks	3
CHAPTER 2	Switching Foundations	23
CHAPTER 3	Basic IP Services	45
CHAPTER 4	IOS and Routing Foundations	67
CHAPTER 5	Wireless and Network Security Concepts	93
CHAPTER 6	Basic WAN Connectivity	111

Part II: ICND2

CHAPTER 7	Advanced Switching Concepts	129
CHAPTER 8	Subnetting, VLSM, and IPv6	159
CHAPTER 9	Advanced Routing Configuration	183
CHAPTER 10	Access Lists and Network Address Translation	209
CHAPTER 11	Frame Relay, PPP, and VPN Connectivity	237
APPENDIX	What's on the CD-ROM	257

Table of Contents

About the Author . . . vi

Introduction . . . ix

Part I: ICND1

Chapter 1:
Operation of Data Networks . . . 3

Quick Answer Key . . . 16
Answers and Explanations . . . 17

Chapter 2:
Switching Foundations . . . 23

Quick Answer Key . . . 39
Answers and Explanations . . . 40

Chapter 3:
Basic IP Services . . . 45

Quick Answer Key . . . 59
Answers and Explanations . . . 60

Chapter 4:
IOS and Routing Foundations . . . 67

Quick Answer Key . . . 87
Answers and Explanations . . . 88

Chapter 5:
Wireless and Network Security Concepts . . . 93

Quick Answer Key . . . 105
Answers and Explanations . . . 106

Chapter 6:
Basic WAN Connectivity . . . 111

Quick Answer Key . . . 122
Answers and Explanations . . . 123

Part II: ICND2

Chapter 7:
Advanced Switching Concepts **129**

Quick Answer Key 150
Answers and Explanations 151

Chapter 8:
Subnetting, VLSM, and IPv6 . . . . **159**

Quick Answer Key 175
Answers and Explanations 176

Chapter 9:
Advanced Routing Configuration **183**

Quick Answer Key 202
Answers and Explanations 203

Chapter 10:
Access Lists and Network Address Translation **209**

Quick Answer Key 230
Answers and Explanations 231

Chapter 11:
Frame Relay, PPP, and VPN Connectivity **237**

Quick Answer Key 251
Answers and Explanations 252

Appendix:
What's on the CD-ROM **257**

Multiple Test Modes 257
Attention to Exam Objectives 258
Installing the CD 258
Creating a Shortcut to the MeasureUp Practice Tests 259
Technical Support 260

About the Author

Jeremy Cioara, CCIE No. 11727, works in many facets of the Cisco networking realm. As an author, he has written multiple books for Cisco Press and *Exam Cram*. As an instructor, he teaches at Interface Technical Training (www.interfacett.com) in Phoenix, Arizona. Likewise, Jeremy has recorded many E-Learning titles at CBTNuggets (www.cbtnuggets.com). Finally, Jeremy is the CIO of AdTEC Networks and works as a network consultant focusing on Cisco network and Voice over IP (VoIP) implementations. Jeremy also runs the Cisco Blog (www.ciscoblog.com) in his "free time." Thankfully, he is married to the Certified Best Wife in the World (CBWW) who helps him manage his time and priorities and prevents him from getting an enormous Cisco logo tattooed across his chest.

Dedication

I'd like to dedicate this book to my newest daughter, Isabella. She's currently ten months old and is staring at me right now from a soft blanket on the floor. By the time she's old enough to read, this book will probably be outdated as we will all have Ethernet ports implanted in our skull. (I'm opting for a wireless connection, myself.) Hopefully, if we remember to pull this book off the shelf and read this dedication I can tell her what amazing joy she has brought me. This tiny, arm-flailing, cooing, cheesy-grinning, soft, delicate, playful yet scandalously sly, giggling little girl has become my addiction. I hope I can always help her know how incredibly special she is to me.

Acknowledgments

My number one acknowledgment always goes to Jesus Christ who has blessed me in more ways than I even realize. Thank you for granting me the talent to be successful in the realm of Cisco networking. Please allow me to use these talents to accomplish more for Your kingdom than an Ethernet cable ever could. Thanks to my darling wife, Susan. You are my eyes and ears that help me to understand what is REALLY going on around me. I love you! And last, but not least: Thank you fish swimming in the big fish tank next to me. You bring me much peace and serenity as I sit here typing these acknowledgments—especially the big yellow Butterfly fish that swims this way and that. Swish, swish, swish. Swish, swish.

We Want to Hear from You!

As the reader of this book, *you* are our most important critic and commentator. We value your opinion and want to know what we're doing right, what we could do better, what areas you'd like to see us publish in, and any other words of wisdom you're willing to pass our way.

As an associate publisher for Que Publishing, I welcome your comments. You can email or write me directly to let me know what you did or didn't like about this book—as well as what we can do to make our books better.

Please note that I cannot help you with technical problems related to the topic of this book. We do have a User Services group, however, where I will forward specific technical questions related to the book.

When you write, please be sure to include this book's title and author as well as your name, email address, and phone number. I will carefully review your comments and share them with the author and editors who worked on the book.

Email: feedback@quepublishing.com

Mail: David Dusthimer
Associate Publisher
Que Publishing
800 East 96th Street
Indianapolis, IN 46240

Reader Services

Visit our website and register this book at www.quepublishing.com/register for convenient access to any updates, downloads, or errata that might be available for this book.

Introduction

What Is This Book About?

Welcome to the *CCNA Practice Questions Exam Cram*! The sole purpose of this book is to provide you with practice questions complete with answers and explanations that will help you learn, drill, and review for the 640-802, 640-822, and 640-816 certification exams. The book offers a large number of questions to practice each exam objective and will help you assess your knowledge before you write the real exam. The detailed answers to every question will help reinforce your knowledge about different issues involving the design and configuration of Cisco networks.

Who Is This Book For?

If you have studied the content for the 640-802, 640-822, or 640-816 exams and feel you are ready to put your knowledge to the test, but you are not sure that you want to take the real exam yet, this book is for you! Maybe you have answered other practice questions or unsuccessfully taken the real exam, reviewed, and want to do more practice questions before retaking the real exam; this book is for you, too! Even when the exam is done and you have passed with flying colors and got the CCENT or CCNA certificate in your pocket, keep the book handy on your desktop to look for answers to your everyday Cisco configuration issues.

What Will You Find In This Book?

As mentioned earlier, this book is all about practice questions! The practice questions in the book, some easy and others containing more complicated problem scenarios, are all aimed at raising your confidence level before writing the real exam. You will find questions that, in fact, you will face in real life.

This book is organized according to the objectives published by Cisco for the following exams:

Exam 640-802: CCNA

Exam 640-822: ICND1

Exam 640-816: ICND2

The book has been organized to help direct your study to specific objectives. If you are studying only for the ICND1 exam (640-822), you only need to review Chapters 1–6. If you are studying for the ICND2 (640-816) exam, you should focus your studies on Chapters 7–11 (although, reviewing Chapters 1–6 may be helpful). If you are studying for the CCNA all-in-one exam, study through the whole book!

Each chapter corresponds to an exam objective, and in every chapter you find the following three elements:

- *Practice Questions*—These are the numerous questions that will help you learn, drill, and review exam objectives. Some of the questions are multiple choice, others are matching (simulating the drag-and-drop style questions on the exam), and others are entering configurations (simulating the simulation style questions on the exam). Choose the correct answer based on your knowledge of Cisco networks.
- *Quick Check Answer Key*—After you have finished answering the questions, you can quickly grade your exam from this section. Only correct answers are given in this section. No explanations are offered yet! Even if you have answered a question incorrectly, do not be discouraged. Just move on! Keep in mind that this is not the real exam. You can always review the topic and do the questions again.
- *Answers and Explanations*—This section provides correct answers as well as further explanations about the content posed in that question. Use this information to learn why an answer is correct and to reinforce the content in your mind for the exam day.

NOTE

It is not possible to reflect a real exam on a paper product. As mentioned earlier, the purpose of the book is to help you prepare for the exam and not provide you with real exam questions. Neither the author nor Que Publishing can guarantee that you will pass the exam only by memorizing the practice questions given in this book.

You will also find a *Cram Sheet* at the beginning of the book specifically written for the exam day. The Cram Sheet contains core knowledge that you need for the exam. The Cram Sheet condenses all the necessary facts found in the exam into an easy-to-handle tear card. It is something you can carry with you to the testing center and use as a last-second study aid. Be aware that you cannot take the Cram Sheet into the exam room, though!

Hints for Using This Book

Because this book is a paper practice product, you might want to complete your exams on a separate piece of paper so that you can reuse the exams over and over without having previous answers in your way. Also, a general rule of thumb across all practice question products is to make sure that you are scoring well into the high 80% to 90% range in all topics before attempting the real exam. The higher percentages you score on practice question products, the better your chances for passing the real exam. Of course, we cannot guarantee a passing score on the real exam, but we can offer you plenty of opportunities to practice and assess your knowledge levels before you enter the real exam.

When you have completed the exam on paper, use the companion MeasureUp CD to take a timed exam. This will further help you gain confidence and make a self-assessment in case you need more study. Your results will indicate the exam objectives in which you need further study or hands-on practice.

Need Further Study?

Are you having a hard time correctly answering these questions? If so, you probably need further review of all exam objectives. Be sure to see the following sister products to this book from Que Publishing:

- *CCNA Exam Prep (Exam 640-802) (2nd Edition)* by Jeremy Cioara, David Minutella, and Heather Stevenson (ISBN 0789737132).
- *CCNA Exam Cram (Exam 640-802) (3rd Edition)* by Michael Valentine and Andrew Whitaker (ISBN 0789737124).

PART I

ICND1

Chapter 1 Operation of Data Networks

Chapter 2 Switching Foundations

Chapter 3 Basic IP Services

Chapter 4 IOS and Routing Foundations

Chapter 5 Wireless and Network Security Concepts

Chapter 6 Basic WAN Connectivity

1

CHAPTER ONE

Operation of Data Networks

This chapter covers the following CCNA objectives that fall under the content area, **Describe how a network works:**

- Describe the purpose and functions of various network devices.
- Select the components required to meet a network specification.
- Use the OSI and TCP/IP models and their associated protocols to explain how data flows in a network.
- Describe common networked applications including web applications.
- Describe the purpose and basic operation of the protocols in the OSI and TCP models.
- Describe the impact of applications (Voice over IP and Video over IP) on a network.
- Interpret network diagrams.
- Determine the path between two hosts across a network.
- Describe the components required for network and Internet communications.
- Identify and correct common network problems at Layers 1, 2, 3, and 7 using a layered model approach.
- Differentiate between LAN/WAN operation and features.

Quick Check

1. You are a network technician at Bubbles, Inc. Your newly appointed trainee is troubleshooting a connectivity problem on the network and would like to test application layer connectivity between devices. What command would you use?

   ❍ **A. ping**

   ❍ **B. telnet**

   ❍ **C. traceroute**

   ❍ **D. verify**

   ❍ **E. trace**

Quick Answer: **16**
Detailed Answer: **17**

2. You are connecting a laptop to a Cisco router to configure it for the first time. After opening your terminal program and selecting COM1, you are prompted for the port settings. What settings should you use?

   ❍ **A.** 9600bps, 8 data bits, no parity, 1 stop bit, hardware flow control

   ❍ **B.** 9600bps, 8 data bits, no parity, 1 stop bit, no flow control

   ❍ **C.** 56000bps, 8 data bits, no parity, 1 stop bit, hardware flow control

   ❍ **D.** 56000bps, 8 data bits, no parity, 1 stop bit, no flow control

Quick Answer: **16**
Detailed Answer: **17**

3. Which of the following is a security concern when configuring a device using Telnet?

   ❍ **A.** All communication is sent in clear text.

   ❍ **B.** Passwords are sent using reversible encryption.

   ❍ **C.** Passwords cannot be changed in a Telnet session.

   ❍ **D.** Passwords are not used during a Telnet session.

Quick Answer: **16**
Detailed Answer: **17**

Quick Check

4. You are attempting to test telnet connectivity to a Cisco router in your company's lab environment, but are unable to create a session. What should you do to resolve the problem?

Quick Answer: **16**
Detailed Answer: **17**

- ❍ **A.** Use a straight-through cable to connect your computer's COM port to the router's console port.
- ❍ **B.** Use a rollover cable to connect your computer's COM port to the router's console port.
- ❍ **C.** Use a straight-through cable to connect your computer's COM port to the router's Ethernet port.
- ❍ **D.** Use a crossover cable to connect your computer's Ethernet port to the router's Ethernet port.
- ❍ **E.** Use a rollover cable to connect your computer's Ethernet port to the router's Ethernet port.
- ❍ **F.** Use a straight-through cable to connect your computer's Ethernet port to the router's Ethernet port.

5. Which of the following is a valid benefit of using a hub in an enterprise network?

Quick Answer: **16**
Detailed Answer: **17**

- ❍ **A.** A network hub could be used to monitor network traffic from multiple sources using a packet sniffer or IDS/IPS appliance.
- ❍ **B.** Because it is hardware-based, a hub can transmit traffic with less latency than a network switch.
- ❍ **C.** A hub provides a better throughput for steady, low-bandwidth streams of traffic such as Voice over IP (VoIP) or Video over IP (VIP).
- ❍ **D.** A hub provides dedicated bandwidth on a per-port basis.

6. You are preparing to discuss the foundations of network communication with a junior administrator at your company. How would you describe the characteristics of TFTP using the OSI model?

Quick Answer: **16**
Detailed Answer: **17**

- ❍ **A.** TFTP is a transport layer protocol that transmits using TCP port 21.
- ❍ **B.** TFTP is an application layer protocol that transmits over the transport layer protocol TCP using port 21.
- ❍ **C.** TFTP is an application layer protocol that transmits over the transport layer protocol UDP using port 69.
- ❍ **D.** TFTP is a network layer protocol that transmits using UDP port 69.

Quick Check

7. You are using Microsoft Internet Explorer on a PC to access the Cisco website (www.cisco.com). What source port will your PC use for communication?

   Quick Answer: **16**
   Detailed Answer: **17**

   - ❍ **A.** UDP port 80.
   - ❍ **B.** TCP port 80.
   - ❍ **C.** The port will be randomly assigned by the operating system.
   - ❍ **D.** Any TCP port under 1024.

8. You are a network consultant for a small, 20-user company. The company has purchased a new building and would like you to design a network infrastructure using Cisco equipment. The company will be using a cable modem Internet connection, multiple mobile laptops, and 15 stationary desktop PCs. The company would also like VPN connectivity remotely to the office. What are the most likely network components you will use? (Choose three.)

   Quick Answer: **16**
   Detailed Answer: **18**

   - ❍ **A.** Cisco switch
   - ❍ **B.** Cisco router
   - ❍ **C.** VLANs
   - ❍ **D.** ASA firewall
   - ❍ **E.** Cisco Wireless Access Point
   - ❍ **F.** Cisco IPS Sensor

9. An interface capable of sending at a T1 speed would be transmitting data at which of the following?

   Quick Answer: **16**
   Detailed Answer: **18**

   - ❍ **A.** 1.544 Mbps
   - ❍ **B.** 1.544 MBps
   - ❍ **C.** 1.544 Gbps
   - ❍ **D.** 1.544 GBps

10. Routing decisions are made at which layer of the OSI model?

    Quick Answer: **16**
    Detailed Answer: **18**

    - ❍ **A.** Application
    - ❍ **B.** Transport
    - ❍ **C.** Session
    - ❍ **D.** Data Link
    - ❍ **E.** Network

Quick Check

11. Which of the following protocols operate solely at Layer 2 of the OSI model? (Choose three.)

Quick Answer: **16**
Detailed Answer: **18**

- ❍ **A.** 802.3 MAC
- ❍ **B.** IP
- ❍ **C.** HDLC
- ❍ **D.** PPP
- ❍ **E.** ISDN
- ❍ **F.** TCP

12. Which of the following are common network applications? (Choose three.)

Quick Answer: **16**
Detailed Answer: **18**

- ❍ **A.** Graphics creation
- ❍ **B.** Email
- ❍ **C.** Spreadsheets
- ❍ **D.** Instant messaging
- ❍ **E.** Database
- ❍ **F.** Word processing

13. What is the primary purpose of a router? (Choose two.)

Quick Answer: **16**
Detailed Answer: **18**

- ❍ **A.** To provide an intermediary device where network signals are transmitted from one device to another
- ❍ **B.** To control broadcast and multicast traffic from flooding through multiple networks
- ❍ **C.** To interconnect networks and provide the best path between them
- ❍ **D.** To protect networks using firewall capabilities implemented by using access lists

Quick Check

14. Refer to Figure 1.1. HostA wants to communicate with ServerB. What destination MAC address will be in the header of the packet at position A (as notated in Figure 1.1)?

Quick Answer: **16**
Detailed Answer: **18**

FIGURE 1.1 Network diagram.

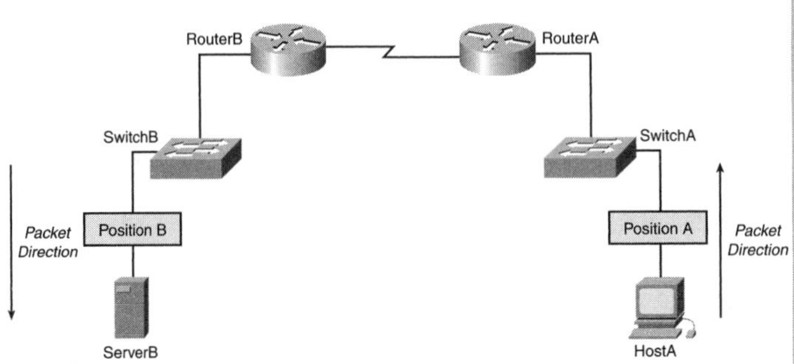

- ❍ **A.** The MAC address of HostA
- ❍ **B.** The MAC address of SwitchA
- ❍ **C.** The MAC address of RouterA
- ❍ **D.** The MAC address of RouterB
- ❍ **E.** The MAC address of SwitchB
- ❍ **F.** The MAC address of ServerB

15. Refer to Figure 1.1. HostA wants to communicate with ServerB. What destination IP address will be in the header of the packet at position A (as notated in Figure 1.1)?

Quick Answer: **16**
Detailed Answer: **19**

- ❍ **A.** The IP address of HostA
- ❍ **B.** The IP address of SwitchA
- ❍ **C.** The IP address of RouterA
- ❍ **D.** The IP address of RouterB
- ❍ **E.** The IP address of SwitchB
- ❍ **F.** The IP address of ServerB

Quick Check

16. Refer to Figure 1.1. HostA wants to communicate with ServerB. What source MAC address will be in the header of the packet at position B (as notated in Figure 1.1)?

Quick Answer: **16**
Detailed Answer: **19**

- ❍ **A.** The MAC address of HostA
- ❍ **B.** The MAC address of SwitchA
- ❍ **C.** The MAC address of RouterA
- ❍ **D.** The MAC address of RouterB
- ❍ **E.** The MAC address of SwitchB
- ❍ **F.** The MAC address of ServerB

17. Refer to Figure 1.2. HostA is unable to communicate with ServerB. Based on the information given in the Figure 1.2, what is the most likely cause of the problem?

Quick Answer: **16**
Detailed Answer: **19**

FIGURE 1.2 Network diagram.

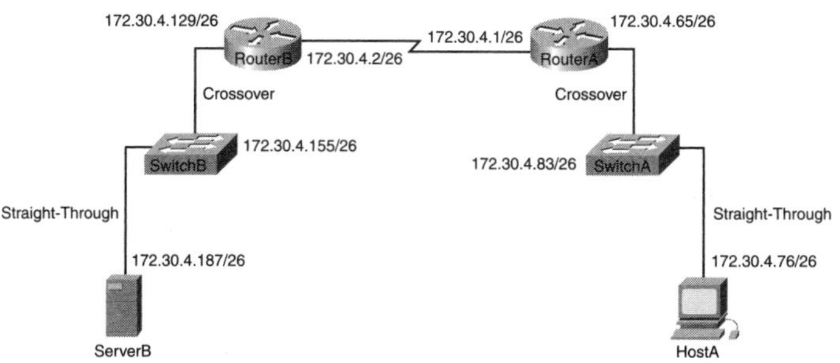

- ❍ **A.** HostA and ServerB are on different subnets.
- ❍ **B.** HostA and ServerB are on the same subnet.
- ❍ **C.** RouterA or RouterB has an access list, which prevents HostA from reaching ServerB.
- ❍ **D.** Crossover cables should be replaced with straight-through cables.

Quick Check

18. Which of the following are valid fields in a TCP header? (Choose four.)

Quick Answer: **16**
Detailed Answer: **19**

- ❍ **A.** Sequence number
- ❍ **B.** Source IP address
- ❍ **C.** Checksum
- ❍ **D.** Acknowledgement number
- ❍ **E.** Destination MAC address
- ❍ **F.** Destination port

19. Refer to Figure 1.3. HostA issues a ping request to HostB. Which of the following outputs would accurately reflect the contents of the ARP table on HostA?

Quick Answer: **16**
Detailed Answer: **19**

FIGURE 1.3 Network diagram.

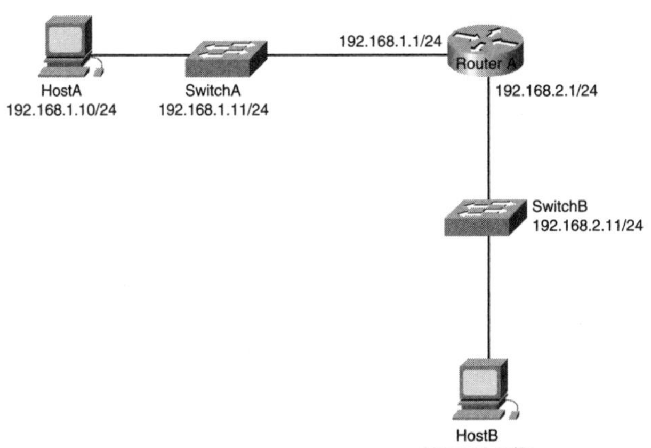

❍ **A.**

```
C:\>arp -a
Interface: 192.168.1.10 on Interface 0x10000003
  Internet Address      Physical Address      Type
  192.168.1.1           00-0c-85-4c-05-00     dynamic
```

❍ **B.**

```
C:\>arp -a
Interface: 192.168.1.10 on Interface 0x10000003
  Internet Address      Physical Address      Type
  192.168.1.1           00-0c-85-4c-05-00     dynamic
  192.168.2.1           00-0c-85-4c-05-01     dynamic
  192.168.2.10          00-b1-33-df-5e-11     dynamic
```

Quick Check

❍ **C.**

```
C:\>arp -a
Interface: 192.168.1.10 on Interface 0x10000003
  Internet Address      Physical Address      Type
  192.168.1.1           00-0c-85-4c-05-00     dynamic
  192.168.2.10          00-b1-33-df-5e-11     dynamic
```

❍ **D.**

```
C:\>arp -a
Interface: 192.168.1.10 on Interface 0x10000003
  Internet Address      Physical Address      Type
  192.168.1.11          00-0a-11-3c-34-01     dynamic
```

20. You are troubleshooting network connectivity issues between a Microsoft Windows client and a server. The server's IP address recently changed and you want to clear the client's ARP table. What command will accomplish this?

Quick Answer: **16**
Detailed Answer: **19**

❍ **A. arp -clear**

❍ **B. arp -a**

❍ **C. arp –c all**

❍ **D. arp –d ***

21. Which of the following commands would allow a network client to test connectivity to a destination device and verify the current delay for each router traversed while making the connection?

Quick Answer: **16**
Detailed Answer: **19**

❍ **A. ping**

❍ **B. test**

❍ **C. tracert**

❍ **D. telnet**

❍ **E. ssh –h -d**

Quick Check

22. Refer to Figure 1.4. HostA just transmitted a certain amount of data to HostB. What does HostB's response indicate?

Quick Answer: **16**
Detailed Answer: **20**

FIGURE 1.4 Network diagram.

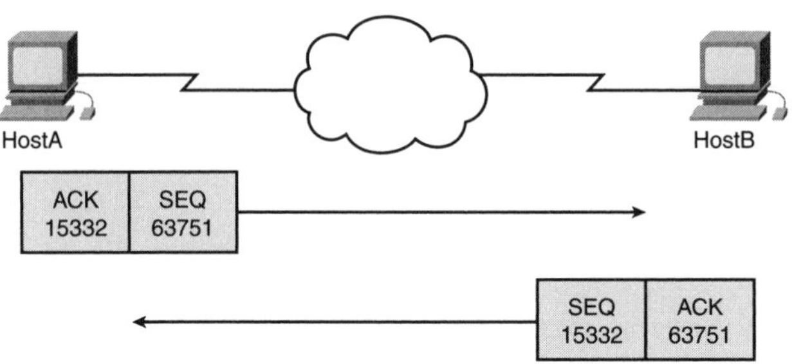

- ❍ **A.** HostB's response is a retransmission of data requested by HostA.
- ❍ **B.** HostB has indicated that a portion of HostA's transmission was not received and needs to be retransmitted.
- ❍ **C.** HostB's response indicates the TCP session will now close.
- ❍ **D.** HostB's response is normal and expected. Network communication will continue unhindered.

23. The following is a list of network functions. Enter the appropriate letter to match the network function to the corresponding OSI layer.

Quick Answer: **16**
Detailed Answer: **20**

A = Data link layer

B = Network layer

- ❍ **A.** ______ Provides error detection
- ❍ **B.** ______ Routes data packets
- ❍ **C.** ______ Finds the best path to use when delivering data
- ❍ **D.** ______ Provides logical addressing
- ❍ **E.** ______ Provides physical addressing
- ❍ **F.** ______ Defines how data is formatted for transmission

Quick Check

24. Match the correct term to the corresponding OSI layer.

Quick Answer: **16**
Detailed Answer: **20**

A = Physical layer

B = Data link layer

C = Network layer

D = Transport layer

- ❍ **A.** ______ Segments
- ❍ **B.** ______ Frames
- ❍ **C.** ______ Bits
- ❍ **D.** ______ Packets

25. The application layer of the TCP/IP stack corresponds to which of the following three OSI model layers? (Choose three.)

Quick Answer: **16**
Detailed Answer: **21**

- ❍ **A.** ______ Physical
- ❍ **B.** ______ Transport
- ❍ **C.** ______ Data link
- ❍ **D.** ______ Segments
- ❍ **E.** ______ Presentation
- ❍ **F.** ______ Session
- ❍ **G.** ______ Network
- ❍ **H.** ______ Application

26. A host is assigned the IP address 10.5.62.173/27. An application on the host attempts to contact a server with the IP address 10.5.62.158/27. What is the next step in the process of network communication?

Quick Answer: **16**
Detailed Answer: **21**

- ❍ **A.** The host will send an ARP message directly to the destination server to obtain its MAC address.
- ❍ **B.** The host will contact the IP address of its default gateway to find the MAC address for the destination server.
- ❍ **C.** The host will send an ARP broadcast to find the MAC address of its default gateway.
- ❍ **D.** The host will send an ARP broadcast to find the MAC address of the destination server.

Quick Check

Quick Answer: **16**
Detailed Answer: **22**

27. Users on a specific network segment in your organization are complaining that they cannot reach the Internet. While working through the troubleshooting process, you discover that all the ports connecting to the PCs in the segment have been set to auto-negotiate speed and duplex. You also gather information from one of the end-user workstations; this information is shown in Figure 1.5. What is the most likely cause of the problem?

FIGURE 1.5 Command prompt output.

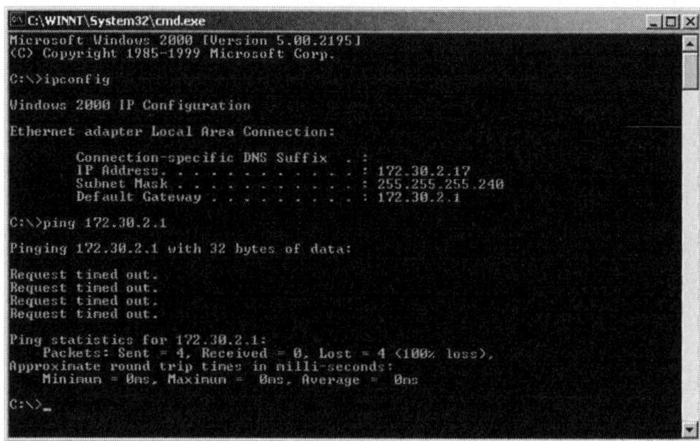

❍ **A.** All host and server connections in the network should have speed and duplex hard coded.

❍ **B.** The connectivity problems are related to an IP addressing issue.

❍ **C.** The default gateway could be blocking ICMP ping traffic.

❍ **D.** All ports should be set for 10Mbps, half-duplex connections for testing purposes.

Quick Check

28. Refer to Figure 1.6. HostA has just sent a ping request to HostB. Based on the information given in Figure 1.6, how will the switch respond?

Quick Answer: **16**
Detailed Answer: **22**

FIGURE 1.6 Network diagram.

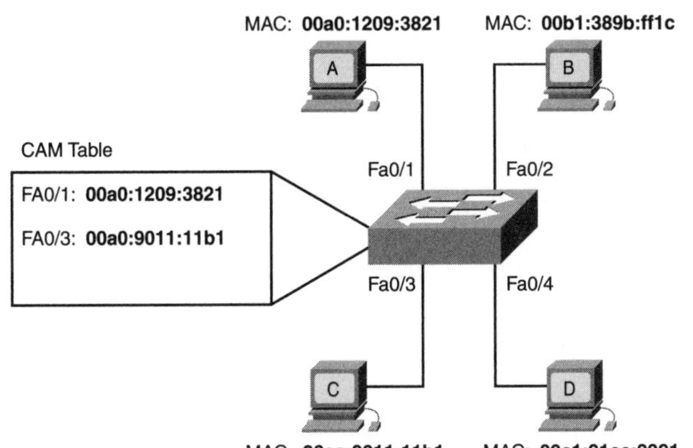

- ❍ **A.** The switch will forward the frame out FA0/2.
- ❍ **B.** The switch will flood the frame out all ports.
- ❍ **C.** The switch will multicast the frame only to unknown ports.
- ❍ **D.** The switch will flood the frame out all ports except FA0/1.

29. When data is being encapsulated, the last piece of information to be added is the ________.

Quick Answer: **16**
Detailed Answer: **22**

- ❍ **A.** TCP source and destination port
- ❍ **B.** Destination IP address
- ❍ **C.** Source IP address
- ❍ **D.** FCS

30. Which of the following are characteristics of the Internet Protocol (IP)? (Choose three.)

Quick Answer: **16**
Detailed Answer: **22**

- ❍ **A.** Best-effort delivery
- ❍ **B.** Reliable
- ❍ **C.** Uses sequence numbers
- ❍ **D.** Operates at the network layer of OSI
- ❍ **E.** Connectionless
- ❍ **F.** Uses a three-way handshake

Quick Check Answer Key

1. B
2. B
3. A
4. D
5. A
6. C
7. C
8. A, D, E
9. A
10. E
11. A, C, D
12. B, D, E
13. B, C
14. C
15. F
16. D
17. D
18. A, C, D, F
19. A
20. D
21. C
22. B
23. a. A, b. B, c. B, d. B, e. A, f. A
24. a. D, b. B, c. A, d. C
25. E, F, H
26. C
27. B
28. D
29. D
30. A, D, E

Answers and Explanations

1. **B.** Even though it is a basic program, Telnet communicates using data that interacts with the application layer of an operating system. Answers A, C, and E are incorrect because these utilities (ping and traceroute) rely on ICMP, which only tests connectivity up to the network layer of the OSI model. Answer D is not a valid command.

2. **B.** Communications software should be configured to communicate at 9600bps, with 8 data bits, 1 stop bit, no parity, and no flow control. This is commonly written 9600 8N1N. The other answers have settings that fail to match this.

3. **A.** One of the major drawbacks to using Telnet to manage your Cisco devices is the fact that all communication is sent in clear text. If a malicious person captures data using a packet sniffer, that person will have no trouble decoding the exact information entered into the remote Cisco device. This includes all password information! Because of this, Cisco has introduced Secure Shell (SSH) support into all modern IOS versions. SSH uses encryption for all communication. Answer B is incorrect because Telnet does not use any encryption. Answers C and D are incorrect because passwords can be changed using Telnet, and passwords are typically used when connecting to a Telnet session.

4. **D.** By connecting a crossover cable from your computer's Ethernet port to the router's Ethernet port, you should have direct network access to the device. You could then assign your PC an IP address from the same subnet as the router interface. This is a tricky question and could lead you to choose answer B. This will allow you to connect to the console port to configure the router, but this will not allow you to test TCP/IP connectivity to the router. All other answers are invalid cable connections.

5. **A.** Because a hub sends all traffic out all ports, it can be a device used for sniffing the network (for information gathering) or for use with an IDS/IPS appliance. Answer B was a true statement until switches used ASIC-based chipsets allowing them to transmit data at line speed. VoIP and VIP traffic will be destroyed because only one device can send or receive at a time when using a hub, making answers C and D incorrect.

6. **C.** The Trivial File Transfer Protocol (TFTP) works at the application layer of the OSI model. This results in it being dependent on lower-layer protocols such as UDP for transmission. TFTP uses UDP port 69 when communicating. All other answers either use the wrong layer of the OSI model, wrong port number (TCP port 21 is used for FTP control signals), or wrong protocol.

7. **C.** When communicating across a network, a TCP/IP client will use both a source and destination port. The well-known *destination port* of HTTP is TCP port 80; however, the source port will be randomly generated by the underlying operating system and will be above port 1024 (as ports below 1024 are considered well-known port numbers—making answers A, B, and D incorrect). This allows a source PC to have many network-capable applications actively communicating at the same time.

8. **A, D, E.** In a small network environment requiring wireless access (for the mobile laptops) and Internet connectivity, all that should be required is a Cisco ASA 5505 firewall (providing protected Internet connectivity and VPN services), a Cisco switch (providing LAN connectivity), and one or more Cisco Wireless Access Points (providing wireless network connectivity). The Cisco 3800 ISR (answer B) would be far too large of a router for a small network environment. VLANs (answer C) is a network concept and not equipment. An IPS Sensor (answer F) is also typically used in larger high-traffic, high-security environments.

9. **A.** A T1-capable interface can transmit data at 1.544 megabits per second (Mbps). The measurement of 1.544 megabytes per second (MBps) (answer B) would be eight times the speed of a T1 interface (12.352 Mbps) because there are eight bits in every byte. Answers C and D represent gigabits per second (Gbps) and gigabytes per second (GBps), which far exceed the capabilities of a T1 interface.

10. **E.** The network layer of the OSI model is responsible for the routing of data packets (selecting the best path to deliver data) and logical addressing (such as IP addressing). Answer A is incorrect because the application layer provides an interface to the network application itself. Answer B is incorrect because the transport layer dictates the reliability of the connection and port numbers. Answer C is incorrect because the session layer starts, ends, and manages network sessions. Answer D is incorrect because the data link layer handles physical addressing and formatting data for the network media.

11. **A, C, D.** 802.3 MAC is a sublayer of the Ethernet standard that provides Layer 2 addressing for clients. PPP and HDLC are Layer 2 WAN encapsulation protocols for communicating over point-to-point WAN links. IP and TCP (answers B and F) work at Layer 3 and 4 of the OSI model, respectively. ISDN (answer E) is a legacy WAN standard that operates at Layer 1, 2, and 3 of the OSI model.

12. **B, D, E.** Email, database communication (such as SQL or Oracle), and instant messaging are common network-based applications. All other answers are applications installed for operation on a local PC rather than network communication.

13. **B, C.** Routers provide connections multiple networks and find the best path between them. Likewise, a router also controls broadcast and multicast traffic. Without this control, broadcast and multicast traffic would flood through the network unbounded. Answer A could be vaguely interpreted as a network proxy, hub, or switch. Answer D demonstrates one capability of Cisco routers, but this is not a router's primary purpose.

14. **C.** HostA can only communicate directly with the devices on its local network segment. When communicating with the remote ServerB, HostA will put its own source IP address and the destination IP address of ServerB into the header. It will then add its own source MAC address and the destination MAC address of its default gateway to allow communication with a network outside its own. All other answers do not apply to this question.

15. **F.** HostA will use its own IP address as the source and the server's IP address as the destination. This is why two layers of addressing are so critical. The MAC address allows devices to communicate on the local network, while the IP address allows communication to the local network AND networks outside the local network. All other answers do not apply to this question.

16. **D.** After the packet has reached the network segment where ServerB is located, the old source and destination MAC addresses are removed by RouterB and replaced by the MAC addresses relevant for the local network. All other answers do not apply to this question.

17. **D.** A router to switch connection should use straight-through cabling rather than crossover. Answers A and B are incorrect because HostA and ServerB are on different subnets by design because they have multiple routers between them. By a slim chance, an access list could be the issue; however, the glaring issue based on the diagram is incorrect cabling, making answer C an unlikely and not the best answer.

18. **A, C, D, F.** In a TCP header, the sequence and acknowledgement numbers allow the receiving machine to dictate how much data can be received at once (the TCP window size) and allow the sending machine to realize whether data has been dropped. The checksum provides a mechanism to ensure that the TCP header information has not been damaged during transmission. The destination port number dictates what services the TCP packet is attempting to reach. Answer B is incorrect because the IP address is not a valid field because this is part of the network layer (Layer 3) header. Answer E is incorrect because the MAC address is part of the data link layer (Layer 2) header.

19. **A.** When HostA attempts to contact HostB, it will realize that HostB is not located on the same network. This causes HostA to send an ARP message for its default gateway (192.168.1.1), whose MAC address is then added to the ARP table. You will *never* see ARP messages for hosts on a network other than the network your computer resides on, which is why answers B and C are incorrect. Answer D is incorrect because the switch IP address (192.168.1.11) will not allow HostA to reach HostB.

20. **D.** Clearing the client ARP table is often done during network changes. This can be accomplished using the syntax "arp –d *" from a command prompt. The asterisk argument instructs the PC to clear all ARP entries rather than just a specific entry. Answers A and C are incorrect because these are not valid arguments for the ARP command. Answer B is incorrect because this command will display the ARP table to the screen.

21. **C.** The **traceroute** command (implemented as **tracert** on a Microsoft Windows machine) can be compared to an enhanced ping. Rather than just testing connectivity to an end device, it tests connectivity to every network layer device in the path, displaying the ping results (delay) for each device as it moves through the network to the destination. Answer A is incorrect because the ping command only tests direct connectivity to a destination device. Answers B and E are incorrect because these commands are not valid. Answer D is incorrect because Telnet invokes a connection rather than testing connectivity.

22. **B.** This tricky question requires an intimate understanding of TCP sequence and acknowledgement numbers. When HostA sends data up to sequence number 63751, the expected acknowledgement (ACK) under normal network conditions would be the next sequence number in line (63752 in this case). However, because HostB responded with the same sequence number, it indicated that some of the data was not received (making answer D incorrect). HostA will respond by resending the last requested sequence number (63751 in this case), followed by whatever maximum amount of data is allowed by the current TCP window size. Answer A is incorrect because there is nothing in the figure to indicate a retransmission. Answer C is incorrect because there is no signal to end the TCP session.

23. **A.**___**A**__ Provides error detection

    B. ___**B**__ Routes data packets

    C. ___**B**__ Finds the best path to use when delivering data

    D. ___**B**__ Provides logical addressing

    E. ___**A**__ Provides physical addressing

    F. ___**A**__ Defines how data is formatted for transmission

24. **A.**___**D**__ Segments

    B. ___**B**__ Frames

    C. ___**A**__ Bits

    D. ___**C**__ Packets

25. **E, F, H.** The TCP/IP stack groups the top three layers into a single application layer, as shown in Figure 1.7. This is because the functions of the top three OSI layers are typically handled within the application layer protocol standard.

FIGURE 1.7 TCP/IP to OSI model mappings.

TCP/IP	OSI
Application Layer	Application Layer
	Presentation Layer
	Session Layer
Transport Layer	Transport Layer
Internet Layer	Network Layer
Network Access Layer	Data Link Layer
	Physical Layer

26. **C.** A quick calculation of the subnet addresses defined in the question shows that the server belongs to the 10.5.62.128/27 subnet (addresses 10.5.62.128-10.5.62.159) while the host belongs to the 10.5.62.160/27 subnet (addresses 10.5.62.160-10.5.62.191). Because of this, the host will need to contact its default gateway. To accomplish this, the host will send an ARP broadcast request to determine the MAC address of its default gateway. Answer A is incorrect because the server is located on a different subnet. Answer B is incorrect because ARP messages are always broadcasts and cannot be sent directly. Answer D is incorrect because an ARP broadcast will be stopped at the router.

27. **B.** The connectivity issues are resulting from the hosts being on a different subnet than the default gateway. Based on the host's IP address (172.30.2.17) and subnet mask (255.255.255.240), you can determine that the network range is 172.30.2.16–172.30.2.31. Because the default gateway falls outside this range, it will be considered unreachable. Answer A is incorrect because speed and duplex being set to auto will work correctly in most cases. While the default gateway could be blocking ICMP traffic, answer B is the "better answer" making answer C incorrect. Answer D is incorrect because this would only degrade network performance in modern networks.

28. **D.** When a switch receives a request for an unknown MAC address, it will flood the frame out all ports with the exception of the port on which the request was received, which makes answer B incorrect. Answer A is incorrect because this will occur only if the switch had already known the MAC address of HostB. Answer C is incorrect because the switch floods an unknown MAC address out all ports.

29. **D.** The headers are added to data in the following order: application, transport, internet, and then data link. The last information to be added during the encapsulation process is the Frame Check Sequence (FCS). This is also called the Cyclical Redundancy Check (CRC) field, which is a hash of the data contained in the frame. If any of the data changes during transmission, the FCS will become invalid, and the data will be dropped at the receiving end. Answers B and C are incorrect because IP address information is added at the network layer. Answer A is incorrect because TCP port numbers are added at the transport layer.

30. **A, D, E.** The IP protocol operates at the network layer of the OSI model. It simply defines addressing standards for the network. Because of this, it does not offer any reliability or session-based communication. For this, it relies on the upper-layer TCP protocol. Answers B, C, and F are characteristics of the TCP protocol.

2

CHAPTER TWO

Switching Foundations

This chapter covers the following ICND1 objectives that fall under the content area, **Implement a small switched network:**

- Select the appropriate media, cables, ports, and connectors to connect switches to other network devices and hosts.
- Explain the technology and media access control method for Ethernet technologies.
- Explain network segmentation and basic traffic management concepts.
- Explain the operation of Cisco switches and basic switching concepts.
- Perform, save, and verify initial switch configuration tasks including remote access management.
- Verify network status and switch operation using basic utilities (including ping, traceroute, telnet, SSH, arp, ipconfig), and the **SHOW** and **DEBUG** commands.
- Implement and verify basic security for a switch (port security, deactivate ports).
- Identify, prescribe, and resolve common switched network media issues, configuration issues, autonegotiation, and switch hardware failures.

Quick Check

1. In today's networks, more and more corporations are replacing hubs with switches. Which of the following is a reason for switching to a Catalyst switch from a hub?

   Quick Answer: **39**
   Detailed Answer: **40**

   ❍ **A.** Catalyst switches take less time to process frames than hubs take.

   ❍ **B.** Catalyst switches decrease the amount of bandwidth available to hosts.

   ❍ **C.** Catalyst switches increase the number of collision domains in the network.

   ❍ **D.** Catalyst switches do not forward broadcasts.

2. You want to configure your Cisco switch for remote access capabilities. Which of the following commands will move you into the correct mode for configuring the switch IP address?

   Quick Answer: **39**
   Detailed Answer: **40**

   ❍ **A. interface fa0/1**

   ❍ **B. interface loopback1**

   ❍ **C. interface vlan1**

   ❍ **D. interface fa0/24**

   ❍ **E. configure terminal**

3. What are the default configuration settings on a Catalyst switch? (Choose three.)

   Quick Answer: **39**
   Detailed Answer: **40**

   ❍ **A.** CDP Enabled

   ❍ **B.** CDP Disabled

   ❍ **C.** Ports set to 100Mbps/full duplex

   ❍ **D.** Ports set to auto-negotiate

   ❍ **E.** IP address set to 192.168.1.10

   ❍ **F.** No IP address set

Quick Check

4. A junior network administrator at your company asks you to brief him on the differences and similarities between bridges and switches. What should you tell him? (Choose two.)

Quick Answer: **39**
Detailed Answer: **40**

❍ **A.** Switches are slower than bridges because they have fewer ports.

❍ **B.** A switch is a multiport bridge.

❍ **C.** Bridges and switches learn MAC addresses by examining the source MAC address of each frame received.

❍ **D.** A bridge forwards a broadcast, but a switch does not.

5. You are configuring a switch for remote access. What command must be issued in Global Configuration mode to allow the switch to be accessed from a subnet other than its own?

Quick Answer: **39**
Detailed Answer: **40**

❍ **A.** **ip default-gateway**

❍ **B.** **router ip**

❍ **C.** **router rip**

❍ **D.** **routing enabled**

6. While verifying some configurations on your switch, you see that the Spanning-Tree Protocol (STP) is enabled. The junior network administrator working with you at the time asks you what STP does. What do you tell her?

Quick Answer: **39**
Detailed Answer: **40**

❍ **A.** STP stops routing loops in your network.

❍ **B.** STP minimizes broadcasts in your network.

❍ **C.** STP allows routing loops in your network.

❍ **D.** STP monitors and prevents loops in your switched network.

Quick Check

7. What is the effective throughput for each of 24 PCs connecting to a Catalyst switch's FastEthernet ports operating in half-duplex mode?

Quick Answer: **39**
Detailed Answer: **40**

❍ **A.** 1Mbps

❍ **B.** 10Mbps

❍ **C.** 100Mbps

❍ **D.** 2400Mbps

8. You want to configure the FastEthernet 0/20 port on your Catalyst switch for port security. If anyone other than the MAC address 0001.3232.AABB connects to the port, it should immediately shut down. Which of the following configurations accomplishes this objective?

Quick Answer: **39**
Detailed Answer: **41**

❍ **A.**

```
interface fa0/20
 switchport mode access
 switchport port-security
 switchport port-security mac-address 0001.3232.AABB
 switchport port-security violation shutdown
```

❍ **B.**

```
interface fa0/20
 switchport mode access
 mac-address 0001.3232.AABB
 port-security violation shutdown
```

❍ **C.**

```
interface fa0/20
 switchport mode access
 port-security
 mac-address 0001.3232.AABB
 port-security violation shutdown
```

❍ **D.**

```
interface fa0/20
 switchport mode access
 switchport port-security
 mac-address 0001.3232.AABB
 switchport port-security violation shutdown
```

Quick Check

9. What command allows you to verify your port security configuration on interface FastEthernet 0/20?

Quick Answer: **39**
Detailed Answer: **41**

- ❍ **A. show interface fa0/20**
- ❍ **B. show ip interface fa0/20**
- ❍ **C. show interface fa0/20 switchport**
- ❍ **D. show port-security interface fa0/20**

10. Your boss asks you to explain why you purchased switches instead of the "cheaper" hubs, because they do the same thing. What do you tell him to justify the purchase of the switches?

Quick Answer: **39**
Detailed Answer: **41**

- ❍ **A.** Hubs do not extend the length of an Ethernet segment.
- ❍ **B.** Hubs do not offer half-duplex connections.
- ❍ **C.** Hubs do not give dedicated bandwidth to each end user.
- ❍ **D.** Hubs do not accept 100Mbps connections.

11. You have been asked to convert the management protocol for all the Cisco switches in your network from Telnet to SSH. You have entered the following configuration on one of the switches:

Quick Answer: **39**
Detailed Answer: **41**

```
Switch(config)# username admin password cisco
Switch(config)# ip domain-name examcram.com
Switch(config)# crypto key generate rsa general-keys modulus 1024
Switch(config)# ip ssh version 2
Switch(config)# line vty 0 4
Switch(config-line)# login local
Switch(config-line)# transport input ssh
```

Does this configuration accomplish your objective?

- ❍ **A.** Yes, this configuration accomplishes the objective.
- ❍ **B.** No, to disable Telnet, you must also enter the command **no transport input telnet**.
- ❍ **C.** No, SSH requires RSA keys that are 512 bits or less.
- ❍ **D.** No, rather than using the VTY lines, you should be configuring SSH lines.

Quick Check

12. You are verifying your port security configuration and notice the following:

Quick Answer: **39**
Detailed Answer: **41**

```
Switch#show port-security interface fa0/5
Port Security              : Enabled
Port Status                : Secure-down
Violation Mode             : Shutdown
Aging Time                 : 0 mins
Aging Type                 : Absolute
SecureStatic Address Aging : Disabled
Maximum MAC Addresses      : 1
Total MAC Addresses        : 1
Configured MAC Addresses   : 0
Sticky MAC Addresses       : 1
Last Source Address:Vlan   : 0015.c5af.ea37:1
Security Violation Count   : 18
```

What does this output indicate?

❍ **A.** A security violation has occurred, and the interface has been shut down.

❍ **B.** There have been security violations in the past, but at present, there is no device connected to the port.

❍ **C.** A MAC address is stuck on the interface and needs to be cleared.

❍ **D.** Port security requires at least one configured MAC address to be entered and is presently keeping the interface in the down state.

13. Your current switch is completely saturated with devices and has no available ports. As a temporary solution, you decide to attach an additional hub to the network to provide more ports. What type of cable should you use when attaching the network switch to the hub?

Quick Answer: **39**
Detailed Answer: **41**

❍ **A.** Straight-through

❍ **B.** Crossover

❍ **C.** Rollover

❍ **D.** Serial

14. What field exists at the end of every Ethernet frame to ensure data corruption does not occur during transmission?

Quick Answer: **39**
Detailed Answer: **41**

❍ **A.** Preamble

❍ **B.** CheckSEQ

❍ **C.** ACK

❍ **D.** FCS

Quick Check

15. Refer to Figure 2.1. HostA sends a single message into the switch. HostB, HostC, and HostD receive the message while HostE and HostF do not. What type of message was sent by HostA?

Quick Answer: **39**
Detailed Answer: **42**

FIGURE 2.1 Network diagram.

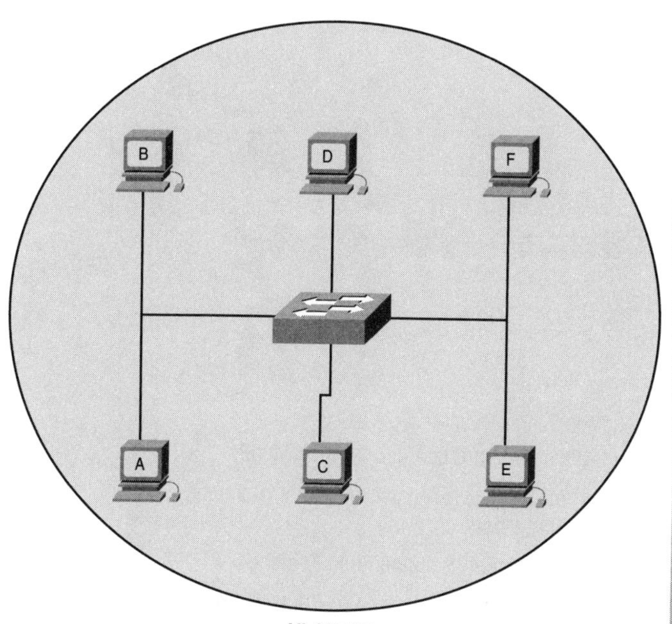

❍ **A.** Unicast
❍ **B.** Multiple unicast
❍ **C.** Multicast
❍ **D.** Broadcast
❍ **E.** VLAN-based

16. Which portion of the MAC address 00-19-D1-22-DC-F3 represents the vendor-assigned component?

Quick Answer: **39**
Detailed Answer: **42**

❍ **A.** 00-19-D1
❍ **B.** 00-19
❍ **C.** 19-D1-22
❍ **D.** D1-22-DC
❍ **E.** 22-DC-F3

Quick Check
Quick Answer: **39**
Detailed Answer: **42**

17. Refer to Figure 2.2. You have just finished configuring SwitchB, shown in the network diagram. You have tested SSH connectivity from HostD successfully; however, the junior network administrator is unable to connect from HostA. Further testing reveals that HostA can ping HostD, but cannot ping SwitchB. What is the most likely cause of the problem?

FIGURE 2.2 Network diagram.

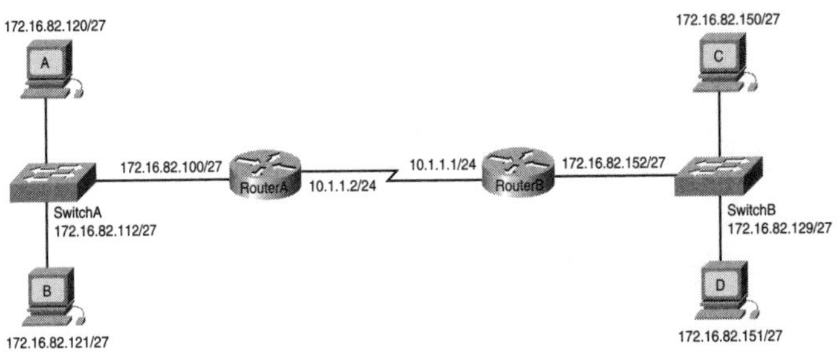

- ❍ **A.** A default-gateway is not configured on SwitchB.
- ❍ **B.** One of the routers is denying access to the IP subnet of SwitchB from HostA.
- ❍ **C.** HostA is on a different IP subnet than SwitchB.
- ❍ **D.** SwitchB and the Ethernet interface of RouterB are on different IP subnets.
- ❍ **E.** SwitchB and the Ethernet interface of RouterA are on different subnets.

Quick Check

Quick Answer: **39**
Detailed Answer: **42**

18. One of your users is reporting a slow connection speed to the corporate server from his PC. Further investigation reveals that the PC is connected to FastEthernet 0/18. You perform the following **show** command from the switch:

```
CAT3550#show interfaces FastEthernet 0/23
FastEthernet0/23 is up, line protocol is up (connected)
  Hardware is Fast Ethernet, address is 000c.854c.0517 (bia
➥000c.854c.0517)
  MTU 1500 bytes, BW 100000 Kbit, DLY 100 usec,
     reliability 255/255, txload 1/255, rxload 1/255
  Encapsulation ARPA, loopback not set
  Keepalive set (10 sec)
  Full-duplex, 100Mb/s, media type is 10/100BaseTX
  input flow-control is off, output flow-control is unsupported
  ARP type: ARPA, ARP Timeout 04:00:00
  Last input 00:00:20, output 00:00:01, output hang never
  Last clearing of "show interface" counters never
  Input queue: 0/75/0/0 (size/max/drops/flushes); Total output
➥drops: 0
  Queueing strategy: fifo
  Output queue: 0/40 (size/max)
  5 minute input rate 376000 bits/sec, 92 packets/sec
  5 minute output rate 79000 bits/sec, 54 packets/sec
     170650256 packets input, 661378431 bytes, 0 no buffer
     Received 206362 broadcasts (0 multicast)
     0 runts, 0 giants, 0 throttles
     0 input errors, 0 CRC, 0 frame, 0 overrun, 0 ignored
     0 watchdog, 26102 multicast, 0 pause input
     0 input packets with dribble condition detected
     246704306 packets output, 3116889248 bytes, 0 underruns
     0 output errors, 0 collisions, 3 interface resets
     0 babbles, 1926502 late collision, 0 deferred
     0 lost carrier, 0 no carrier, 0 PAUSE output
     0 output buffer failures, 0 output buffers swapped out
```

Based on this output, what is the most likely cause of the problem?

- ❍ **A.** The user is sending too much traffic and is likely saturating the link.
- ❍ **B.** The Ethernet cable length between the host and the server is too long.
- ❍ **C.** The switch is not configured to handle the multicast messages it is receiving.
- ❍ **D.** The keepalive has not been set.

Quick Check

19. How do two devices connected to a LAN respond when a collision is detected?

Quick Answer: **39**
Detailed Answer: **42**

- ❍ **A.** The devices will first transmit a jam signal.
- ❍ **B.** The devices will wait a specific amount of time and then retransmit their data.
- ❍ **C.** The devices will ignore the collision and continue to transmit data.
- ❍ **D.** One device will transmit a specialized beam using the Ethernet cable, which causes the other device to melt.

20. Some users in your organization have reported network connectivity issues from their PCs. While physically inspecting the switch, you notice that the System LED is blinking green. What does this indicate?

Quick Answer: **39**
Detailed Answer: **42**

- ❍ **A.** The switch has experienced a hardware failure.
- ❍ **B.** One or more of the ports on the switch are experiencing a speed or duplex mismatch.
- ❍ **C.** The devices attached to the switch have flapping interfaces.
- ❍ **D.** The switch is currently rebooting.

Quick Check

21. Telnet sessions to one of your switches in your organization continually fail. After connecting to the console port of your switch, you execute the following command:

Quick Answer: 39
Detailed Answer: 42

```
CAT3550#show interfaces vlan 1
Vlan1 is administratively down, line protocol is down
  Hardware is EtherSVI, address is 000c.854c.0500 (bia
➥000c.854c.0500)
  Internet address is 172.30.1.1/24
  MTU 1500 bytes, BW 1000000 Kbit, DLY 10 usec,
     reliability 255/255, txload 1/255, rxload 1/255
  Encapsulation ARPA, loopback not set
  ARP type: ARPA, ARP Timeout 04:00:00
  Last input 02:18:34, output 00:00:04, output hang never
  Last clearing of "show interface" counters never
  Input queue: 0/75/0/0 (size/max/drops/flushes); Total output
➥drops: 4
  Queueing strategy: fifo
  Output queue: 0/40 (size/max)
  5 minute input rate 0 bits/sec, 0 packets/sec
  5 minute output rate 0 bits/sec, 0 packets/sec
     27283 packets input, 6886373 bytes, 0 no buffer
     Received 0 broadcasts (0 IP multicast)
     0 runts, 0 giants, 0 throttles
     0 input errors, 0 CRC, 0 frame, 0 overrun, 0 ignored
     1017635 packets output, 76798877 bytes, 0 underruns
     0 output errors, 0 interface resets
     0 output buffer failures, 0 output buffers swapped out
```

What is the cause of the problem?

❍ **A.** The interface has an unusually high number of output drops.

❍ **B.** The management interface has been moved from VLAN 1.

❍ **C.** The management interface is shutdown.

❍ **D.** The Catalyst 3550 supports only SSH connections.

22. You want to configure the IP default gateway to 192.168.1.1 on your Catalyst switch. Which of the following commands will accomplish this objective?

Quick Answer: 39
Detailed Answer: 43

❍ **A.** Switch(config)#**ip default-gateway 192.168.1.1**

❍ **B.** Switch(config)#**default-gateway 192.168.1.1 255.255.255.0**

❍ **C.** Switch(config)#**default-gateway 192.168.1.1**

❍ **D.** Switch(config-if)#**ip address 192.168.1.1 255.255.255.0**

Quick Check

Quick Answer: **39**
Detailed Answer: **43**

23. Observe the following output:

```
Cisco IOS Software, C3550 Software (C3550-I5K91L2Q3-M),
➥Version 12.2(25)SEA, RELEASE SOFTWARE (fc)
Copyright (c) 1986-2005 by Cisco Systems, Inc.
Compiled Tue 25-Jan-05 23:50 by antonino
ROM: Bootstrap program is C3550 boot loader

CAT3550 uptime is 7 weeks, 3 days, 20 hours, 28 minutes
System returned to ROM by power-on
System image file is "flash:c3550-i5k91l2q3-mz.122-
➥25.SEA/c3550-i5k91l2q3-mz.122-25.S"

Cisco WS-C3550-24-PWR (PowerPC) processor (revision B0)
➥with 65526K/8192K bytes
of memory.
Processor board ID CAT0711Z0WH
Last reset from warm-reset
Running Layer2/3 Switching Image

The password-recovery mechanism is enabled.
384K bytes of flash-simulated NVRAM.
Base ethernet MAC Address: 00:0C:85:4C:05:00
Motherboard assembly number: 73-8100-06
Power supply part number: 341-0029-01
Motherboard serial number: CAT071105Z3
Power supply serial number: DTH0710060S
Model revision number: B0
Motherboard revision number: A0
Model number: WS-C3550-24PWR-SMI
System serial number: CAT0711Z0WH
Configuration register is 0x10F
```

Which of the following commands generated this output?

- ❍ **A.** Switch#**show config**
- ❍ **B.** Switch#**show run**
- ❍ **C.** Switch#**show ios**
- ❍ **D.** Switch#**show version**
- ❍ **E.** Switch#**show uptime**

Quick Check
Quick Answer: **39**
Detailed Answer: **43**

24. Observe the following output:

```
CAT3550#show mac-address-table
          Mac Address Table
-----------------------------------------

Vlan    Mac Address       Type        Ports
----    -----------       --------    -----
 All    000c.854c.0500    STATIC      CPU
 All    000c.854c.0501    STATIC      CPU
 All    000c.854c.0502    STATIC      CPU
 All    000c.854c.0503    STATIC      CPU
 All    000c.854c.0504    STATIC      CPU
 All    000c.854c.0505    STATIC      CPU
 All    000c.854c.0506    STATIC      CPU
 All    000c.854c.0507    STATIC      CPU
 All    000c.854c.0508    STATIC      CPU
 200    0012.1723.01da    DYNAMIC     Fa0/13
 200    0012.17fc.a3db    DYNAMIC     Fa0/13
 200    0014.1c48.e6d1    DYNAMIC     Fa0/7
 200    0014.1c48.e71a    DYNAMIC     Fa0/10
 200    0014.6a9c.3309    DYNAMIC     Fa0/16
 200    0014.a89e.f845    DYNAMIC     Fa0/8
 200    0018.8b7c.3712    DYNAMIC     Fa0/7
 200    0019.d122.dcf3    DYNAMIC     Fa0/9
```

How did the Static and Dynamic MAC addresses end up in the CAM table?

❍ **A.** The Static MAC addresses had to be input by an administrator; the Dynamic MAC addresses were learned by the switch.

❍ **B.** The Static MAC addresses belong to the switch itself; the Dynamic MAC addresses were learned by the switch.

❍ **C.** The Static MAC addresses had to be learned by the switch; the Dynamic MAC addresses were input by an administrator.

❍ **D.** The Static MAC addresses are reversed duplicates of the Dynamic MAC addresses and were learned by the switch.

Quick Check

25. The switch pictured in Figure 2.3 receives a frame destined for the MAC address 00aa:911b:9cc3. How is this frame handled?

Quick Answer: **39**
Detailed Answer: **43**

FIGURE 2.3 Network diagram.

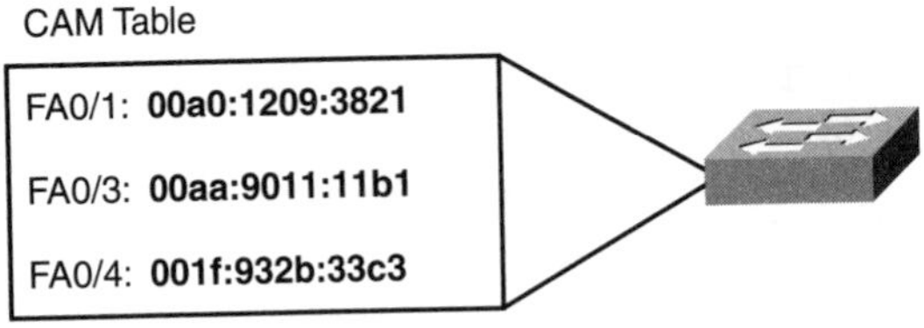

CAM Table

FA0/1: **00a0:1209:3821**

FA0/3: **00aa:9011:11b1**

FA0/4: **001f:932b:33c3**

- ❍ **A.** The frame is dropped.
- ❍ **B.** The frame is sent out Fa0/3.
- ❍ **C.** The frame is sent out all ports.
- ❍ **D.** The frame is sent out all ports with the exception of the port on which it was received.

26. You want to implement port security in your company to protect against unauthorized network access. After logging in to the switch, you enter the following commands:

Quick Answer: **39**
Detailed Answer: **43**

```
Switch(config)#interface range fa0/1-20
Switch(config-if-range)#switchport mode access
Switch(config-if-range)#switchport port-security
Switch(config-if-range)#switchport port-security maximum 1
Switch(config-if-range)#switchport port-security mac-address
➥sticky
Switch(config-if-range)#switchport port-security violation
➥shutdown
```

What does this configuration accomplish?

- ❍ **A.** Port security is enabled, and ports are limited to a maximum of one violation per port. The first MAC address to transmit data on the port will be the only MAC address allowed. After a second violation has occurred, the interface will shut down.
- ❍ **B.** Port security is enabled, and the port is limited to an access port, which can only be used between switches. Only one upstream switch is allowed to connect to the port. All MAC addresses learned on the port will "stick" to the interface. If more than one upstream switch is attached, the port will shut down.

Quick Check

❍ **C.** Port security is enabled, and ports are limited to a maximum of one MAC address each. The first MAC address to transmit data on the port will be the only MAC address allowed. Any other MAC addresses will cause the interface to enter an err-disabled state.

❍ **D.** Port security is not enabled because the syntax "switchport port-security on" was not used. All other port-security commands will not take effect until this command is entered.

27. The switch pictured in Figure 2.4 does not have a green or amber light on the FastEthernet ports shown in the figure. What areas would you inspect on the switch? (Choose three.)

Quick Answer: **39**
Detailed Answer: **43**

FIGURE 2.4 Network diagram.

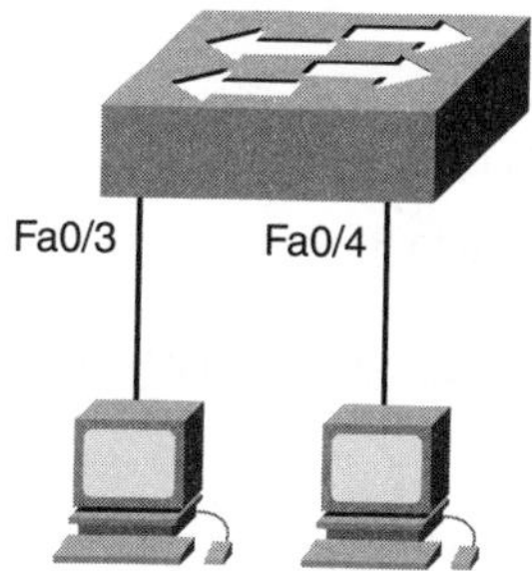

❍ **A.** Ensure the cables being used are crossover cables.

❍ **B.** Ensure the ports are configured as trunk ports.

❍ **C.** Ensure the cables being used are straight-through cables.

❍ **D.** Ensure the switch has power.

❍ **E.** Reboot all devices pictured.

❍ **F.** Reseat all cables pictured.

Quick Check

28. Workstation A needs to be able to telnet to SW_B (shown in Figure 2.5). What must be configured to make this connection possible?

Quick Answer: **39**
Detailed Answer: **43**

FIGURE 2.5 Network diagram.

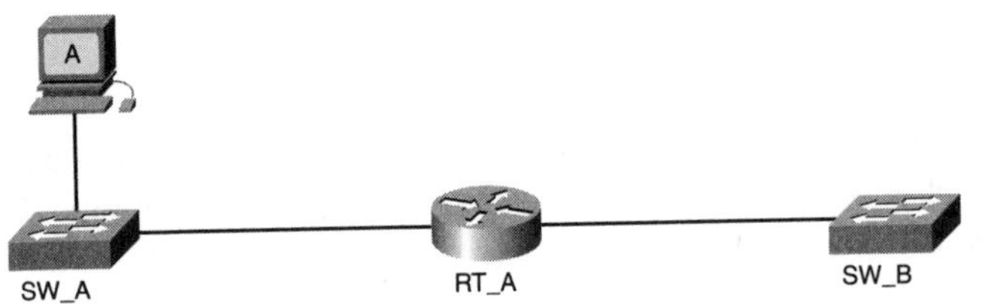

- ❍ **A.** VLAN 1 on RT_A
- ❍ **B.** VLAN 1 on SW_A
- ❍ **C.** Default gateway on SW_B
- ❍ **D.** Crossover cable connecting SW_B to RT_A
- ❍ **E.** Trunk port connecting SW_B to RT_A

29. What are two advantages of switches over hubs? (Choose two.)

Quick Answer: **39**
Detailed Answer: **44**

- ❍ **A.** Decreased collision domains
- ❍ **B.** Increasing the maximum length of Category 5 UTP cable between devices
- ❍ **C.** Increasing the broadcast domain size
- ❍ **D.** Allowing simultaneous transmissions from multiple devices
- ❍ **E.** Filtering frames based on the MAC address fields in the header

30. What is the effect of entering the following command on a switch?

Quick Answer: **39**
Detailed Answer: **44**

```
Switch(config)#service password-encryption
```

- ❍ **A.** The enable secret password is encrypted.
- ❍ **B.** Only the enable password is encrypted.
- ❍ **C.** The telnet and console passwords are encrypted.
- ❍ **D.** The enable secret will now supersede the enable password.
- ❍ **E.** All passwords are encrypted.

Quick Check Answer Key

1. C
2. C
3. A, D, F
4. B, C
5. A
6. D
7. C
8. A
9. D
10. C
11. A
12. B
13. B
14. D
15. C
16. E
17. A
18. B
19. A
20. D
21. C
22. A
23. D
24. B
25. D
26. C
27. C, D, F
28. C
29. D, E
30. E

Answers and Explanations

1. **C.** Switches provide a separate circuit for each interface, and thus provide a separate collision domain for each interface. Answer A is incorrect because hubs do not process frames. Answer B is incorrect because hubs suffer from collisions that decrease bandwidth. Answer D is incorrect, as switches flood received broadcasts.

2. **C.** By default, all physical interfaces on a Cisco switch are assigned to VLAN 1. Because of that, you can enter the configuration mode for the VLAN 1 virtual interface by typing **interface vlan 1** from Global Configuration mode. From the VLAN interface configuration mode, you can assign an IP address to the switch. Answers A and D are incorrect because you do not assign the IP address to a physical interface. Answer B is incorrect because loopback interfaces are not reachable through telnet on a Layer 2 switch.

3. **A, D, F.** By default, a switch boots up with the following configuration:

   No IP address

   CDP enabled

   Ports auto-negotiate

   Spanning-tree enabled

   No console password

4. **B, C.** Bridges build the bridge table by listening to incoming frames and examining the source MAC address in the frame. Switches are multiport bridges that allow you to create multiple collision domains. Answer A is incorrect, as bridges are software-based, and switches have hardware that assists in speeding up transactions. Answer D is incorrect because both bridges and switches forward broadcasts.

5. **A.** By issuing the **ip default-gateway** command, you are specifying a router that the switch can send frames to if they are sent outside the network segment. This is necessary whenever you want to telnet to a switch from a remote network. Answer B is a nonexistent command on a switch. Answer C is used only on routers and is irrelevant to a Layer 2 switch. Answer D is a nonexistent command.

6. **D.** Spanning-Tree Protocol was developed by DEC and updated by the IEEE 802.1d standard. It dynamically monitors your switched environment and blocks ports to stop switching loops (not routing loops) from happening in your switched environment. Answers A and C are incorrect, as they do not contain or create routing loops. Answer B is incorrect because STP does not stop or minimize broadcasts.

7. **C.** The 24 FastEthernet Ports operate at 100Mbps in either full- or half-duplex mode. In half-duplex mode, they have 100Mbps to send or receive traffic. If changed to full-duplex mode, the hosts have 100Mbps to send and 100Mbps to receive (theoretically doubling the amount of bandwidth). Answers A, B, and D are incorrect values.

8. **A.** When you are configuring port security, all commands begin with the **switchport port-security** syntax. In addition, the port must be configured as a hard-coded access port before the port-security features will function (by typing **switchport mode access**). The **switchport port-security** command enables the port-security feature. You must then add your MAC addresses using the **switchport port-security mac-address** command. Finally, using the **switchport port-security violation shutdown** command instructs the port to shut down when it sees a bad MAC address. All other answers are missing one or more critical pieces of this syntax.

9. **D.** The **show port-security interface** command allows you to see any port security features you have enabled on an interface. Answer A is incorrect because the **show interface** command just shows you port statistics such as the number of packets and bytes sent and received. Answer B is incorrect because this command shows you layer 3 statistics for the interface and is typically used for routed interfaces. Answer C is incorrect because this command displays the access or trunking characteristics of the port.

10. **C.** Hubs do not separate each port into a separate collision domain. Separate collision domains grant dedicated bandwidth to each port, and thus each end user plugged into that port. Answer A is not correct, as hubs can extend the length of an Ethernet segment. Hubs are also known as *multiport repeaters*. Answer B is incorrect, as hubs do offer half-duplex connections. Answer D is incorrect, as there are hubs that support FastEthernet connections.

11. **A.** The syntax shown is a complete configuration of SSH on a switch. Answer B is incorrect because typing the command **transport input ssh** automatically disables Telnet. If you wanted to support both Telnet and SSH, you could enter **transport input telnet ssh**. Answer C is incorrect because SSH works with any RSA encryption keys you can generate on a Cisco device; the stronger the modulus (key length), the stronger the encryption. Answer D is incorrect because both SSH and Telnet connect using VTY lines. No SSH lines are available on Cisco devices.

12. **B.** Based on the Security Violation Count field in the output, you can gather that the interface has experienced violations in the past, but because of the current Port Status (Secure-Down) we can see that there is currently no device attached. If a valid device was attached, the Port Status would show Secure-Up. If an invalid device was attached (one with a disallowed MAC address), the Port Status would show Secure-Shutdown. Answer A is incorrect because the Port Status does not show Secure-Shutdown. Answer C is incorrect because a MAC address cannot get "stuck" on an interface. The Sticky MAC address feature allows a switch to dynamically hard-code allowed MAC addresses. Answer D is incorrect because Cisco switches do not require a configured MAC address.

13. **B.** When attaching a hub to a switch, a crossover cable is required. This is because they are considered "like devices." Answers A, C, and D are incorrect because these cable types do not meet the requirement.

14. **D.** The Frame Check Sequence (FCS) field at the end of a frame is the calculated hash of the entire packet. If anything changes in the packet during transmission, the FCS hash calculation at the other end will not match and the packet will be dropped. Answer A is incorrect because the Preamble exists at the front of the frame and is used to synchronize the signals of the communicating computers. Answer C is incorrect because the ACK field is part of a TCP segment. Answer B does not exist.

15. **C.** Multicast messages are sent to a *group* of devices. They do not reach *all* devices like a broadcast message or just a single device like a unicast message. Answers A and B are incorrect because the question stated that only a single message was sent. Answer E is incorrect because a broadcast message would have reached everyone (including HostE and HostF). Answer F is incorrect because there is not a specific "VLAN-based" message type.

16. **E.** The vendor-assigned portion of the MAC address is the second half—technically, the last 24 bits. The first half (technically, the first 24 bits) represents the Organizational Unique Identifier (OUI), which are assigned to specific network manufacturing organizations. In this case, the second half of the MAC address is 22-DC-F3. The other answers do not correspond to the question.

17. **A.** The most likely cause of this failure is because the default gateway is not configured on SwitchB. By configuring an IP address, all the hosts on the local subnet (172.16.82.128-159/28) will be able to reach SwitchB via Telnet and SSH (if configured). All IP addresses (and subnets) in Figure 2.2 are correctly assigned, which eliminates answers C, D, and E. Finally, if one of the routers were denying access to SwitchB's IP subnet, HostA would not have been able to ping HostD, making answer B incorrect.

18. **B.** The **show interface** output reveals many late collision packets. These types of collisions are typically caused by an Ethernet cable being too long or the total distance between the host and server being too long. While the host is currently sending data, the link is far from saturated, making answer A incorrect. Answers C and D are incorrect because the answers do not apply to this scenario.

19. **A.** When devices detect a collision on a cable, they will initially transmit a jam signal. This signal indicates to the rest of the devices connected to the hub that a collision was detected and data transmissions need to stop until the data can be successfully retransmitted. Answer B is incorrect because the jam signal is transmitted first and the machines will then wait a random amount of time before retransmitting the packet. Answer C is incorrect because collisions are never ignored. Answer D is incorrect because this only occurs in Sci-Fi movies.

20. **D.** The System LED blinks green when the switch is rebooting. This could have been caused by a power outage, a loose power cable, or many other reasons. Answer A is incorrect because the System LED would turn amber if a hardware failure occurred. Answer B is incorrect because there is no physical indication of a speed or duplex mismatch (other than the port LED going dark due to the port disabling itself). Answer C is incorrect because the ports would blink on and off if one of the devices had a flapping interface.

21. **C.** The output **Vlan1 is administratively down, line protocol is down** is a clear indication that the interface is shutdown. To correct this issue, you should enter the interface configuration mode and issue the **no shutdown** command. Answers A and B would be worth looking into if this output did not exist. Answer D is incorrect because the Catalyst 3550 always supports telnet connections (as do all Cisco devices).

22. **A.** The correct command to configure the default gateway on a switch is **ip default-gateway** *ip address* from global configuration mode. The other answers either have the wrong mode or the wrong command.

23. **D.** The output displayed is generated by the **show version** command. This command is commonly used to inspect the uptime and IOS version running on the switch. The **show config** command is an older command you could substitute for the **show running-config** command. Both commands would return the running configuration, making answers A and B incorrect. Answers C and E are incorrect because there is no **show ios** or **show uptime** command.

24. **B.** On observing the output from the **show mac-address-table** command you can see that all the MAC addresses that are of the type STATIC belong to the CPU ports. This means they belong to the switch itself. Although Static MAC addresses can be assigned by an administrator on a per-port basis, they would reflect this port number under the Ports column of the output. The Dynamic MAC addresses are always learned by the switch itself. All other answers do not apply once this definition is understood.

25. **D.** When the switch receives a broadcast or a frame destined for an unknown MAC address, it will flood the frame out all ports with the exception of the port on which the frame was received. All other answers do not apply to this question.

26. **C.** The syntax shown is the ideal way to enable port security on a switch. Answer A is incorrect because a single violation will shut down the port immediately. Answer B is incorrect because a switch does not have any way of telling whether another switch attaches to another PC. If an additional switch is connected, more than one MAC address will enter the port, and it will shut down. Answer D is incorrect because the command **switchport port-security** enables port security on an interface.

27. **C, D, F.** When troubleshooting switchport connections, first examine the physical layer. PCs should connect using straight-through cables. Cables can commonly come loose, so reseating the cables is also a good idea. Although it may seem obvious, the switch might not be plugged in. Answer A is invalid because crossover cables are used to uplink other switches. Answer B is not correct because trunk ports do not connect to end PCs; rather, they are typically used to uplink between switches. Finally, if the lights are out on the switch, rebooting the devices will not solve the problem, making answer E inaccurate.

28. **C.** Because SW_B is on a different subnet, it will need a default gateway to reach devices not on its own network. Answers A and B are incorrect because the VLAN 1 interface on RT_A or SW_A do not play a role in this network scenario (although, SW_B would also need an IP address assigned to its VLAN 1 interface). Answers D and E are incorrect because switches do not connect to routers using crossover cables or trunk ports.

29. **D, E.** Switches allow all connected devices to send and receive at the same time if the switch is running in full duplex. If the switch is running in half duplex, all connected devices can send or receive at the same time. Either way, the switch has a major benefit over hubs because hubs only allow a single device to send or receive at a time (hubs only run in half-duplex mode). Switches also have the capability to learn and filter data based on MAC address information. Answer A is incorrect because switches increase the number of collision domains. Answer B is incorrect because the maximum distance a Category 5 UTP cable can travel is based on the cable, not the hub or switch. Answer C is incorrect because both hubs and switches have the same broadcast domain size.

30. **E.** Entering the **service password-encryption** command encrypts all clear-text passwords on the switch. All other answers do not apply to this question.

CHAPTER THREE

Basic IP Services

This chapter covers the following ICND1 objectives that fall under the content area, **Implement an IP addressing scheme and IP services to meet network requirements for a small branch office:**

- Describe the need and role of addressing in a network.
- Create and apply an addressing scheme to a network.
- Assign and verify valid IP addresses to hosts, servers, and networking devices in a LAN environment.
- Explain the basic uses and operation of NAT in a small network connecting to one ISP.
- Describe and verify DNS operation.
- Describe the operation and benefits of using private and public IP addressing.
- Enable NAT for a small network with a single ISP and connection using SDM and verify operation using CLI and ping.
- Configure, verify, and troubleshoot DHCP and DNS operation on a router.
- Implement static and dynamic addressing services for hosts in a LAN environment.
- Identify and correct IP addressing issues.

Quick Check

1. You are designing a network that needs to support 55 users. You don't plan to extend the segment beyond the current number of users. Which subnet mask would best meet your needs?

   ❍ **A.** 255.255.0.0
   ❍ **B.** 255.255.255.0
   ❍ **C.** 255.255.255.192
   ❍ **D.** 255.255.255.160

Quick Answer: **59**
Detailed Answer: **60**

2. You have added a new switch to your network. You want to manage it remotely, so you need to assign it an IP address. Your router that connects to the switch has an IP address of 172.16.12.33/27. Which of the following addresses can you assign to this switch?

   ❍ **A.** 172.16.12.33/28
   ❍ **B.** 172.16.12.32/27
   ❍ **C.** 172.16.12.33/27
   ❍ **D.** 172.16.12.34/27
   ❍ **E.** 172.16.12.35/28
   ❍ **F.** 172.16.12.38/28
   ❍ **G.** 172.16.12.63/27

Quick Answer: **59**
Detailed Answer: **60**

3. You are designing an IP address scheme for your brand-new remote office. The vice president of IT calls to tell you that you will be in charge of the 192.168.1.64/26 subnetwork. This supplies you with a single subnetwork with 62 hosts. You need to have at least two subnets with 14 hosts in each subnet. What custom subnet mask should you use?

   ❍ **A.** 255.255.255.128
   ❍ **B.** 255.255.255.192
   ❍ **C.** 255.255.255.224
   ❍ **D.** 255.255.255.240
   ❍ **E.** 255.255.255.248

Quick Answer: **59**
Detailed Answer: **60**

Quick Check

4. Identify three valid host addresses in any subnet of the 201.168.27.0 network, assuming a fixed subnet mask of 255.255.255.240. (Choose three.)

Quick Answer: **59**
Detailed Answer: **60**

- ❍ **A.** 201.168.27.33
- ❍ **B.** 201.168.27.112
- ❍ **C.** 201.168.27.119
- ❍ **D.** 201.168.27.126
- ❍ **E.** 201.168.27.175
- ❍ **F.** 201.168.27.208

5. You have an internal web server that has the IP address 172.16.5.9. You need to enable this server to be accessed on TCP port 80 from the Internet; what would be the best solution for this situation?

Quick Answer: **59**
Detailed Answer: **60**

- ❍ **A.** Static NAT
- ❍ **B.** Dynamic NAT
- ❍ **C.** NAT Overload
- ❍ **D.** Standard Routing
- ❍ **E.** Port NAT

6. Which of the following represent a private IP address? (Choose two.)

Quick Answer: **59**
Detailed Answer: **60**

- ❍ **A.** 192.168.5.205
- ❍ **B.** 172.32.65.31
- ❍ **C.** 10.168.5.205
- ❍ **D.** 224.16.23.1

Quick Check

Refer to Figure 3.1 for the following three questions.

FIGURE 3.1 Network diagram.

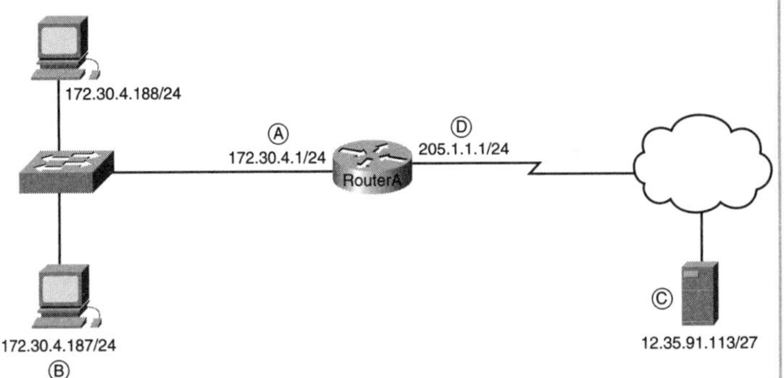

7. You have configured NAT to share a single public IP address (205.1.1.1/24) with many internal private addresses (172.30.4.0/24 network) for Internet access. Which of the following terms does the IP address at position B in Figure 3.1 represent?

Quick Answer: **59**
Detailed Answer: **61**

- ❍ **A.** Inside Local
- ❍ **B.** Inside Global
- ❍ **C.** Outside Local
- ❍ **D.** Outside Global

8. You have configured NAT to share a single public IP address (205.1.1.1/24) with many internal private addresses (172.30.4.0/24 network) for Internet access. Which of the following terms does the IP address at position A in Figure 3.1 represent?

Quick Answer: **59**
Detailed Answer: **61**

- ❍ **A.** Inside Local
- ❍ **B.** Inside Global
- ❍ **C.** Outside Local
- ❍ **D.** Outside Global

Quick Check

9. You have configured NAT to share a single public IP address (205.1.1.1/24) with many internal private addresses (172.30.4.0/24 network) for Internet access. Which of the following terms does the IP address at position D in Figure 3.1 represent?

Quick Answer: **59**
Detailed Answer: **61**

- ❍ **A.** Inside Local
- ❍ **B.** Inside Global
- ❍ **C.** Outside Local
- ❍ **D.** Outside Global

10. You have been allocated the address space 174.82.10.0/24 for the network shown in Figure 3.2. All devices in this network are required to use the same subnet mask, and all subnets are considered usable. What is the most appropriate subnet mask for the network that is shown?

Quick Answer: **59**
Detailed Answer: **62**

FIGURE 3.2 Network diagram.

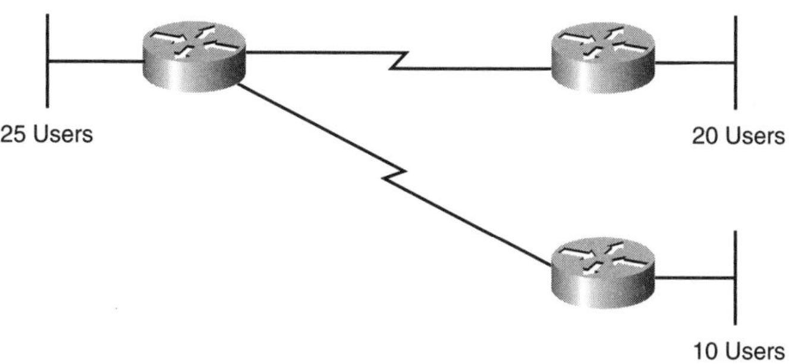

- ❍ **A.** 255.255.252.0
- ❍ **B.** 255.255.255.0
- ❍ **C.** 255.255.255.128
- ❍ **D.** 255.255.255.192
- ❍ **E.** 255.255.255.224
- ❍ **F.** 255.255.255.240

Quick Check

11. What form of NAT maps multiple private IP addresses to a single public address by using different port numbers?

Quick Answer: **59**
Detailed Answer: **62**

❍ **A.** Static NAT
❍ **B.** Dynamic NAT
❍ **C.** Port NAT
❍ **D.** Overload
❍ **E.** Port load

12. What two statements describe the IP address 12.51.5.65/23? (Choose two.)

Quick Answer: **59**
Detailed Answer: **62**

❍ **A.** It is a private IP address.
❍ **B.** The subnet address is 12.51.5.0 255.255.254.0.
❍ **C.** The last usable host address is 12.51.5.254.
❍ **D.** The lowest usable host address is 12.51.4.1.
❍ **E.** The range of usable addresses is from 12.51.5.1 to 12.51.5.254.

13. After the routers shown in Figure 3.3 have been configured, it is discovered that the hosts in the branch office network cannot access the Internet. Further testing reveals additional connectivity issues. What is the most likely solution to this problem?

Quick Answer: **59**
Detailed Answer: **62**

FIGURE 3.3 Network diagram.

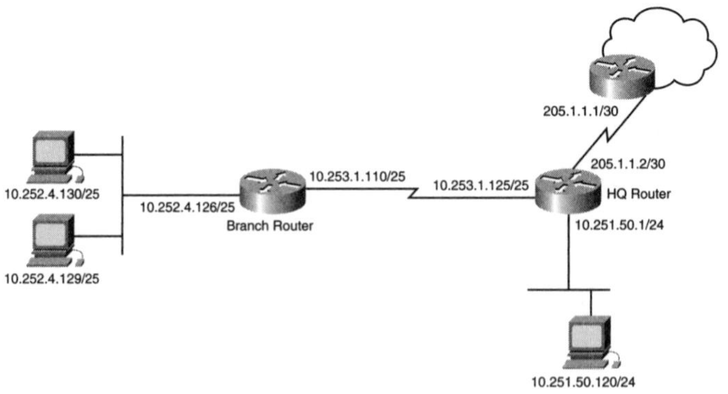

Quick Check

- ❍ **A.** Change the address of the Branch router LAN interface.
- ❍ **B.** Change the subnet mask of the Branch router LAN interface.
- ❍ **C.** Change the address of the Branch router WAN interface.
- ❍ **D.** Change the address of the HQ router WAN interface.
- ❍ **E.** Change the subnet mask of the HQ router LAN interface.
- ❍ **F.** Change the address of the HQ router Internet interface.
- ❍ **G.** Change the subnet mask of the HQ router Internet interface.

14. Which of the following statements describe the network shown in Figure 3.4? (Choose two.)

Quick Answer: **59**
Detailed Answer: **62**

FIGURE 3.4 Network diagram.

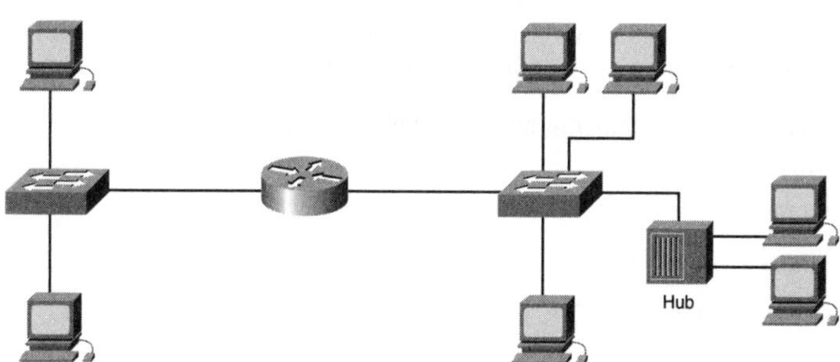

- ❍ **A.** There are seven collision domains.
- ❍ **B.** There are eight collision domains.
- ❍ **C.** There are nine collision domains.
- ❍ **D.** There are ten collision domains.
- ❍ **E.** There is one broadcast domain.
- ❍ **F.** There are two broadcast domains.
- ❍ **G.** There are three broadcast domains.

Quick Check

15. What two statements accurately describe private IP addresses? (Choose two.)

Quick Answer: **59**
Detailed Answer: **62**

- ❍ **A.** Addresses that are nonroutable
- ❍ **B.** Addresses that are assigned to an organization by the IANA
- ❍ **C.** Addresses that cannot be routed on the Internet
- ❍ **D.** An addressing scheme devised to conserve the public IP address space
- ❍ **E.** Addresses that begin with 169.253.0.0/16

16. RFC 1918 defines the private IP address ranges. Which of the following IP addresses are considered part of these ranges? (Choose three.)

Quick Answer: **59**
Detailed Answer: **63**

- ❍ **A.** 10.23.45.67
- ❍ **B.** 126.21.34.56
- ❍ **C.** 172.16.32.1
- ❍ **D.** 172.31.234.55
- ❍ **E.** 192.169.4.5

17. You give your IT department a spreadsheet of IP addresses and their subnets. You receive a call from one of the junior techs asking what the /26 means next to the IP addresses. You tell her:

Quick Answer: **59**
Detailed Answer: **63**

- ❍ **A.** It represents the number of hosts possible on that subnetwork.
- ❍ **B.** It represents the number of subnetworks being used.
- ❍ **C.** It represents the class of IP address being used.
- ❍ **D.** It represents the number of bits in the subnet mask that are set to 1.

18. Which of the following protocols use both TCP and UDP ports?

Quick Answer: **59**
Detailed Answer: **63**

- ❍ **A.** HTTP
- ❍ **B.** DNS
- ❍ **C.** FTP
- ❍ **D.** Telnet
- ❍ **E.** TFTP

Quick Check

Quick Answer: **59**
Detailed Answer: **63**

19. Based on Figure 3.5, what information could you assume about this IP address information? (Choose two.)

FIGURE 3. 5 Command prompt window.

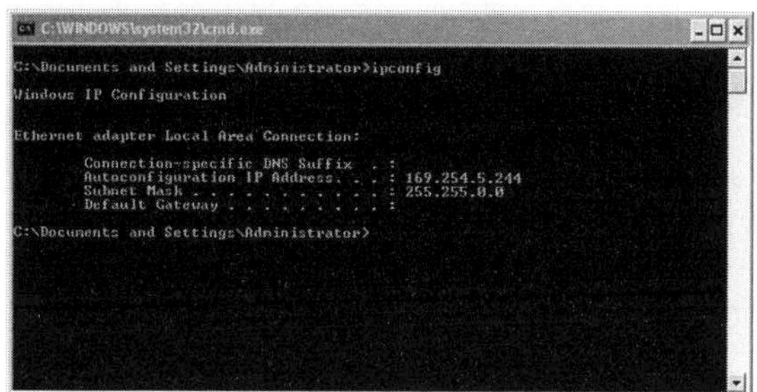

- ❍ **A.** The client is using a private address that was most likely statically assigned by a network administrator.
- ❍ **B.** The client is using a public address that was most likely statically assigned by a network administrator.
- ❍ **C.** The client does not have an assigned IP default gateway.
- ❍ **D.** The client is using a private address that was most likely assigned using DHCP.
- ❍ **E.** The client is using a public address that was most likely assigned using DHCP.
- ❍ **F.** The client could not contact a DHCP server and generated its own IP address.

Quick Check

20. Based on the following output, what form of NAT is being used on this router?

Quick Answer: **59**
Detailed Answer: **63**

```
Pro  Inside global           Inside local          Outside local          Outside global
tcp  71.209.254.131:1433   192.168.1.25:1433     64.12.189.217:443      64.12.189.217:443
tcp  71.209.254.131:1434   192.168.1.25:1434     205.188.8.237:443      205.188.8.237:443
tcp  71.209.254.131:1435   192.168.1.25:1435     205.188.248.168:443    205.188.248.168:443
tcp  71.209.254.131:1436   192.168.1.25:1436     207.200.94.66:80       207.200.94.66:80
tcp  71.209.254.131:1437   192.168.1.25:1437     205.188.216.1:80       205.188.216.1:80
tcp  71.209.254.131:1438   192.168.1.25:1438     207.200.94.66:80       207.200.94.66:80
tcp  71.209.254.131:1440   192.168.1.25:1440     64.12.174.185:80       64.12.174.185:80
tcp  71.209.254.131:1442   192.168.1.25:1442     207.200.74.12:80       207.200.74.12:80
tcp  71.209.254.131:1443   192.168.1.25:1443     64.12.187.25:80        64.12.187.25:80
tcp  71.209.254.131:1444   192.168.1.25:1444     207.200.74.66:80       207.200.74.66:80
tcp  71.209.254.131:1445   192.168.1.25:1445     209.62.180.90:80       209.62.180.90:80
tcp  71.209.254.131:1446   192.168.1.25:1446     8.7.28.81:80           8.7.28.81:80
tcp  71.209.254.131:1447   192.168.1.25:1447     209.62.180.90:80       209.62.180.90:80
tcp  71.209.254.131:52811  192.168.1.26:52811    205.240.85.61:80       205.240.85.61:80
tcp  71.209.254.131:52813  192.168.1.26:52813    205.240.85.61:80       205.240.85.61:80
udp  71.209.254.131:1035   192.168.1.225:1035    63.236.1.135:53        63.236.1.135:53
udp  71.209.254.131:1035   192.168.1.225:1035    64.236.1.107:53        64.236.1.107:53
```

- ❍ **A.** Static NAT
- ❍ **B.** Port-based NAT
- ❍ **C.** Dynamic NAT
- ❍ **D.** NAT Overload

Quick Check

21. Using the following options, select the necessary IP addresses that would accurately complete the network depicted in Figure 3.6. (Choose three.)

Quick Answer: **59**
Detailed Answer: **63**

FIGURE 3. 6 Network diagram.

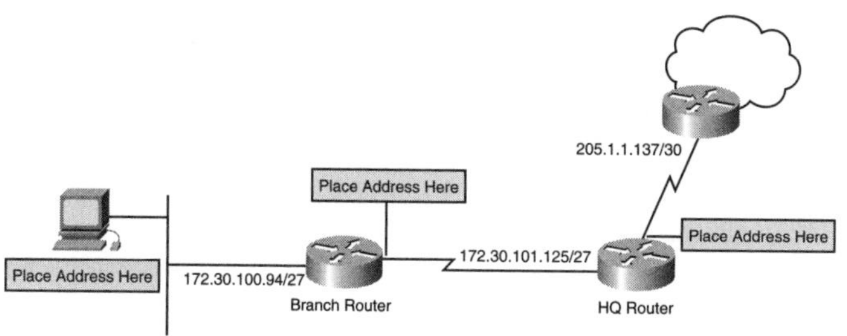

- ❍ **A.** 172.30.101.98/27
- ❍ **B.** 172.30.101.129/27
- ❍ **C.** 172.30.101.163/27
- ❍ **D.** 172.30.100.58/27
- ❍ **E.** 172.30.100.65/27
- ❍ **F.** 172.30.100.95/27
- ❍ **G.** 172.30.100.97/27
- ❍ **H.** 205.1.1.136/30
- ❍ **I.** 205.1.1.138/30
- ❍ **J.** 205.1.1.139/30

22. You have recently changed configuration settings on your DHCP server and network infrastructure. Some of the DHCP clients no longer have access to network resources. What would be the best option to troubleshoot this issue?

Quick Answer: **59**
Detailed Answer: **64**

- ❍ **A.** Reboot the DHCP server.
- ❍ **B.** Use the **tracert** command to determine the location of the network outage.
- ❍ **C.** Verify the ARP cache on the clients by using the **arp –a** command.
- ❍ **D.** Issue the **ipconfig /release** followed by the **ipconfig /renew** commands from a command prompt.

Quick Check

23. Which of the following are true of the DHCP Discover message? (Choose two.)

Quick Answer: **59**
Detailed Answer: **64**

- ❍ **A.** It uses TCP as the transport layer protocol.
- ❍ **B.** It uses UDP as the transport layer protocol.
- ❍ **C.** It uses a reserved multicast MAC address.
- ❍ **D.** It uses a unicast data link and network layer address to reach the DHCP server.
- ❍ **E.** It uses a destination MAC address of FFFF.FFFF.FFFF.
- ❍ **F.** It is commonly ignored and discarded by the DHCP server.

24. How many valid host addresses are provided in the 10.55.128.0/22 subnet?

Quick Answer: **59**
Detailed Answer: **64**

- ❍ **A.** 254
- ❍ **B.** 255
- ❍ **C.** 510
- ❍ **D.** 512
- ❍ **E.** 1022

25. What two statements describe the IP address 172.16.3.68/23? (Choose two.)

Quick Answer: **59**
Detailed Answer: **64**

- ❍ **A.** It is from the subnet 172.16.3.0 255.255.254.0.
- ❍ **B.** The broadcast address of the subnet is 172.16.3.255.
- ❍ **C.** The broadcast address of the subnet is 172.16.4.255.
- ❍ **D.** The first valid IP address of the subnet is 172.16.2.1.
- ❍ **E.** The last valid IP address of the subnet is 172.16.4.254.

26. You are a network technician at Acme, Inc. You have subnetted the 192.168.72.0 network with a /30 mask for connections between your routers. Your boss asks you how many usable subnetworks and usable host addresses per subnet this will provide. What should you tell her, assuming your router can use all possible subnets?

Quick Answer: **59**
Detailed Answer: **64**

- ❍ **A.** 64 networks and 2 hosts
- ❍ **B.** 8 networks and 30 hosts
- ❍ **C.** 8 networks and 32 hosts
- ❍ **D.** 16 networks and 16 hosts
- ❍ **E.** 16 networks and 14 hosts

Quick Check

27. You are configuring a subnet for the Acme, Inc., branch office in Beijing. You need to assign IP addresses to hosts in this subnet. You have been given the subnet mask of 255.255.255.224. Which of these IP addresses would be valid? (Choose three.)

Quick Answer: **59**
Detailed Answer: **65**

- ❍ **A.** 15.234.118.63
- ❍ **B.** 92.11.178.93
- ❍ **C.** 134.178.18.56
- ❍ **D.** 192.168.16.87
- ❍ **E.** 201.45.116.159
- ❍ **F.** 217.63.12.192

28. What is the most likely cause of the problem shown in Figure 3.7 given that your organization is using a private addressing scheme?

Quick Answer: **59**
Detailed Answer: **65**

FIGURE 3.7 Command prompt window.

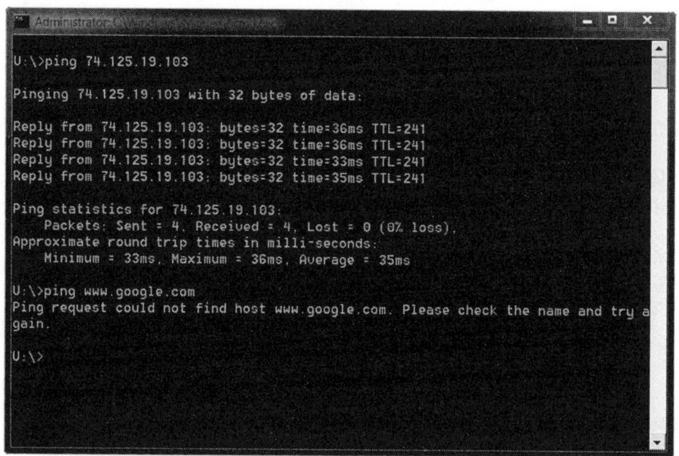

- ❍ **A.** DHCP server scope issues.
- ❍ **B.** The client's default gateway should be set to 74.125.19.103.
- ❍ **C.** DNS server is unreachable.
- ❍ **D.** A routing loop.

Quick Check

29. You need to assign the IP address 192.168.6.1/23 to the FastEthernet0/0 interface of your router. Place the numbers of the following commands in the correct order below. NOTE: Not all commands will be used. You are currently at the following prompt:

Quick Answer: **59**
Detailed Answer: **65**

```
Router>
```

1 = config memory

2 = int fa0/0

3 = configure terminal

4 = enable

5 = fastethernet 0/0

6 = ip 192.168.6.1 255.255.254.0

7 = ip address 192.168.6.1 /23

8 = ip address 192.168.6.1 255.255.254.0

❍ **A.** ______
❍ **B.** ______
❍ **C.** ______
❍ **D.** ______

30. An administrator pings the IP address 127.0.0.1 from a command prompt on a server. If he receives reply messages, what does this indicate?

Quick Answer: **59**
Detailed Answer: **65**

❍ **A.** The server has connected successfully to a device using IP.
❍ **B.** The server has connectivity with local devices.
❍ **C.** The server can reach the Internet.
❍ **D.** TCP and UDP operations are working successfully.
❍ **E.** TCP/IP is operating on the server.

Quick Check Answer Key

1. C
2. D
3. D
4. A, C, D
5. A
6. A, C
7. A
8. A
9. B
10. E
11. D
12. C, D
13. A
14. B, F
15. C, D
16. A, C, D
17. D
18. B
19. C, F
20. D
21. A, E, I
22. D
23. B, E
24. E
25. B, D
26. A
27. B, C, and D
28. C
29. A. 4, B. 3, C. 2, D. 8
30. E

Answers and Explanations

1. **C.** This particular subnet mask allows for up to 62 hosts per network. Answer A is incorrect, as it allows for 65,534 hosts. Answer B is incorrect, as it allows up to 254 hosts. Answer D is incorrect, as it is not a valid subnet mask.

2. **D.** The next valid IP host address in the 172.16.12.32 network is 172.16.12.34. Answer A is incorrect, as it is on a different subnetwork with a /28 mask. Answer B is incorrect, as it is the network address for that particular subnetwork. Answer C is incorrect, as it is the same IP address as the router interface. Answers E and F are incorrect as well, as they are on different subnets than the router interface. Answer G is incorrect because it represents the broadcast address for the 172.16.12.32 subnetwork and cannot be used as a host address.

3. **D.** The subnet mask 255.255.255.240 gives you two additional subnets, with up to 14 hosts per subnetwork. Answer A is incorrect, as it is a higher subnet mask than your original /26, which is actually called *supernetting*. Answer B is incorrect because it is your original subnet mask. Answer C is incorrect, as it does not give you enough subnets. Answer E is incorrect, as it gives you enough subnets (six), but you would have only six hosts per network.

4. **A, C, D.** A subnet mask of 255.255.255.240 divides the fourth octet into subnet parts: the highest four bits and a host part (the lowest four bits). You simply check the fourth octet to ensure that all subnet and host parts are okay. The host bit portion cannot be 0000 or 1111. Answers A, C, and D are correct because 33 in decimal is 00100001, 119 in decimal is 01110111, and 126 in decimal is 01111110. Answer B is incorrect, as 112 in decimal is 01110000 in binary. This is not a valid host address in this network. All its host bits are zero. Answer E is incorrect, as 175 in decimal is 10101111 in binary. All host bits are ones. This is the local broadcast address and cannot be used as a host address. Answer F is incorrect, as 208 in decimal is 11010000 in binary. This is not a valid host address in this network, and all its host bits are zero.

5. **A.** Static NAT provides the best solution when you need a 1:1 translation from a private address or port number to a public address or port number. Answer B is incorrect because Dynamic NAT allows many hosts to be translated at the same time. Answer C is incorrect because NAT Overload allows many internal hosts to share a single Internet IP address. Answer D is also incorrect. Standard routing does not work because private addresses are blocked from traversing the Internet. Finally, Answer E is incorrect because there is no such thing as Port NAT.

6. **A, C.** The private address ranges are 10.x.x.x, 172.16.x.x–172.31.x.x, and 192.168.x.x. Answers B and D fall outside these ranges.

Refer to Figure 3.8 for the following three answer explanations.

FIGURE 3.8 Network diagram.

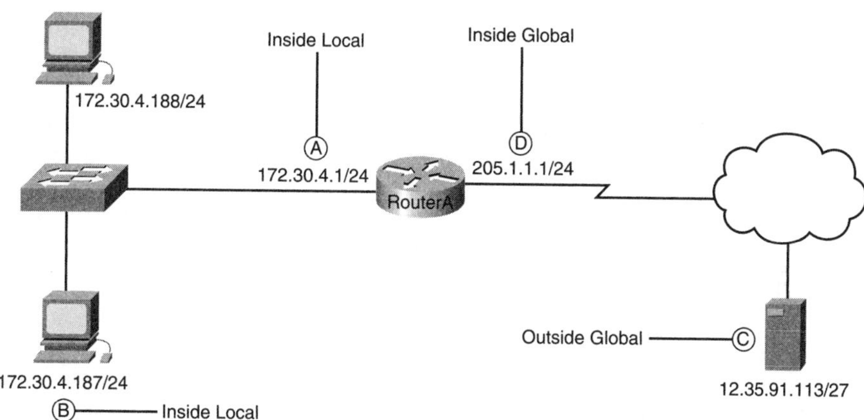

7. **A.** Inside local addresses encompass any address on your internal network that is translated to the outside network via NAT. Answer B is incorrect because the inside global addresses are the IP addresses of the inside hosts as seen by the outside world (after translation). Answer C is incorrect because the outside local addresses are outside (Internet) addresses as they appear to the hosts behind a NAT device. Answer D is incorrect because the outside global addresses are standard Internet-attached devices.

8. **A.** Inside local addresses encompass any address on your internal network that is translated to the outside network via NAT. Even though this IP address is assigned to the router, it still needs to be translated via NAT before being forwarded on to the Internet. Answer B is incorrect because the inside global addresses are the IP addresses of the inside hosts as seen by the outside world (after translation). Answer C is incorrect because the outside local addresses are outside (Internet) addresses as they appear to the hosts behind a NAT device. Answer D is incorrect because the outside global addresses are standard Internet-attached devices.

9. **B.** Inside global addresses are the IP addresses of the inside hosts as seen by the outside world (after translation). These are typically public IP addresses that are used to access the Internet. Answer A is incorrect because inside local addresses encompass any address on your internal network that is translated to the outside network via NAT. Answer C is incorrect because the outside local addresses are outside (Internet) addresses as they appear to the hosts behind a NAT device. Answer D is incorrect because the outside global addresses are standard Internet-attached devices.

10. **E.** The subnet mask 255.255.255.224 provides 8 subnets of 30 usable host IP addresses per subnet. This will address each of the three LANs shown in the diagram along with the two WAN connections. Answer A is incorrect because you cannot move the subnet mask backward on a given network, which is known as supernetting. Answer B is incorrect because this is the original subnet mask and only provides a single network. Answers C and D are incorrect because these masks only provide two or four subnets, respectively, which is short of the five needed. Answer F is incorrect because this subnet mask meets the network requirements, but only allows 14 usable host addresses per network.

11. **D.** NAT Overload allows multiple private addresses to share a single public address by using unique source port numbers for each request. Answer A is incorrect because Static NAT provides a 1:1 mapping between public and private IP addresses. Answer B is incorrect because Dynamic NAT translates one pool of addresses to another, also in 1:1 fashion. Answers C and E are incorrect because there is no such thing as Port NAT or Port load.

12. **C, D.** Given the 12.51.5.65/23 address, you can work backward to find the network range as 12.51.4.0 to 12.51.5.255 (which makes answer E incorrect). The first usable address from this range is 12.51.4.1 and the last is 12.51.5.254. Answer B is incorrect because the subnet address is 12.51.4.0/23. Answer A is incorrect because the 12.0.0.0/8 network is considered public addressing space.

13. **A.** The IP address on the LAN interface of the Branch router is 10.252.4.126/25. This IP address comes from the network range 10.252.4.0 to 10.252.4.127. The hosts on the Branch office LAN are assigned the IP addresses 10.252.4.129 and 10.252.4.130. These IP addresses come from the network range 10.252.4.128 to 10.252.4.255. Adjusting the IP address of the Branch office router to this range would solve the problem, provided the default gateway of all PCs in the Branch office pointed to this new IP address. All other IP addresses and subnet masks in the network diagram are valid.

14. **B, F.** Each active port on a switch is considered its own collision domain. Figure 3.4 shows eight active switch ports, which allows up to eight devices to simultaneously transmit data. The hub in the figure represents only a single collision domain, which is linked to the switch port to which it is connected. Likewise, every active interface of a router represents a broadcast domain. Based on Figure 3.4, there are two active broadcast domains. All other answers do not apply.

15. **C, D.** Private IP addresses are prevented from routing on the Internet because they are duplicated in organizations around the world. The private addressing scheme was designed to be used with NAT to provide Internet access while conserving public address space. Answer A is incorrect because private IP addresses are able to route; they are just unable to route on the Internet. Answer B is incorrect because the Internet Assigned Numbers Authority (IANA) handles public IP address assignments rather than private IP address assignments. Answer E is incorrect because addresses that begin with 169.253.0.0/16 are perfectly valid, public addresses. The range 169.254.0.0/16 is considered the auto-configured IP address range (which is non-routable).

16. **A, C, D.** These addresses are all part of the private ranges of 10.x.x.x and 172.16.x.x–172.31.x.x. Answer B is incorrect, as it does not fall into any of the RFC 1918-specified private ranges. Instead, it is a public IP address that is routable on the Internet. Answer E is incorrect, as it is not a part of the private IP address range. It falls outside the 192.168.x.x range and thus is a public IP address.

17. **D.** Prefix notation, or / notation, shows the number of subnet mask bits that are turned to one, signifying a network portion of the address. Answer A is incorrect, as it does not show the number of hosts on a subnetwork. Answer B is incorrect, as it does not show the number of subnetworks in use. Answer C is incorrect because, even though you can figure out whether it is a Class A, B, or C address based on the prefixes of /8, /16, or /24, it does not necessarily show the class of the address.

18. **B.** DNS uses both TCP and UDP port 53. The TCP form of DNS is typically used to replicate domain records between DNS servers. The UDP form of DNS is typically used for domain lookups from network clients. Answers A, C, D, and E are incorrect because HTTP uses TCP port 80, FTP uses TCP port 21, Telnet uses TCP port 23, and TFTP uses UDP port 69.

19. **C, F.** The 169.254.0.0/16 address range is reserved for auto-configuration IP addresses. These addresses are auto-generated by a client when it is unable to contact a DHCP server to allow minimal LAN-based communication. These IP address configurations never have default gateways assigned because they are not routable. Answers A, B, D, and E are incorrect because network administrators rarely, if ever, assign clients IP addresses from the 169.254.0.0/16 range statically or via DHCP.

20. **D.** The output is demonstrating NAT Overload because it shows many Inside Local (internal) IP addresses being translated to a single Inside Global (external) IP address using unique source port numbers. Answer A is incorrect because Static NAT would show 1:1 mappings between Inside Local and Inside Global IP addresses. Answer B is incorrect because there is no such thing as port-based NAT. Answer C is incorrect because Dynamic NAT would also show many 1:1 mappings between pools of IP addresses.

21. **A, E, I.** The best way to approach this type of problem is to reverse-engineer the given IP addresses on the diagram to determine their network range. For the WAN link between the Branch and HQ routers, you can find the network range to be 172.30.101.96 to 172.30.101.127. Because 172.30.101.96 represents the network and 172.30.100.127 represents the subnet broadcast address, you cannot assign them to the router interfaces. Answers B and C are incorrect because they are from other subnets. For the Branch Router LAN, you can find the network range to be 172.30.100.64 to 172.30.100.95. Because 172.30.100.64 represents the network and 172.30.100.95 represents the subnet broadcast address, you cannot assign them to clients. Answer E is correct because it is from the same subnet as the router (172.30.100.94). Answer F is not correct because it is the broadcast address, and answers D and G are not correct because they are from different subnets. Finally, for the HQ Router Internet interface, you can find the network range to be 205.1.1.136 to 205.1.1.139. Because 205.1.1.136 represents the network and 205.1.1.139 represents the subnet broadcast address, you cannot assign them to the router interface. This makes answers H and J incorrect.

22. **D.** When making changes to an IP scope on a DHCP server, you may need to release and renew IP addresses on the network clients. This will allow them to get any new scope options that were implemented, such as new IP addresses, DNS server settings, or a default gateway. Answer A is incorrect because DHCP servers should not have to be rebooted anytime configuration settings are changed. Answer B is incorrect because **tracert** is typically used to find router issues in a communication path. Answer C is incorrect because DHCP server settings should not affect the client's ARP cache. As a side note, the ARP cache will be cleared on releasing and renewing an IP address.

23. **B, E.** The DHCP Discover message is a broadcast packet generated by a DHCP client when attempting to obtain an IP address. Every broadcast message that uses the IP protocol suite will use UDP as a transport layer protocol (because TCP requires a three-way handshake to establish communication, making answer A incorrect). Likewise, broadcast messages are always sent to the destination MAC address FFFF.FFFF.FFFF (or FF-FF-FF-FF-FF-FF, depending on the format you are more familiar with). This forces the Layer 2 switch to send the message out all ports. Answers C and D are incorrect because DHCP Discover packets use broadcast rather than multicast or unicast to communicate. Answer F is incorrect because DHCP servers process and respond to DHCP Discover packets.

24. **E.** The formula used to calculate the maximum number of hosts per subnet is (2^x) – 2, where "x" is the number of host bits in the subnet mask. A /22 subnet mask has 10 host bits, so (2^10) – 2 = 1022. Keep in mind that you will not have access to a calculator on any Cisco exam, so it may be beneficial to become familiar with common exponential values. All other answers do not apply to this question.

25. **B, D.** By reverse-engineering the subnet mask, you can find the original network range for this address as 172.16.2.0 to 172.16.3.255. Because the first and last addresses in the range are reserved, the first usable address becomes 172.16.2.1, and the last usable address becomes 172.16.3.254. Answer A is incorrect because this address is from the 172.16.2.0 255.255.254.0 subnet. Answer C is incorrect because the broadcast address is 172.16.3.255. Answer E is incorrect because the last valid address for the subnet is 172.16.3.254.

26. **A.** The mask /30 gives you 64 subnetworks using the (2^n) formula, where n equals the number of bits borrowed for the subnet. You also find that there are two available hosts per subnet using the ($2^n - 2$) formula, where n equals the number of bits borrowed for the hosts. Because all subnets are usable, you do not need to subtract 2 from the subnetworks. Answer B is incorrect, as that would be a /27 mask. Answer C is incorrect, as there would never be 32 hosts per subnet; you always have to subtract 2 from the 2^n formula because of the network ID and the directed broadcast address on each subnetwork. Answer D is incorrect, as you would never have 16 hosts per subnet; you always have to subtract 2 from the 2^n formula because of the network ID and the directed broadcast address on each subnetwork. Answer E is incorrect, as the /28 subnet mask gives you 16 subnetworks and 14 possible hosts.

27. **B, C, and D.** These three are valid host addresses when using a 255.255.255.224 subnet mask against the address. Answer A is incorrect, as it is a broadcast address on the 16.234.118.32 network. Answer E is incorrect, as it is a broadcast address on the 210.45.116.128 network. Answer F is incorrect, as it is the network address for 237.63.12.192.

28. **C.** Based on the information given, the most likely cause of the problem is DNS-related. By examining the command prompt output you can see that the client is able to ping a public IP address, which indicates the organization's Internet routing is operating correctly. However, when the client attempts to ping by using the hostname, the ping request fails in indicating that it could not find the host www.google.com. Answer A is incorrect because there is nothing shown to indicate a DHCP server issue. Answer B is incorrect because the question indicates the organization is using a private IP address scheme. Answer D is incorrect because successful pings to the Internet eliminate routing issues.

29. The correct order of the commands is as follows:

    a.___4__

    b.___3__

    c.___2__

    d.___8__

30. **E.** 127.0.0.1 is a reserved loopback address for testing connectivity to the local device (in this case, the server). Being able to successfully ping the loopback address does not indicate any connectivity capabilities outside the local system, making answers A, B, and C incorrect. Answer D is incorrect because pinging a local loopback address tests the ICMP protocol rather than TCP or UDP.

CHAPTER FOUR

IOS and Routing Foundations

This chapter covers the following ICND1 objectives that fall under the content area, **Implement a small, routed network:**

- Describe basic routing concepts (including packet forwarding, router lookup process).
- Describe the operation of Cisco routers (including router bootup process, POST, router components).
- Select the appropriate media, cables, ports, and connectors to connect routers to other network devices and hosts.
- Configure, verify, and troubleshoot RIPv2.
- Access and utilize the router CLI to set basic parameters.
- Connect, configure, and verify operation status of a device interface.
- Verify device configuration and network connectivity using ping, traceroute, Telnet, SSH, or other utilities.
- Perform and verify routing configuration tasks for a static or default route given specific routing requirements.
- Manage IOS configuration files (including save, edit, upgrade, restore).
- Manage Cisco IOS.
- Implement password and physical security.
- Verify network status and router operation using basic utilities (including ping, traceroute, Telnet, SSH, arp, ipconfig), and the **SHOW** and **DEBUG** commands.

Quick Check

1. You need to establish an EXEC session and access the command-line interface of your Cisco router. Which of the following access methods meet your requirements? (Choose three.)

   - ❍ **A.** Console connection
   - ❍ **B.** TFTP session
   - ❍ **C.** Telnet session
   - ❍ **D.** Modem connection
   - ❍ **E.** FTP session

Quick Answer: **87**
Detailed Answer: **88**

2. You are logged in to a router and want to view the IP address of neighboring Cisco routers. What IOS command gives this information for the directly connected neighbors?

   - ❍ **A.** **show ip clients**
   - ❍ **B.** **show cdp neighbor**
   - ❍ **C.** **show cdp neighbor detail**
   - ❍ **D.** **show ip links**
   - ❍ **E.** **show ip route**

Quick Answer: **87**
Detailed Answer: **88**

3. You want to assign an IP address to the FastEthernet 0/0 interface of a router. In Figure 4.1, draw lines connecting the modes of the router to the order of steps you would use to complete this task. Not all modes will be used.

Quick Answer: **87**
Detailed Answer: **88**

FIGURE 4.1 IOS command steps.

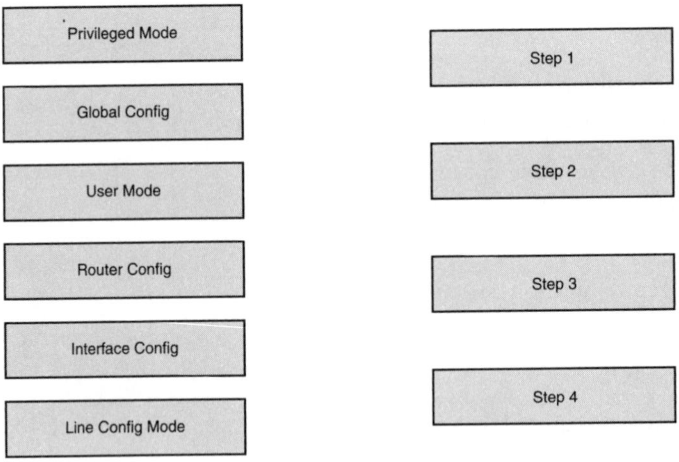

Modes	Steps
Privileged Mode	Step 1
Global Config	Step 2
User Mode	Step 3
Router Config	Step 4
Interface Config	
Line Config Mode	

Quick Check

4. During the boot process, your router stops at a ROMMON prompt. You suspect that the IOS has become corrupt. Which router component should you examine to verify your suspicions?

Quick Answer: **87**
Detailed Answer: **88**

- ❍ **A.** RAM
- ❍ **B.** NVRAM
- ❍ **C.** Hard Drive
- ❍ **D.** Flash
- ❍ **E.** ROM
- ❍ **F.** TFTP server connectivity

5. You connect to a router console port and press the Enter key. The router returns the following prompt:

Quick Answer: **87**
Detailed Answer: **89**

Router(config-line)#

What function is typically accomplished from this mode?

- ❍ **A.** Assigning passwords to the console or vty ports
- ❍ **B.** Assigning an IP address to the router
- ❍ **C.** Adjusting IOS location values
- ❍ **D.** Configuring logging to an external server

6. When working in the Cisco IOS, which commands move your cursor to the beginning of the line and end of the line, respectively?

Quick Answer: **87**
Detailed Answer: **89**

- ❍ **A.** CTRL-A, CTRL-Z
- ❍ **B.** CTRL-1, CTRL-9
- ❍ **C.** CTRL-A, CTRL-E
- ❍ **D.** CTRL-S, CTRL-Z

Quick Check

7. You are troubleshooting a Cisco router at one of your offices. The router seems to lose its configuration each time it is rebooted. You study the output shown below. What is the cause of the problem?

Quick Answer: **87**
Detailed Answer: **89**

```
Cisco 2801 (revision 5.0) with 238592K/23552K bytes of memory.
Processor board ID FTX0922W160
2 FastEthernet interfaces
1 terminal line
1 Virtual Private Network (VPN) Module
4 Voice FXO interfaces
1 DSP, 8 Voice resources
1 cisco service engine(s)
DRAM configuration is 64 bits wide with parity disabled.
191K bytes of NVRAM.
62592K bytes of ATA CompactFlash (Read/Write)
Configuration register is 0x2142
```

❍ **A.** The NVRAM is not marked as Read/Write.

❍ **B.** The configuration register is incorrect.

❍ **C.** The router has an insufficient DRAM configuration.

❍ **D.** 28XX series routers no longer save their configuration to NVRAM. Boot register settings should be modified to reflect this.

8. You are attempting to telnet to a router named CiscoWest as shown here:

Quick Answer: **87**
Detailed Answer: **89**

```
Router-1#telnet CiscoWest
Trying CiscoWest (10.3.3.1) ... Open
Password required, but none set
[Connection to CiscoWest closed by foreign host]
```

Which of the following is true?

❍ **A.** Your router does not currently have a Telnet password set.

❍ **B.** The CiscoWest router does not currently have a Telnet password set.

❍ **C.** Your router does not currently have an enable secret password set.

❍ **D.** The CiscoWest router does not currently have an enable secret password set.

Quick Check

9. Where does the router store its current configuration file while in operation?

Quick Answer: **87**
Detailed Answer: **89**

- ❍ **A.** NVRAM
- ❍ **B.** Flash
- ❍ **C.** RAM
- ❍ **D.** TFTP server
- ❍ **E.** ROM

10. You are a network technician at ACME Inc. A junior administrator at the company wants to know the sequence of events that occur when you power on a router. What is your reply?

Quick Answer: **87**
Detailed Answer: **89**

- ❍ **A.** POST, locate configuration, apply configuration, locate IOS, load IOS
- ❍ **B.** POST, locate IOS, load IOS, locate configuration, apply configuration
- ❍ **C.** Test memory consistency, run software routines, load IOS, apply configuration
- ❍ **D.** Test memory consistency, run software routines, apply configuration, load IOS

11. You notice by using a show version command that your Cisco router booted using the IOS image c2801-adventerprisek9-mz.124-4.XC.bin. What does the c2801 portion of the filename represent?

Quick Answer: **87**
Detailed Answer: **89**

- ❍ **A.** The memory requirements
- ❍ **B.** The boot register settings
- ❍ **C.** The configuration register
- ❍ **D.** The feature set
- ❍ **E.** The format of the IOS file
- ❍ **F.** The platform
- ❍ **G.** The version number

12. Which prompt displays the configuration mode that allows you to configure multiple virtual interfaces on a single physical interface?

Quick Answer: **87**
Detailed Answer: **89**

- ❍ **A.** router(config-if)#
- ❍ **B.** router(config-subif)#
- ❍ **C.** router(config-line)#
- ❍ **D.** router(config)#
- ❍ **E.** router(vt-int)#

Quick Check

Quick Answer: **87**
Detailed Answer: **89**

13. You are verifying the configuration of your Cisco router and notice the following:

```
Router-1#show running-config
...
line vty 0 4
 password cisco
 logging synchronous
 login
 transport input all
```

You want to prevent your vty password from being displayed in clear text in the running-configuration. How can this be accomplished?

- ❍ **A.** By entering the password using the command **secret cisco** rather than **password cisco**.
- ❍ **B.** By entering the command **service password-encryption** in global configuration mode, the password will be encrypted in both the running-configuration and when typed in Telnet sessions.
- ❍ **C.** By entering the command **service password-encryption** in global configuration mode, the password will be encrypted in the running-configuration but not when typed in Telnet sessions.
- ❍ **D.** Passwords entered under vty, con, and aux ports cannot be encrypted. Only passwords entered using the **enable secret** command can be encrypted.
- ❍ **E.** Passwords entered under vty, con, and aux ports cannot be encrypted. Only passwords entered using the **enable password** command can be encrypted.

Quick Check

14. You have installed a new WAN link to a remote office. After some initial testing, you find that the connection is not functional. Based on the following output, what is the most likely cause of the problem?

Quick Answer: **87**
Detailed Answer: **90**

```
RouterAZ#show interfaces serial 0
Serial0 is down, line protocol is down
  Hardware is HD64570
  Internet address is 10.1.1.1/24
  MTU 1500 bytes, BW 1544 Kbit, DLY 20000 usec,
     reliability 255/255, txload 1/255, rxload 1/255
  Encapsulation HDLC, loopback not set
  Keepalive set (10 sec)
  Last input never, output never, output hang never
  Last clearing of "show interface" counters never
  Input queue: 0/75/0/0 (size/max/drops/flushes); Total output drops: 0
  Queueing strategy: weighted fair
  Output queue: 0/1000/64/0 (size/max total/threshold/drops)
     Conversations  0/0/256 (active/max active/max total)
     Reserved Conversations 0/0 (allocated/max allocated)
  5 minute input rate 0 bits/sec, 0 packets/sec
  5 minute output rate 0 bits/sec, 0 packets/sec
     0 packets input, 0 bytes, 0 no buffer
     Received 0 broadcasts, 0 runts, 0 giants, 0 throttles
     0 input errors, 0 CRC, 0 frame, 0 overrun, 0 ignored, 0 abort
     0 packets output, 0 bytes, 0 underruns
     0 output errors, 0 collisions, 5 interface resets
     0 output buffer failures, 0 output buffers swapped out
     0 carrier transitions
     DCD=down  DSR=down  DTR=down  RTS=down  CTS=down
```

- ❍ **A.** The IP address assigned to the interface is invalid.
- ❍ **B.** The interface is shutdown.
- ❍ **C.** The interface does not have a cable attached.
- ❍ **D.** The interface is using HDLC encapsulation, whereas the remote end equipment is using PPP.

Quick Check

15. You have just installed and configured a new branch office, shown in Figure 4.2. The organization would prefer to use static routing between the Branch and HQ routers to save on overhead. In addition, the organization wants you to create a single static route on the Branch router that allows the users to access both the HQ LAN and the Internet. Write in the commands necessary to accomplish this configuration; the command prompts have been provided for you.

Quick Answer: **87**
Detailed Answer: **90**

FIGURE 4.2 Network diagram.

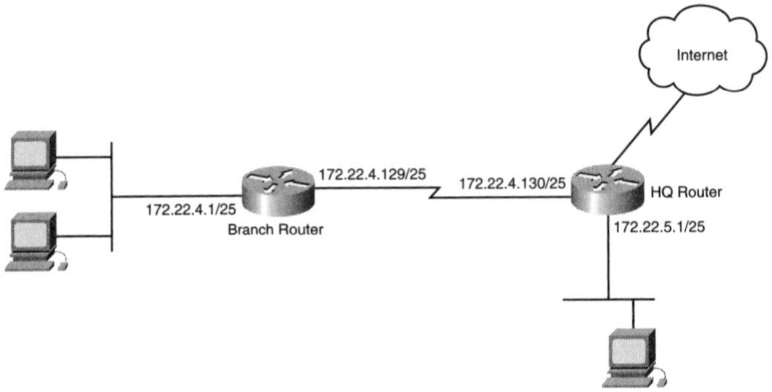

BranchRTR> ____

BranchRTR# ____

BranchRTR(config)#____

HQ_RTR> ____

HQ_RTR# ____

HQ_RTR(config)#____

Quick Check

Quick Answer: **87**
Detailed Answer: **90**

16. Your organization wants to run version 2 of the RIP protocol *only* on the 172.31.4.0/24 network, as shown in Figure 4.3. Which of the following configurations will accomplish this objective?

FIGURE 4.3 Network diagram.

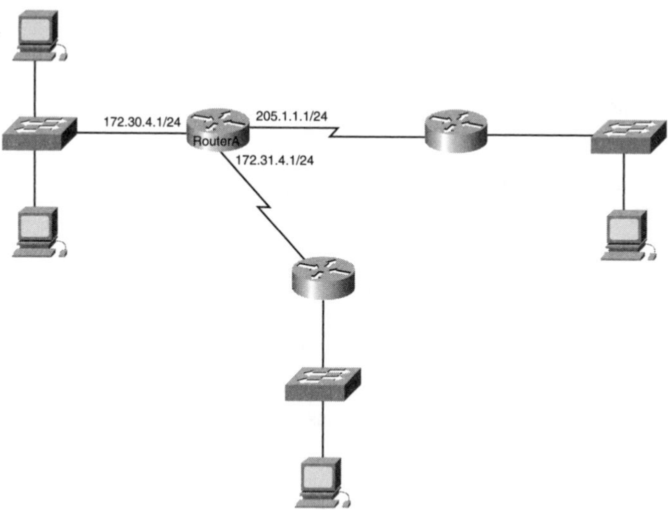

❍ **A.**

```
RouterA(config)#router rip
RouterA(config-router)#network 172.31.4.0
RouterA(config-router)#version 2
```

❍ **B.**

```
RouterA(config)#router rip 2
RouterA(config-router)#network 172.31.4.0
```

❍ **C.**

```
RouterA(config)#router rip
RouterA(config-router)#network 172.31.4.0 255.255.255.0
RouterA(config-router)#version 2
```

❍ **D.**

```
RouterA(config)#router rip
RouterA(config-router)#network 172.31.0.0
RouterA(config-router)#version 2
```

❍ **E.**

```
RouterA(config)#router rip 2
RouterA(config-router)#network 172.31.4.0 /24
```

Quick Check

17. One of the network administrators from your organization comes to you for help. When working on the Cisco router, he often has messages that interrupt what he is typing as shown in the following:

Quick Answer: **87**
Detailed Answer: **90**

```
AccessServer(config)#^Z
AccessServer#show ip
05:36:14: %SYS-5-CONFIG_I: Configured from console by consoleinterface
```

What methods can he use to keep this from happening? (Choose two.)

❍ **A.** Disable logging to the console port by typing **no logging console** from global configuration mode.

❍ **B.** Turn on the service interrupt by typing the command **service interrupt** from global configuration mode.

❍ **C.** Turn on the service interrupt by typing the command **service interrupt** from line configuration mode.

❍ **D.** Enable synchronous logging for the console port by typing the command **logging synchronous** from line configuration mode.

18. One of your organization's routers is experiencing issues with keeping its routing table consistent with the rest of the other routers. What command will allow you to see RIP updates as they are sent from and received by the router?

Quick Answer: **87**
Detailed Answer: **90**

❍ **A. show ip route**

❍ **B. show ip rip**

❍ **C. show ip protocol**

❍ **D. debug ip route**

❍ **E. debug ip rip**

❍ **F. debug rip updates**

Quick Check

19. You want to upgrade your IOS on your Cisco router. Before you do, you need to back up the existing IOS version from your router to a network server. Which of the following series of steps depicts the correct process?

Quick Answer: **87**
Detailed Answer: **90**

❍ **A.**

Step 1: Enable RCP server software on a client PC.

Step 2: Test connectivity between the router and PC.

Step 3: Verify the IOS filename in the router system: drive.

Step 4: Type the command **copy system rcp** from Privileged EXEC.

Step 5: Enter the correct IOS filename and RCP server address.

❍ **B.**

Step 1: Obtain a valid Cisco CCO backup license.

Step 2: Ensure the router is able to reach the Internet.

Step 3: Enter the command **backup CCO**.

Step 4: Enter your CCO account number when prompted.

❍ **C.**

Step 1: Insert a USB key in the provided USB port on the router.

Step 2: Verify the IOS filename.

Step 3: Type the command **flashusb** from Privileged EXEC.

Step 4: When the copy completes, remove the USB key and store in a safe place.

❍ **D.**

Step 1: Enable TFTP server software on a client PC.

Step 2: Test connectivity between the router and PC.

Step 3: Verify the IOS filename in the router Flash.

Step 4: Type the command **copy flash tftp** from Privileged EXEC.

Step 5: Enter the correct IOS filename and TFTP server address.

Quick Check

Quick Answer: **87**
Detailed Answer: **90**

20. You have pasted the configurations shown into the two new routers shown in Figure 4.4. HostA can connect to the Serial 0/0 interface of RouterA, but cannot reach HostB. RouterA can successfully ping the S1/0 interface of RouterB. The host configurations are verified as good. What could be the cause of the problem?

FIGURE 4.4 Network diagram.

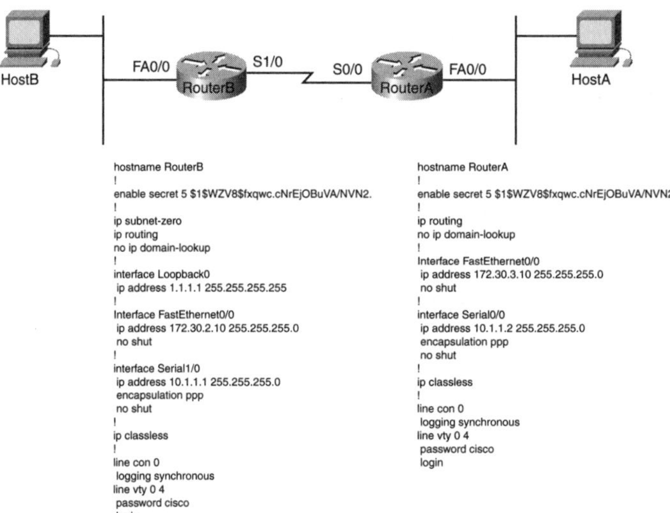


```
hostname RouterB
!
enable secret 5 $1$WZV8$fxqwc.cNrEjOBuVA/NVN2.
!
ip subnet-zero
ip routing
no ip domain-lookup
!
interface Loopback0
 ip address 1.1.1.1 255.255.255.255
!
Interface FastEthernet0/0
 ip address 172.30.2.10 255.255.255.0
 no shut
!
interface Serial1/0
 ip address 10.1.1.1 255.255.255.0
 encapsulation ppp
 no shut
!
ip classless
!
line con 0
 logging synchronous
line vty 0 4
 password cisco
 login
```

```
hostname RouterA
!
enable secret 5 $1$WZV8$fxqwc.cNrEjOBuVA/NVN2.
!
ip routing
no ip domain-lookup
!
Interface FastEthernet0/0
 ip address 172.30.3.10 255.255.255.0
 no shut
!
interface Serial0/0
 ip address 10.1.1.2 255.255.255.0
 encapsulation ppp
 no shut
!
ip classless
!
line con 0
 logging synchronous
line vty 0 4
 password cisco
 login
```

❍ **A.** RouterA is missing the **ip subnet-zero** command.

❍ **B.** The routers do not have any routes other than connected interfaces.

❍ **C.** Cisco routers should use HDLC encapsulation when communicating over WAN connections.

❍ **D.** RouterB has an invalid loopback interface.

Quick Check
Quick Answer: **87**
Detailed Answer: **91**

21. Based on the following output, which of the following networks represent an invalid route?

```
RouterAZ#show ip route
Codes: C - connected, S - static, R - RIP, M - mobile, B - BGP
       D - EIGRP, EX - EIGRP external, O - OSPF, IA - OSPF inter area
       N1 - OSPF NSSA external type 1, N2 - OSPF NSSA external type 2
       E1 - OSPF external type 1, E2 - OSPF external type 2, E - EGP
       i - IS-IS, su - IS-IS summary, L1 - IS-IS level-1, L2 - IS-IS level-2
       ia - IS-IS inter area, * - candidate default, U - per-user static route
       o - ODR, P - periodic downloaded static route

Gateway of last resort is 10.1.2.1 to network 0.0.0.0

     10.0.0.0/24 is subnetted, 2 subnets
C       10.1.1.0 is directly connected, FastEthernet0/0
C       10.1.2.0 is directly connected, FastEthernet0/1
     5.0.0.0/24 is subnetted, 3 subnets
R    5.1.1.0 [120/16] via 10.1.1.5, 00:00:10, FastEthernet0/0
R    5.2.1.0 [120/15] via 10.1.1.5, 00:00:10, FastEthernet0/0
R    5.3.1.0 [120/10] via 10.1.1.5, 00:00:10, FastEthernet0/0
R    192.168.1.0/24 [120/10] via 10.1.2.1, 00:00:10, FastEthernet0/1
R    192.168.2.0/24 [120/15] via 10.1.2.1, 00:00:10, FastEthernet0/1
R    192.169.3.0/24 [120/10] via 10.1.2.1, 00:00:10, FastEthernet0/1
S*   0.0.0.0/0 [1/0] via 10.1.2.1
```

- ❍ **A.** 10.1.1.0/24
- ❍ **B.** 5.1.1.0/24
- ❍ **C.** 5.2.1.0/24
- ❍ **D.** 5.3.1.0/24
- ❍ **E.** 192.168.1.0/24
- ❍ **F.** 192.168.2.0/24
- ❍ **G.** 192.169.3.0/24
- ❍ **H.** 0.0.0.0/0

Quick Check

22. Which of the connections shown in Figure 4.5 represent invalid cabling connections? (Choose three.)

Quick Answer: **87**
Detailed Answer: **91**

FIGURE 4.5 Network diagram.

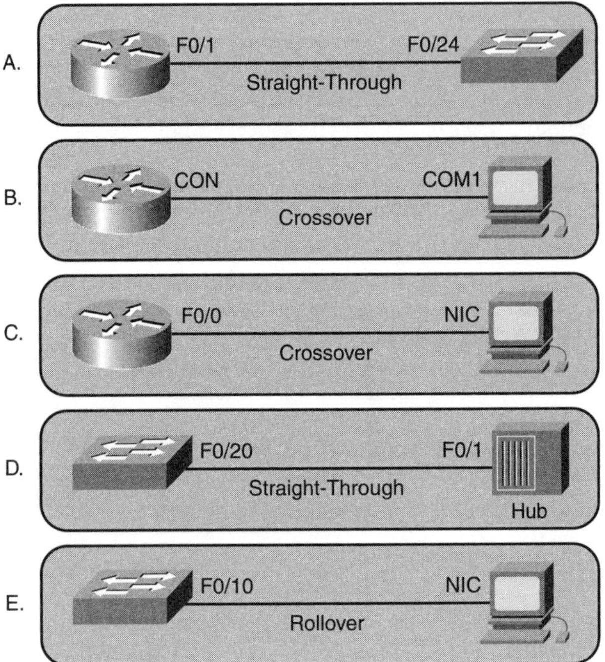

23. RouterB is connected to four upstream routers, as shown in Figure 4.6. It has just received a packet from the LAN with the destination IP address 192.168.5.5/24. Based on the following routing table output, what output interface will the router choose?

Quick Answer: **87**
Detailed Answer: **91**

```
RouterB#show ip route
Codes:C - connected, S - static, R - RIP, M - mobile, B - BGP
      D - EIGRP, EX - EIGRP external, O - OSPF, IA - OSPF inter area
      N1 - OSPF NSSA external type 1, N2 - OSPF NSSA external type 2
      E1 - OSPF external type 1, E2 - OSPF external type 2, E - EGP
      i - IS-IS, su - IS-IS summary, L1 - IS-IS level-1, L2 - IS-IS level-2
      ia - IS-IS inter area, * - candidate default, U - per-user static route
      o - ODR, P - periodic downloaded static route
```

Quick Check

```
Gateway of last resort is 192.168.4.1 to network 0.0.0.0

C    192.168.55.0/24 is directly connected, FastEthernet0/1
C    192.168.10.0/24 is directly connected, Serial0/0
C    192.168.50.0/24 is directly connected, Serial0/1
C    192.168.80.0/24 is directly connected, Serial1/0
C    192.168.4.0/24 is directly connected, Serial1/1
R    192.168.1.0/24 [120/2] via 192.168.10.1, 00:00:10, Serial0/0
R    192.168.2.0/24 [120/15] via 192.168.50.1, 00:00:11, Serial0/1

R    192.169.3.0/24 [120/10] via 192.168.80.2, 00:00:22, Serial1/0
S*   0.0.0.0/0 [1/0] via 192.168.4.1
```

FIGURE 4.6 Network diagram.

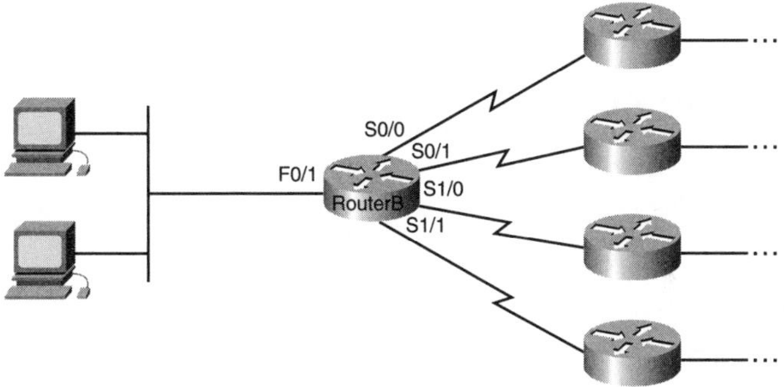

❍ **A.** F0/1

❍ **B.** S0/0

❍ **C.** S0/1

❍ **D.** S1/0

❍ **E.** S1/1

❍ **F.** The packet will be dropped.

Quick Check

24. In Figure 4.7, draw lines connecting the router memory components to their function.

Quick Answer: **87**
Detailed Answer: **91**

FIGURE 4.7 Memory components.

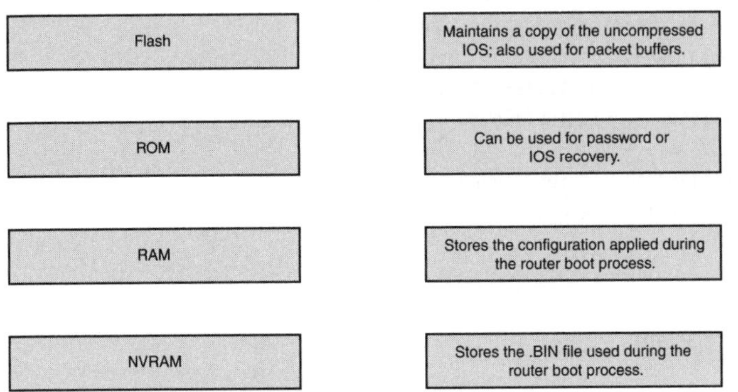

25. Your organization wants you to set all the Privileged EXEC passwords on the Cisco devices in the network to "appl3s33d!" using the most secure password storage available. What command will you use to accomplish this?

    - ❍ **A. privileged password appl3s33d!**
    - ❍ **B. privileged secret password appl3s33d!**
    - ❍ **C. enable password appl3s33d!**
    - ❍ **D. enable secret appl3s33d!**
    - ❍ **E. enable secret password appl3s33d!**
    - ❍ **F. service password-encryption appl3s33d!**

Quick Answer: **87**
Detailed Answer: **92**

26. You want to test the network connection between your corporate router (R1, shown in Figure 4.8) and ServerA. Which of the following results represent an accurate output for the **traceroute** command?

Quick Answer: **87**
Detailed Answer: **92**

FIGURE 4.8 Network diagram.

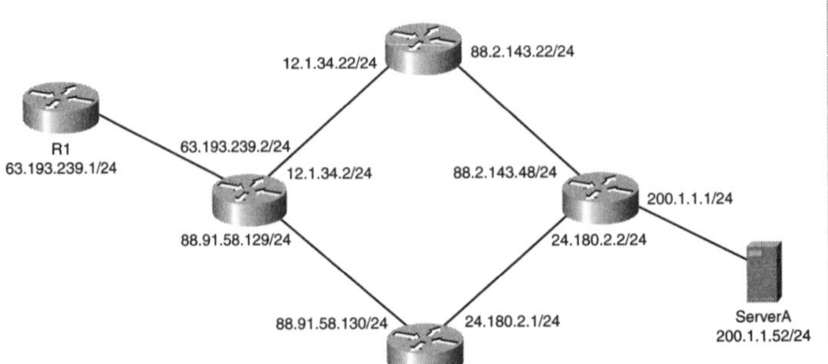

Quick Check

○ **A.**

```
R1#traceroute 200.1.1.52
Type escape sequence to abort.
Tracing the route to 200.1.1.52
  1 63.193.239.2 8 msec 12 msec 12 msec
  2 12.1.34.22 8 msec 12 msec 12 msec
  3 88.2.143.48 12 msec 12 msec 14 msec
  4 200.1.1.52 18 msec 13 msec 13 msec
```

○ **B.**

```
R1#traceroute 200.1.1.52
Type escape sequence to abort.
Tracing the route to 200.1.1.52
  1 63.193.239.1 12 msec 12 msec 12 msec
  2 63.193.239.2 8 msec 12 msec 12 msec
  3 12.1.34.22 8 msec 12 msec 12 msec
  4 88.2.143.48 12 msec 12 msec 14 msec
  5 200.1.1.52 18 msec 13 msec 13 msec
```

○ **C.**

```
R1#traceroute 200.1.1.52
Type escape sequence to abort.
Tracing the route to 200.1.1.52
  1 63.193.239.1 12 msec 12 msec 12 msec
  2 63.193.239.2 8 msec 12 msec 12 msec
  3 12.1.34.2 8 msec 12 msec 12 msec
  4 12.1.34.22 12 msec 12 msec 14 msec
  5 88.2.143.22 18 msec 13 msec 13 msec
  6 88.2.143.48 12 msec 12 msec 14 msec
  7 200.1.1.1 6 msec 14 msec 13 msec
  8 200.1.1.52 18 msec 13 msec 13 msec
```

○ **D.**

```
R1#traceroute 200.1.1.52
Type escape sequence to abort.
Tracing the route to 200.1.1.52
  1 63.193.239.2 8 msec 12 msec 12 msec
  2 12.1.34.2 8 msec 12 msec 12 msec
  3 12.1.34.22 12 msec 12 msec 14 msec
  4 88.2.143.22 18 msec 13 msec 13 msec
  5 88.2.143.48 12 msec 12 msec 14 msec
  6 200.1.1.1 6 msec 14 msec 13 msec
  7 200.1.1.52 18 msec 13 msec 13 msec
```

Quick Check

Quick Answer: **87**
Detailed Answer: **92**

27. You want to implement a logon banner on all of the Cisco routers in your network. Which of the following represent valid syntax to implement these logon banners? (Choose two.)

❍ **A.**

```
Router(config)#banner motd *
********************************
Unauthorized access prohibited
********************************
```

❍ **B.**

```
Router(config)#banner motd *Unauthorized access prohibited*
```

❍ **C.**

```
Router(config)#banner motd ##
********************************
Unauthorized access prohibited
********************************##
```

❍ **D.**

```
Router(config)#logon banner :
********************************
Unauthorized access prohibited
********************************:
```

❍ **E.**

```
Router(config)#banner begin &
********************************
Unauthorized access prohibited
********************************&
```

❍ **F.**

```
Router(config)#banner login ^
********************************
Unauthorized access prohibited
********************************^
```

Quick Check

Use Figure 4.9 to answer the following three questions.

FIGURE 4.9 Network diagram.

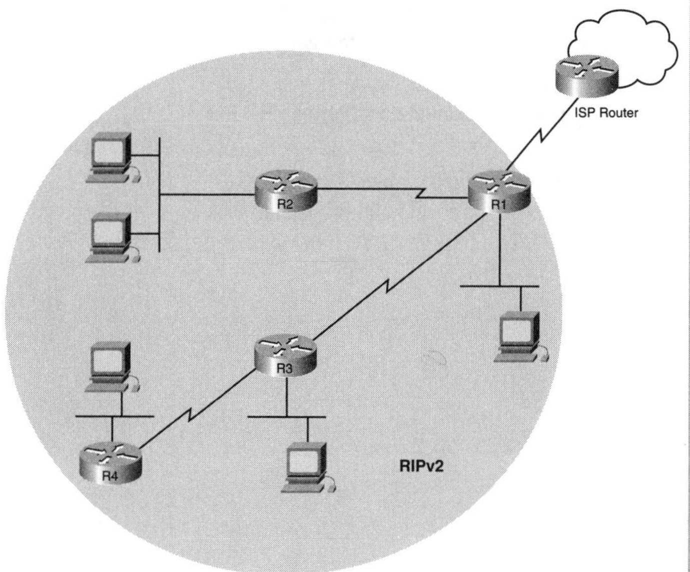

28. Which one of the routers shown in Figure 4.9 should have a static, default route?

Quick Answer: **87**
Detailed Answer: **92**

- ❍ **A.** R1
- ❍ **B.** R2
- ❍ **C.** R3
- ❍ **D.** R4
- ❍ **E.** ISP Router

29. After network convergence occurs, messages sent between routers would follow what guidelines?

Quick Answer: **87**
Detailed Answer: **92**

- ❍ **A.** Broadcasts sent once every 30 seconds
- ❍ **B.** Multicasts sent once every 30 seconds
- ❍ **C.** Hello messages sent once every 5 seconds
- ❍ **D.** Hello messages sent once every 10 seconds
- ❍ **E.** Messages sent only when the network topology changes

Quick Check

Quick Answer: **87**
Detailed Answer: **92**

30. If R3 only had RIPv1 capabilities and all other routers were running only RIPv2, what would be the result?

- ❍ **A.** RIPv2 is backward-compatible with RIPv1. Network operations would proceed as normal.
- ❍ **B.** R1 and R4 would detect the RIPv1 updates from R3 and would adjust their RIP versions to match.
- ❍ **C.** R3 would not understand RIPv2 updates and would create a "black hole" in the network between R1 and R4.
- ❍ **D.** Because RIPv1 is classful, R3 would automatically summarize routes sent from R1 and R4 back to their classful boundaries.

Quick Check Answer Key

1. A, C, D
2. C
3. See detailed answer
4. D
5. A
6. C
7. B
8. B
9. C
10. B
11. F
12. B
13. C
14. C
15. See detailed answer
16. D
17. A, D
18. E
19. D
20. B
21. B
22. B, D, E
23. E
24. See detailed answer
25. D
26. A
27. B, F
28. A
29. B
30. C

Answers and Explanations

1. **A, C, and D.** Command-line interfaces can be established through a Telnet session, modem connection, and console connection. Answer B is incorrect. Although TFTP is used to load a new IOS image onto a router, it does not allow you to establish a command-line interface session. Answer E is incorrect, as FTP sessions are not used to establish command-line interface sessions with Cisco routers.

2. **C.** Typing **show cdp neighbors** from user or privileged mode uses the Cisco Discovery Protocol (CDP) to discover any directly connected Cisco device. By adding the **detail** variable to the command, the router displays the IP address information of the remote devices. This powerful command works at the data link layer of the OSI model and can discover directly connected devices even if no IP address is configured on the local or remote interface! Answers A and B are incorrect because they are not valid commands. Answer E is incorrect because it shows the IP routing table for the device rather than the neighboring router IP address information.

3.

FIGURE 4.10 IOS command steps.

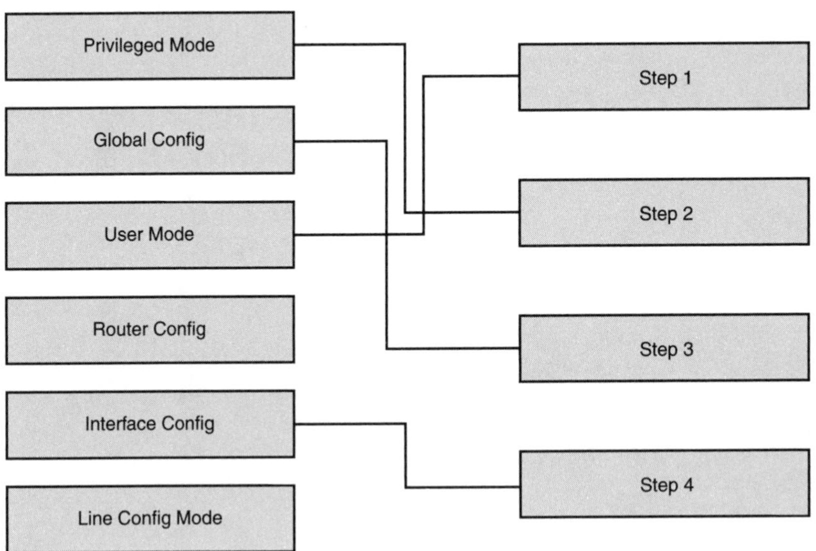

4. **D.** The IOS is stored in the flash of the router in a compressed format. During the boot sequence, the router decompresses the IOS into RAM. If the router is unable to find the IOS in flash, it will boot into ROMMON mode, allowing you to attempt an IOS recovery through TFTP or XMODEM.

5. **A.** An administrator will enter the line configuration mode to access the Console, AUX, or VTY ports of the router. This mode is typically accessed to assign login or password information to the ports. Answer B is incorrect because assigning IP addresses is done from interface configuration mode. Answers C and D are incorrect because these functions are performed from global configuration mode.

6. **C.** A helpful way to remember this is that the letter A is the beginning of the alphabet, and the letter E is the first letter in the word "end."

7. **B.** The default configuration register on a Cisco router is 0x2102. By changing it to 0x2142, the router ignores the startup configuration stored in NVRAM. You would typically change the configuration register to 0x2142 to perform password recovery on your router.

8. **B.** By default, Cisco routers do not have a password set under the VTY ports. To prevent users from reaching the unconfigured router, the IOS will display the **Password required, but none set** message to any host attempting to connect remotely through Telnet or SSH. If a router does not have an enable secret password set but has a password set under the VTY ports, a remote user will be able to telnet into user mode but will not be able to enter privileged mode.

9. **C.** The current configuration file is stored in RAM. If the router loses power or is rebooted, this configuration is lost. That is why it is important to save your configuration to NVRAM often by using the **copy running-config startup-config** command.

10. **B.** All Cisco devices initially complete a Power-On Self Test (POST) to discover and verify the installed hardware. From there, the device uses the configuration register settings to locate and load the Cisco IOS software followed by locating (using the configuration register) and applying the configuration to the router.

11. **F.** The IOS filename is typically divided into the following form: xxxx-yyyy-ww.aaa-bb.bin, where:

    xxxx = the platform

    yyyy = the feature set

    ww = the format (such as compression types)

    aaa = major version number

    bb = minor version number

12. **B.** Sub-interface config mode is typically used to allow the router to believe it has multiple logical connections out a single physical interface. These configurations are especially handy when routing between VLANs using a router-on-a-stick design or in Frame Relay environments. Answer A is incorrect because it only allows you to configure the physical interface.

13. **C.** The **service password-encryption** command encrypts *all* clear-text passwords on the router. While this encryption algorithm is considered weak in comparison to the hashing algorithm used for the **enable secret** command, it is better than having passwords stored in clear text. Answer B is incorrect because encryption is not applied to anything entered using the Telnet application, which is sent over the network in clear text.

14. **C.** Most likely, the interface does not have a cable attached. This is evidenced by the output "Serial0 is down, line protocol is down." If the problem was related to an IP addressing (Layer 3) issue, the Serial0 would show up and the line protocol would be up, making answer A incorrect. If the interface were shut down, the output would display "Serial0 is administratively down," making answer B incorrect. If the issue were related to an encapsulation mismatch, the output would display "Serial0 is up, line protocol is down," making answer D incorrect.

15.

```
BranchRTR> enable
BranchRTR# configure terminal
BranchRTR(config)# ip route 0.0.0.0 0.0.0.0 172.22.4.130

HQ_RTR> enable
HQ_RTR# configure terminal
HQ_RTR(config)# ip route 172.22.4.0 255.255.255.128 172.22.4.129
```

16. **D.** Version 1 of the RIP routing protocol is enabled by typing **router rip** from Global Configuration mode. To convert it to version 2, you simply enter the command **version 2** from Router Configuration mode. Finally, RIP network statements are always entered as though you were using a classful networking strategy. Because 172.31.4.0/24 was originally a class B address, the **network** statement must be entered as **network 172.31.0.0**. All other answers either enter this network command incorrectly (subnet masks are never used with the **network** command) or incorrectly assign the version number.

17. **A, D.** The preferred remedy for this issue is to turn on synchronous logging because many of the messages that are displayed are helpful to a network administrator. By turning off console logging, all log messages that are typically sent through the console port are suppressed. Answers B and C are incorrect because there is no **service interrupt** concept or command.

18. **E.** The **debug ip rip** command allows you to see real-time updates to the RIP process. Answers A, B, and C are incorrect because show commands do not display information as it happens. Rather, show commands display a snapshot of a router process at the time of execution. Answers D and F are incorrect because these debug commands are invalid syntax.

19. **D.** The five-step process shown depicts the steps to back up the Cisco IOS to a TFTP server. Answer A is incorrect because the system: drive of the router represents the router's RAM; the IOS is stored in Flash. Answer B is incorrect because this process is completely invalid (but quite creative). Answer C is incorrect because there is no "flashusb" command; although, newer routers do support external USB connectivity.

20. **B.** Based on the configurations shown, the routers do not know about each other's LAN networks. This is because there is no dynamic protocol configuration, nor are any static routes installed. Answer A is incorrect because the **ip subnet-zero** command allows the router to use the first and last subnet of a subnetted address. It will not have any impact on this scenario. Answer C is incorrect because Cisco routers can use HDLC or PPP without any adverse effect. Answer D is incorrect because the loopback interface configured on RouterB is a perfectly valid and common configuration to assign the router a virtual IP address.

21. **B.** 5.1.1.0/24 is the invalid route because the routing table shows it as 16 hops away—[120/16] (where 120 is the administrative distance and 16 is the hop count). RIP can support networks up to 15 hops away; 16 hops are considered unreachable. All other answers (even 192.169.3.0/24) represent valid networks.

22. **B, D, E.** Answer B is invalid because connections from the COM (serial) port of a PC to the Console (CON) of the router should use a rollover cable. Answer D is invalid because switch-to-switch, switch-to-hub, or hub-to-hub connections all use crossover cables. Answer E is invalid because connections from the network card (NIC) of a PC to a FastEthernet port of a switch should use straight-through Ethernet cabling. Answers A and C represent valid connections.

23. **E.** The packet will exit the S1/1 interface. This is because the router does not have a specific route for the 192.168.5.0/24 network, so it will rely on the default route. Based on the routing table, the default route next hop IP address is 192.168.4.1. Examining the routing table further reveals that the 192.168.4.0/24 network is a route directly connected to the Serial 1/1 interface. Answers A, B, C, and D represent interfaces connected to other networks that are not valid for this question. Answer F is incorrect because the packet would only be dropped in this if there was not a default route installed in the routing table.

24.

FIGURE 4.11 Memory components.

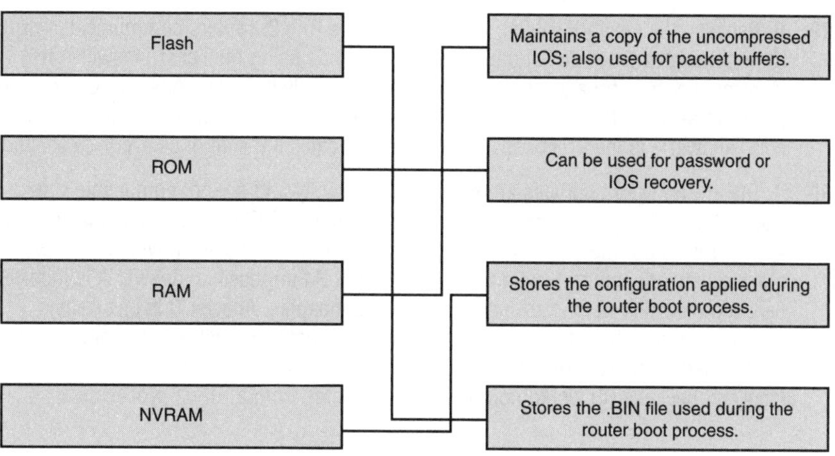

25. **D.** The **enable secret** command uses MD5 hashing to securely store the password in the running configuration. You can either enter the command **enable secret** *password* or **enable secret 0** *password* to enter the password into the IOS. The extra zero in the latter syntax form instructs the router that a clear text password, rather than a hashed form of the password, will follow. Answers A, B, E, and F are invalid commands. Answer C stores the Privileged EXEC password in the configuration in clear text, which is not the most secure storage available.

26. **A.** The **traceroute** command allows you to see all of the routers between your device and the destination device. Answer B is incorrect because the first hop that will be displayed from the **traceroute** command is the IP address of the next router, not your router. Answers C and D are incorrect because each router is only represented with a single IP address rather than the incoming and outgoing IP address of each interface.

27. **B, F.** You can add logon banners to a Cisco device by using either the **banner motd** *delimiting character* or **banner login** *delimiting character* syntax. The *delimiting character* variable should be a character that indicates the beginning and end of your logon banner. Answer A is incorrect because the delimiting character was used multiple times in the logon banner. Answer C is incorrect because the delimiting character must be a single character. Answers D and E are incorrect because the commands **logon banner** and **banner begin** produce invalid syntax messages.

28. **A.** Because R1 is directly connected to the Internet, it needs a default route to access Internet resources. Other routers in the network can either receive this default route via RIP, statically have their own default route, or not have access to Internet resources. All other answers to this question do not apply.

29. **B.** Because the network routing protocol in use is RIPv2, routers communicate normal routing updates (keepalives) once every 30 seconds using multicast. Answer A is incorrect because broadcast messaging was used only in RIPv1. Answers C and D are incorrect because the Hello protocol is used by the OSPF and EIGRP routing protocols. Answer E is incorrect because multicast updates are sent once every 30 seconds.

30. **C.** RIPv1 and RIPv2 updates are formatted differently and are not compatible with each other. Although a router can run both versions of RIP at a time, the question stated that this is not the case. This will cause R3 to become a black hole in the network, making network communication between R1 and R4 impossible. Answer A is incorrect because the RIP versions are not backwards compatible. Answer B is incorrect because routers are not able to detect version mismatches. Instead, the routers are hard-coded to the versions they will run by the network administrator. Answer D is incorrect because R3 would not understand updates from a RIPv2 process.

CHAPTER FIVE

Wireless and Network Security Concepts

This chapter covers the following ICND1 objectives that fall under the content areas, **Explain and select the appropriate administrative tasks required for a WLAN and Identify security threats to a network and describe general methods to mitigate those threats:**

- Describe standards associated with wireless media (including: IEEE WI-FI Alliance, ITU/FCC).
- Identify and describe the purpose of the components in a small wireless network (including SSID, BSS, and ESS).
- Identify the basic parameters to configure on a wireless network to ensure that devices connect to the correct access point.
- Compare and contrast wireless security features and capabilities of WPA security (including open, WEP, WPA-1/2).
- Identify common issues with implementing wireless networks.
- Explain today's increasing network security threats and the need to implement a comprehensive security policy to mitigate the threats.
- Explain general methods to mitigate common security threats to network devices, hosts, and applications.
- Describe the functions of common security appliances and applications.
- Describe security recommended practices including initial steps to secure network devices.

Quick Check

1. An intruder breaks into a network and retrieves an Excel spreadsheet detailing confidential corporate information. What type of network attack is this considered?

   ❍ **A.** Retrieval attack
   ❍ **B.** Reconnaissance attack
   ❍ **C.** Access attack
   ❍ **D.** Intrusion attack

Quick Answer: **105**
Detailed Answer: **106**

2. Which of the following should be a part of an organization's network security plan?

   ❍ **A.** Physically securing network equipment
   ❍ **B.** Designating specific dates for operating system patches or upgrades to allow patches or upgrades to be fully tested
   ❍ **C.** A password policy suggesting that users should use personal information in passwords to avoid forgetting or writing down password information
   ❍ **D.** Minimizing network overhead by breaking larger networks into VLANs

Quick Answer: **105**
Detailed Answer: **106**

3. After installing a central 802.11g wireless network, a few users are complaining about slow performance or signal drops. Other users on the same wireless network seem to be operating at peak efficiency. What are the most likely causes of this issue? (Choose three.)

   ❍ **A.** Mismatched AES encryption settings
   ❍ **B.** Invalid WEP key
   ❍ **C.** Cordless phones
   ❍ **D.** Metal file cabinets
   ❍ **E.** Incorrect SSID information
   ❍ **F.** Direction of the wireless antenna

Quick Answer: **105**
Detailed Answer: **106**

Quick Check

Use Figure 5.1 to answer the following three questions

FIGURE 5.1 Wireless network diagram.

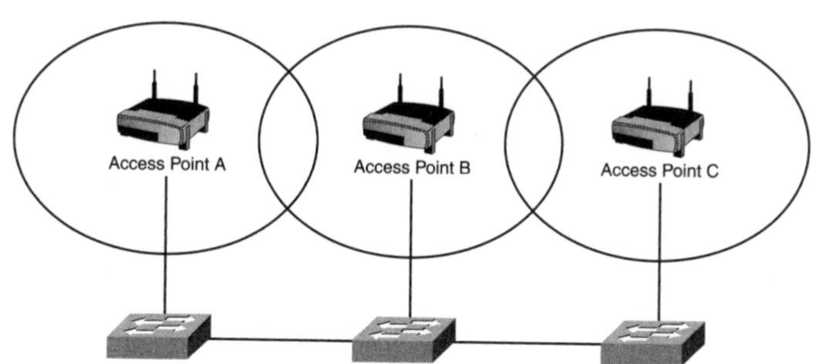

4. You have been assigned to manage the 802.11g wireless network shown in Figure 5.1. How should the wireless channels be configured on Access Points A, B, and C?

   Quick Answer: **105**
   Detailed Answer: **106**

   ❍ **A.** All access points should use the same channel.
   ❍ **B.** All access points should use different channels.
   ❍ **C.** Access points should use different wireless standards.
   ❍ **D.** Access point should use channels with nonoverlapping frequencies.

5. What amount of overlapping signal should you have between the different wireless access points?

   Quick Answer: **105**
   Detailed Answer: **106**

   ❍ **A.** Because overlapping signals interfere with each other, the amount of overlap should be minimized to less than 2 percent.
   ❍ **B.** The overlap should be between 5 to 10 percent.
   ❍ **C.** The overlap should be between 10 to 15 percent.
   ❍ **D.** The overlap should be between 15 to 20 percent.

6. Assuming the 802.11g wireless network shown in Figure 5.1 was deployed in the United States, what would be an ideal channel configuration?

   Quick Answer: **105**
   Detailed Answer: **106**

   ❍ **A.** All access points should use channel 1 or 3.
   ❍ **B.** All access points should use channel 3 or 6.
   ❍ **C.** The access points should use channels 1, 3, and 6, respectively.
   ❍ **D.** The access points should use channels 1, 6, and 11, respectively.

Quick Check

7. Four wireless access points have been installed and configured to provide wireless access to clients in a small office network. What type of network topology is in use?

Quick Answer: **105**
Detailed Answer: **106**

❍ **A.** BSS
❍ **B.** SSID
❍ **C.** ESS
❍ **D.** RFD
❍ **E.** RF

8. What statements accurately describe wireless network communication? (Choose three.)

Quick Answer: **105**
Detailed Answer: **107**

❍ **A.** Because it uses half-duplex, it is similar to hub-based communication.
❍ **B.** Clients use CSMA/CD communication.
❍ **C.** Clients may experience more interference issues than cable-based communication.
❍ **D.** Because of the WEP standard, communication is considered as secure as or more secure than wired communication.
❍ **E.** RF regulations may change depending on the country where wireless access is used.

9. While working through some network issues with a junior network administrator, you decide to add port security to one of the switches in the network. The junior network administrator asks why you would choose to configure port security. What do you answer?

Quick Answer: **105**
Detailed Answer: **107**

❍ **A.** To restrict unauthorized Telnet or SSH access
❍ **B.** To restrict unauthorized access to the network
❍ **C.** To restrict Internet access for specific network hosts
❍ **D.** To minimize the number of broadcasts on a given switch
❍ **E.** To minimize the number of DHCP requests on a given switch

Quick Check

10. What are two ways that you can protect your device configurations from being compromised from external security threats? (Choose two.)

- ❍ **A.** Use Telnet when managing devices from the Internet and SSH when managing devices locally.
- ❍ **B.** Use the command **transport input encrypted telnet** under all VTY lines.
- ❍ **C.** Configure a firewall that restricts external access to internal network equipment.
- ❍ **D.** Enter the command **exec-timeout 0 0** on the CON, AUX, and VTY ports.
- ❍ **E.** Use SSH to manage devices at all times.

Quick Answer: **105**
Detailed Answer: **107**

11. Which of the following organizations ensures interoperability between vendors of 802.11 products?

- ❍ **A.** Cisco
- ❍ **B.** IEEE
- ❍ **C.** ITU-T
- ❍ **D.** Wi-Fi Alliance
- ❍ **E.** ITU-11 Annex

Quick Answer: **105**
Detailed Answer: **107**

Quick Check

12. UserA (shown in Figure 5.2) would like to SSH to SwitchA. Given the network configuration, how would he accomplish this?

Quick Answer: **105**
Detailed Answer: **107**

FIGURE 5.2 Network diagram.

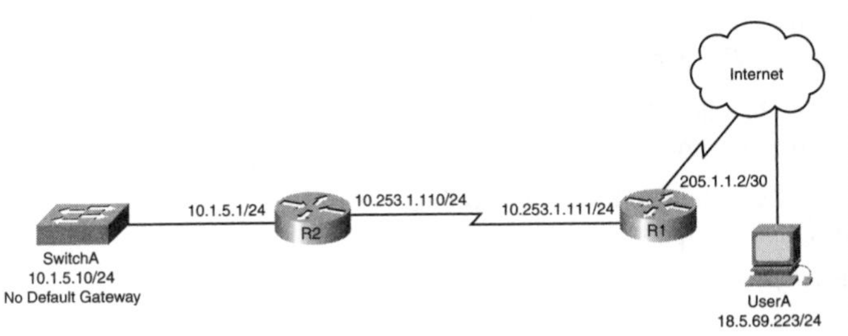

- ❍ **A.** UserA could SSH directly to SwitchA's IP address of 10.1.5.10.
- ❍ **B.** UserA would need to SSH directly to R2 first, and then SSH from R2 to SwitchA.
- ❍ **C.** UserA would need to SSH first to R1, then SSH to R2, and then SSH from R2 to SwitchA.
- ❍ **D.** Because the organization is using private addressing, UserA will not be able to reach SwitchA.
- ❍ **E.** For UserA to reach SwitchA, R1 would need to use Static NAT.

13. 802.11b/g equipment uses which of the following wireless RF bands?

Quick Answer: **105**
Detailed Answer: **107**

- ❍ **A.** 900-MHz
- ❍ **B.** 2.4-GHz
- ❍ **C.** 5-GHz
- ❍ **D.** 6.3-GHz

14. Your organization want to deploy a wireless network that uses the strongest possible security but still supports the use of a PSK. Which of the following security algorithms would you choose?

Quick Answer: **105**
Detailed Answer: **108**

- ❍ **A.** WEP 64-bit
- ❍ **B.** WEP 128-bit
- ❍ **C.** WPA
- ❍ **D.** WPA2

Quick Check

15. You have been asked to configure three new wireless laptops for the corporate network. After booting the laptop into its operating system, you are presented with a list of wireless networks to join. How did the client obtain this list of wireless networks?

Quick Answer: **105**
Detailed Answer: **108**

- ❍ **A.** The network wireless access points send out beacons at a regular interval announcing the SSIDs and data rates for the available wireless networks.
- ❍ **B.** The wireless client sent out probes on all channels to identify the available wireless networks.
- ❍ **C.** After its wireless card initializes, the wireless client sends out beacons announcing itself to the network. The wireless access points respond to the beacons with the available SSIDs.
- ❍ **D.** The client scans for the access point with the strongest signal and obtains a list of available SSIDs from that access point.

16. Which of the following represent network security appliances? (Choose two.)

Quick Answer: **105**
Detailed Answer: **108**

- ❍ **A.** ASA
- ❍ **B.** IOS
- ❍ **C.** IPS
- ❍ **D.** TCP
- ❍ **E.** ITF

17. Which of the following standards provides authentication for the LAN and WLAN?

Quick Answer: **105**
Detailed Answer: **108**

- ❍ **A.** WEP
- ❍ **B.** WPA
- ❍ **C.** WPA2
- ❍ **D.** 802.1x
- ❍ **E.** 802.3
- ❍ **F.** AES

18. What type of encryption does WPA2 use?

Quick Answer: **105**
Detailed Answer: **108**

- ❍ **A.** AES
- ❍ **B.** TKIP
- ❍ **C.** PSK
- ❍ **D.** TKIP with rotating IV

Quick Check

19. You are determining the best location for a wireless access point in your organization. Which of these materials would allow the LEAST amount of wireless signal to pass through?

- ❍ **A.** A drywall
- ❍ **B.** A wooden barrier
- ❍ **C.** A cubicle wall reinforced with sheet metal
- ❍ **D.** A brick wall

Quick Answer: **105**
Detailed Answer: **108**

20. For security reasons, CDP information from RouterA (shown in Figure 5.3) should be restricted from being sent to the Internet. However, this information should be accessible from the internal network. What command or series of commands will accomplish this objective?

Quick Answer: **105**
Detailed Answer: **108**

FIGURE 5.3 Network diagram.

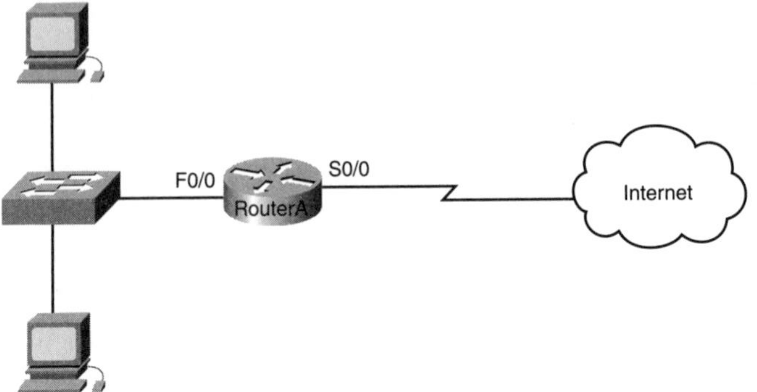

❍ **A.**

```
RouterA(config)#no cdp run
```

❍ **B.**

```
RouterA(config)#no cdp enable
```

❍ **C.**

```
RouterA(config)#interface s0/0
RouterA(config-if)#no cdp run
```

❍ **D.**

```
RouterA(config)#interface s0/0
RouterA(config-if)#no cdp enable
```

Quick Check

21. A network administrator plugged the office printer into port Fa0/24 of the Catalyst switch. The administrator wants to ensure that devices other than the printer will be prevented from accessing the switch. How can this be accomplished? (Choose two.)

Quick Answer: **105**
Detailed Answer: **108**

❍ **A.** Use a physical adapter on the port that is incompatible with other Ethernet cables.

❍ **B.** Configure an IP address restriction on the port to allow only the IP address assigned to the printer.

❍ **C.** Configure MAC address security on the port using the "sticky" option.

❍ **D.** Limit the number of MAC addresses allowed on the port to one.

❍ **E.** Create a static MAC to IP address mapping on the switch linking the MAC address on Fa0/24 to the static IP address assigned to the printer.

22. What are two characteristics of Telnet?

Quick Answer: **105**
Detailed Answer: **109**

❍ **A.** It should be used over SSH when managing devices on the internal network.

❍ **B.** It should be used over SSH when managing devices on the external network.

❍ **C.** All communication is transmitted in clear text.

❍ **D.** It is no longer supported on newer Cisco devices.

❍ **E.** It requires that the destination device be configured to receive incoming Telnet connections.

Quick Check

Quick Answer: **105**
Detailed Answer: **109**

23. You have just finished physically installing a new router in your organization. You must now work through the initial configuration and security of the router. This initial configuration should meet these objectives:

- The router should be named "CCNARouter".
- Privileged EXEC is accessible only after entering the password "ci$co".
- The logon banner should read "**Unauthorized access prohibited**".
- VTY, CON, and AUX ports all require the password "Cisco".
- Idle Telnet/SSH sessions to the router should terminate after 15 minutes.
- Configuration should be committed to NVRAM.

Write in the commands necessary to accomplish this configuration; the command prompts and a few key configuration mode changes have been provided for you.

Router>____________________

Router#____________________

Router(config)#____________________

CCNARouter(config)#____________________

CCNARouter(config)#____________________

CCNARouter(config)#**line con 0**

CCNARouter(config-line)#____________________

CCNARouter(config-line)#____________________

CCNARouter(config-line)#**exit**

CCNARouter(config)#**line aux 0**

CCNARouter(config-line)#____________________

CCNARouter(config-line)#____________________

CCNARouter(config-line)#**exit**

CCNARouter(config)#**line vty 0 4**

CCNARouter(config-line)#____________________

CCNARouter(config-line)#____________________

CCNARouter(config-line)#____________________

CCNARouter(config-line)#**^Z**

CCNARouter#____________________

Quick Check

24. Which of the following would be considered the strongest passwords? (Choose two.)

Quick Answer: **105**
Detailed Answer: **109**

- ❍ **A.** FidoTheDogAteMyLUNCH
- ❍ **B.** #Enabl3S
- ❍ **C.** 4acce552mySysteMz
- ❍ **D.** stormyweather5!
- ❍ **E.** 5up3rS3cur3)

25. While sitting at a conference table, you and a co-worker establish wireless connectivity directly between your laptops. What type of wireless topology has been created?

Quick Answer: **105**
Detailed Answer: **109**

- ❍ **A.** BSS
- ❍ **B.** IBSS
- ❍ **C.** ESS
- ❍ **D.** WPA
- ❍ **E.** SSID

26. Your network security policy indicates that only one device may attach to each switchport. Ports that violate this policy should immediately shut down. What three commands must you use on your Catalyst switch to implement these parameters on all switchports? (Choose three.)

Quick Answer: **105**
Detailed Answer: **110**

- ❍ **A.** Switch(config)#**mac-address maximum 1**
- ❍ **B.** Switch(config-if)#**switchport port-security**
- ❍ **C.** Switch(config-if)#**mac-address maximum 1**
- ❍ **D.** Switch(config-if)#**switchport port-security maximum 1**
- ❍ **E.** Switch(config)#**mac-address violation shutdown**
- ❍ **F.** Switch(config-if)#**switchport port-security violation shutdown**

27. What is the maximum data rate specified for 802.11g wireless networks?

Quick Answer: **105**
Detailed Answer: **110**

- ❍ **A.** 10Mbps
- ❍ **B.** 11Mbps
- ❍ **C.** 54Mbps
- ❍ **D.** 100Mbps

Quick Check

28. Which of the following are characteristics of WEP wireless security? (Choose four.)

Quick Answer: **105**
Detailed Answer: **110**

- ❍ **A.** Static encryption keys
- ❍ **B.** Dynamic encryption keys
- ❍ **C.** No strong authentication capabilities
- ❍ **D.** Strong authentication capabilities
- ❍ **E.** Compatible with MAC address filtering
- ❍ **F.** Incompatible with MAC address filtering
- ❍ **G.** Uses TKIP encryption with rotating IV
- ❍ **H.** Uses RC4-based encryption
- ❍ **I.** Uses AES encryption

29. What two modes are supported by WPA and WPA2 security?

Quick Answer: **105**
Detailed Answer: **110**

- ❍ **A.** Authentication mode
- ❍ **B.** Personal mode
- ❍ **C.** Enterprise mode
- ❍ **D.** Supplicant mode
- ❍ **E.** Authenticator mode

30. Which of the following encryption strategies offers more security?

Quick Answer: **105**
Detailed Answer: **110**

```
enable secret 5 $1$xJI4$zr8uhNfb5.uRdlVz45q/7/
enable password 7
➥08205F4A0F1801111D0A050E2E2A2B71633431170D171005
```

- ❍ **A.** The **enable secret 5** encryption scheme offers stronger security.
- ❍ **B.** The **enable password 7** encryption scheme offers stronger security.
- ❍ **C.** Because the **service password-encryption** command was entered on this device, both passwords are equally secure.
- ❍ **D.** The encryption algorithms are equally secure; however, because the enable secret uses special characters, it is more difficult to break.

Quick Check Answer Key

1. C
2. A
3. C, D, F
4. D
5. C
6. D
7. C
8. A, C, E
9. B
10. C, E
11. D
12. C
13. B
14. D
15. A
16. A, C
17. D
18. A
19. C
20. D
21. C, D
22. C, E
23. See detailed answer
24. B, E
25. B
26. B, D, F
27. C
28. A, C, E, H
29. B, C
30. A

Answers and Explanations

1. **C.** Attacks designed to retrieve data, gain access to resources, or escalate access privileges are typically known as access attacks. Answers A and D are incorrect because these are not known attack categories. Answer B is incorrect because reconnaissance attacks are designed to learn information about a target network.

2. **A.** Physically securing network equipment should always be part of an organization's security plan. If network devices are not physically secure, the passwords on those devices can be quickly removed. Answers B and D are incorrect because, although these are good recommendations for a Microsoft Windows deployment, they should not be part of a network security plan. Answer C is incorrect because using personal information in passwords is exactly the opposite of a good security policy.

3. **C, D, F.** If some users are experiencing great wireless network performance, you can assume the access point is operating correctly. You should begin focusing on interference issues with the clients experiencing performance issues. Cordless phones, metal file cabinets, and the direction of the wireless antenna can all have an impact on a user's wireless signal and performance. Answers A, B, and E are incorrect because any of these issues would result in the user's inability to use the corporate wireless network.

4. **D.** The wireless access points should use channels with nonoverlapping frequencies. This is not the same as using different channels, since many of the channels share the same radio frequency between them (which is why answer B is incorrect). Answer A is incorrect because using the same channel will cause the wireless access points to interfere with each other, causing poor network performance in the areas where the signal overlaps. Answer C is incorrect because using different wireless standards (such as 802.11a, b, g, or n) would prevent wireless clients from seamlessly roaming between access points.

5. **C.** Providing an overlapping wireless signal of 10 to 15 percent between access points is one step toward allowing seamless wireless client roaming around the network. As long as you are using nonoverlapping channels, the signals should not cause interference with each other. All other answers to this question do not apply.

6. **D.** In the USA, the 802.11b/g channels 1, 6, and 11 are the only nonoverlapping channels available for close-proximity wireless access points. Using other channels will cause frequency overlap and thus, network interference. All other answers do not apply to this question.

7. **C.** An Extended Service Set (ESS) wireless network topology describes one or more Basic Service Sets (BSSs) combined into a single system. Answer A is incorrect because a BSS describes a wireless network managed by a single access point. Answer B is incorrect because the Service Set Identifier (SSID) describes the name of the wireless network. Answers D and E are incorrect because they are acronyms that do not apply to this question.

8. **A, C, E.** Wireless network communication is half-duplex because the RF signal cannot support full-duplex communication. In this way, it is similar to a hub. Wireless clients may experience more interference than wired devices because many more devices (such as cordless phones or microwaves) share the same RF band. Answer B is incorrect because wireless clients use CSMA/CA communication rather than CSMA/CD. Answer D is incorrect because WEP has many security vulnerabilities that can be easily exploited.

9. **B.** Port security allows you to specify the maximum number of MAC addresses or even what MAC addresses will be able to use a given switchport. This gives you more control over what hosts are able to access the network. Answer A is incorrect because port security does not affect Telnet or SSH access specifically. Answer C is incorrect because port security limits all access rather than just Internet access. Answer D is incorrect because VLANs help minimize broadcasts. Answer E is incorrect because port security does not affect DHCP requests.

10. **C, E.** Using a firewall to protect your internal network from outside access is one of the best preventions to external security threats. In addition, using SSH to manage devices ensures encrypted communication that cannot be easily viewed using a packet sniffer. Answer A is incorrect because Telnet sends all communication in clear text. Answer B is incorrect because this is invalid syntax. Answer D is incorrect because the **exec-timeout 0 0** command prevents an idle CON, AUX, or VTY session from disconnecting, which poses many security threats.

11. **D.** The Wi-Fi Alliance is a global, nonprofit industry association, which owns the rights to the "WiFi Certified" logo. The Wi-Fi Alliance certifies interoperability between vendors of 802.11 products. Answer A is incorrect because Cisco does not take on this responsibility itself. Answer B is incorrect because the IEEE is the group that manages the 802.11 standards rather than vendor compatibility. Answer C is incorrect because the ITU-T regulates the RF signals used by wireless devices. Answer E is an organization that does not exist.

12. **C.** Because the organization is using private addressing, UserA would first need to SSH directly to R1 (which has an Internet-accessible address). Once logged into R1, UserA would need to SSH to R2. This is because SwitchA is not assigned a default gateway and cannot respond outside its own network. Once on R2, UserA could then SSH to SwitchA because R2 is plugged into the same network. Answer A is incorrect because private addresses are inaccessible from the Internet. Answer B is incorrect because SwitchA does not have a default gateway. Answer D is incorrect because UserA can reach R1's public address and then move from R1 into the privately addressed network. Answer E is incorrect because UserA can accomplish the task without Static NAT mappings.

13. **B.** 802.11b/g wireless equipment uses the unlicensed 2.4-GHz RF band. Many other cordless and wireless devices also share this same band and can interfere with wireless communication. Answer C is incorrect because 802.11a uses the 5-GHz RF band. Answers A and D are RF bands not used by modern wireless networking equipment.

14. **D.** All the security algorithms shown support pre-shared key (PSK) methods of encryption. WPA2 is the strongest of the group because it uses AES encryption methods. Answers A and B are incorrect because the WEP algorithm is considered the weakest of the group. Answer C is incorrect because the initial WPA method used TKIP encryption, which is backwards-compatible with older wireless hardware and stronger than WEP but still not as strong as AES.

15. **A.** Wireless access points send beacons announcing the available wireless SSIDs. The wireless client scans all wireless channels listening for these beacons and builds a list of available wireless networks as the beacons are received. Answer B is incorrect because the client listens to beacons rather than sending out probes. Answer C is incorrect because the access point sends out beacons rather than the client. Answer D is incorrect because the client is passive, not active in the SSID-identification process.

16. **A, C.** The Cisco Adaptive Security Appliance (ASA) acts as a firewall and VPN appliance while the Cisco Intrusion Prevention System (IPS) appliance identifies, classifies, and stops malicious activity in your network. Answer B is incorrect because the Cisco IOS is software rather than an appliance. Answers D and E do not apply to this question.

17. **D.** 802.1X, which is also known as EAP over LAN (EAPoL), is a security method that brings authentication to the LAN and WLAN environments. Answers A, B, and C are incorrect because these are security standards used for wireless technology. Answer E is incorrect because 802.3 is the standard for Ethernet technology. Answer F is incorrect because AES is an encryption standard used in many network technologies.

18. **A.** WPA2 uses AES encryption, which is currently one of the most secure encryption types widely available for wireless networking. Answer B is incorrect because WPA uses TKIP encryption. Answer C is incorrect because PSK simply stands for "pre-shared key" and does not directly correlate to an encryption type. Answer D is incorrect because this is also related to WPA.

19. **C.** Metal objects completely reflect wireless signals, which is why you should never mount wireless access points next to objects like metal file cabinets. Answers A, B, and D are incorrect. All these materials will absorb the wireless signal in varying degrees (with the brick wall being the greatest).

20. **D.** By entering the command **no cdp enable** from Interface Configuration mode, you will disable CDP multicasts from that single interface without affecting the rest of the router. Answers A and C are incorrect because typing **no cdp run** from Global Configuration mode (or Interface Configuration mode, which moves you back to Global Configuration mode) disables CDP on the entire router. Answer B will produce invalid syntax because this command is executed from the wrong mode.

21. **C, D.** Using the command **switchport port-security mac-address sticky** from Interface Configuration mode of a switch allows the switch to hard-code any MAC addresses dynamically learned under the interface into the running configuration. When combined with the command **switchport port-security maximum 1**, the first MAC address learned on the interface will be the only allowed MAC address. Answer A describes a device that does not exist. Answers B and E are possible, but would require much more work than the simpler answers C and D.

22. **C, E.** When using the Telnet protocol, all communication is sent in clear text. It should never be used when an SSH connection is available (making answers A and B incorrect). Because of its ease of use and widespread client support, old and new Cisco devices can receive Telnet connections when configured to do so, making answer D incorrect.

23. The correct configuration is as follows:

```
Router>enable
Router#configure terminal
Router(config)#hostname CCNARouter
CCNARouter(config)#enable secret ci$co (could also use "enable password")
CCNARouter(config)#banner motd %**Unauthorized access prohibited**%
CCNARouter(config)#line con 0
CCNARouter(config-line)#login
CCNARouter(config-line)#password Cisco
CCNARouter(config-line)#exit
CCNARouter(config)#line aux 0
CCNARouter(config-line)#login
CCNARouter(config-line)#password Cisco
CCNARouter(config-line)#exit
CCNARouter(config)#line vty 0 4
CCNARouter(config-line)#login
CCNARouter(config-line)#password Cisco
CCNARouter(config-line)#exec-timeout 15 0 (could also use "exec-timeout
15"
CCNARouter(config-line)#^Z
CCNARouter#copy running-config startup-config
```

24. **B, E.** Strong passwords are defined as having at least eight characters, containing uppercase letters, lowercase letters, numbers, and special characters. This combination makes scripted brute force and dictionary attack mechanisms much less efficient at breaking the password. Answers A, C, and D are each missing one of these criteria.

25. **B.** An Independent Basic Service Set (IBSS) describes a wireless network directly connecting mobile clients without the need for an intermediary access point. Answer A is incorrect because a BSS is a wireless network managed by a single access point. Answer C is incorrect because an ESS is a wireless network managed by two or more access points. Answer D is incorrect because WPA is a wireless security standard. Answer E is incorrect because an SSID simply identifies the wireless network.

26. **B, D, F.** To configure port security on a switch to only allow a single MAC address per port, the following commands must be entered on a per-interface basis:

```
Switch(config)#interface fa0/1
Switch(config-if)#switchport port-security !enables port-security
Switch(config-if)#switchport port-security maximum 1 !limits interface
➥to one MAC address
Switch(config-if)#switchport port-security violation shutdown !diables
➥port if violated
```

This process can be configured on all ports by using the **interface range** command:

```
Switch(config)#interface range fa0/1 - 24
Switch(config-range)#switchport port-security !enables port-security
Switch(config-range)#switchport port-security maximum 1 !limits interface
➥to one MAC address
Switch(config-range)#switchport port-security violation shutdown !diables
➥port if violated
```

Answers A, C, and E produce invalid syntax.

27. **C.** Both 802.11g and 802.11a support a maximum data rate of 54Mbps. 802.11b supports a maximum data rate of 11Mbps. All other answers do not apply.

28. **A, C, E, H.** All of these criteria apply to WEP encryption keys. Answer B is incorrect because dynamic encryption keys are a feature available in WPA and WPA2 wireless security. Answer D is incorrect because WEP does not support strong authentication; rather, it only supports Open and Shared authentication (Shared is considered weaker than Open authentication). Answer F is incorrect because WEP can be used in combination with MAC address filtering. Answers G and I are incorrect because WPA uses TKIP encryption, and WPA2 uses AES encryption.

29. **B, C.** WPA and WPA2 support Personal and Enterprise modes. Personal mode uses a pre-shared key (PSK) for authentication while Enterprise mode integrates with 802.1x/EAP for authentication. Answers A, D, and E are incorrect because these are not valid modes; rather, they are components of the 802.1x authentication strategy.

30. **A.** The **enable secret** command uses a form of hashing rather than encryption and is considered much more secure than the encryption employed by the **service password-encryption** command. In turn, this makes answers B, C, and D incorrect.

CHAPTER SIX

Basic WAN Connectivity

This chapter covers the following ICND1 objectives that fall under the content areas, **Implement and verify WAN links:**

- Describe different methods for connecting to a WAN.
- Configure and verify a basic WAN serial connection.

Quick Check

Quick Answer: **122**
Detailed Answer: **123**

1. What physical WAN cabling plugs into a Cisco serial port?

   ❍ **A.** EIA/TIA-232

   ❍ **B.** EIA/TIA-449

   ❍ **C.** V.35

   ❍ **D.** DB-60

Quick Check

2. Your organization has just installed a new WAN connection to a remote office. Draw lines to match the appropriate term to its location on the network diagram shown in Figure 6.1. Each term will be used only once, and not all terms will be used.

Quick Answer: **122**
Detailed Answer: **123**

FIGURE 6.1 Network diagram.

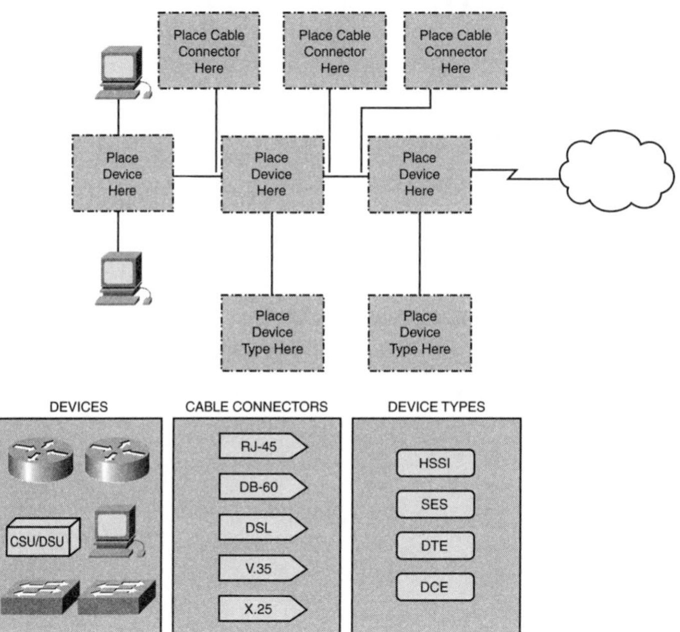

3. You have been asked to configure a Frame Relay connection between two offices. One of the junior network administrators is assisting with a remote router. He asks what layer of the OSI model Frame Relay communication uses. How do you respond?

   ❍ **A.** The physical layer
   ❍ **B.** The data link layer
   ❍ **C.** The network layer
   ❍ **D.** The OSI model describes LAN communication and does not apply to WAN networks.

Quick Answer: **122**
Detailed Answer: **123**

Quick Check

4. Which of the following represent WAN protocols? (Choose three.)

Quick Answer: **122**
Detailed Answer: **124**

- ❍ **A.** Fiber optic
- ❍ **B.** ATM
- ❍ **C.** HDLC
- ❍ **D.** T1
- ❍ **E.** Leased lines
- ❍ **F.** Packet switched
- ❍ **G.** PPP

5. Your organization has ordered a Fractional T1 connection that will consist of six DS0 channels. How much bandwidth is provided by this connection?

Quick Answer: **122**
Detailed Answer: **124**

- ❍ **A.** 56Kbps
- ❍ **B.** 64Kbps
- ❍ **C.** 336Kbps
- ❍ **D.** 384Kbps
- ❍ **E.** 672Kbps
- ❍ **F.** 768Kbps
- ❍ **G.** 1.544Mbps

6. How many DS0s are contained in a T1 and a T3 connection, respectively?

Quick Answer: **122**
Detailed Answer: **124**

- ❍ **A.** 12, 24
- ❍ **B.** 24, 72
- ❍ **C.** 24, 672
- ❍ **D.** 30, 90

7. To test WAN connectivity, you have connected two Cisco routers in a lab environment using a serial crossover cable. What command would you use to set the speed of the connection to 250Kbps?

Quick Answer: **122**
Detailed Answer: **124**

- ❍ **A.** **bandwidth 250**
- ❍ **B.** **bandwidth 250000**
- ❍ **C.** **clock rate 250**
- ❍ **D.** **clock rate 250000**
- ❍ **E.** **clockrate 250**
- ❍ **F.** **clockrate 250000**

Quick Check
Quick Answer: **122**
Detailed Answer: **124**

8. You are configuring R2 (shown in Figure 6.2) to connect using a leased T1 line to R1. Until now, R2's serial interface has not been configured. What three commands do you need to enter to bring up the WAN connection between R1 and R2? (Choose three.)

FIGURE 6.2 Network diagram.

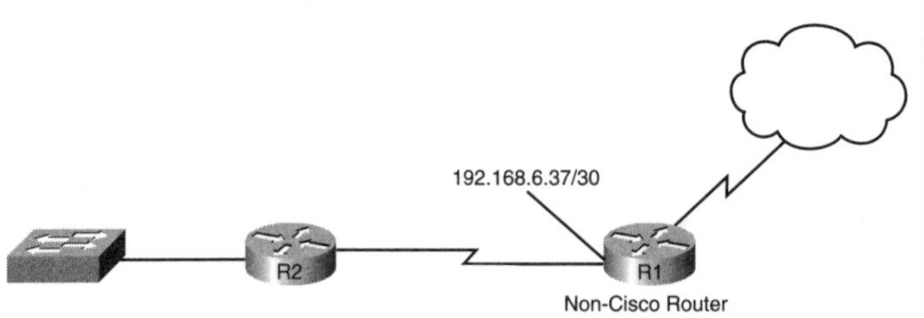

- ❍ **A.** R2(config-if)#**enable**
- ❍ **B.** R2(config-if)#**no shutdown**
- ❍ **C.** R2(config-if)#**ip address 192.168.6.35 255.255.255.252**
- ❍ **D.** R2(config-if)#**ip address 192.168.6.36 255.255.255.252**
- ❍ **E.** R2(config-if)#**ip address 192.168.6.38 255.255.255.252**
- ❍ **F.** R2(config-if)#**encapsulation ppp**
- ❍ **G.** R2(config-if)#**encapsulation hdlc**
- ❍ **H.** R2(config-if)#**encapsulation frame-relay**

Use the following command output to answer the following three questions:

```
Interface Serial0/1/0
Hardware is GT96K
DTE V.35 clocks stopped.
idb at 0x6613D454, driver data structure at 0x66144B98
wic_info 0x661451AC
Physical Port 0, SCC Num 0
MPSC Registers:
MMCR_L=0x000304C0, MMCR_H=0x00000000, MPCR=0x00000000
CHR1=0x00FE007E, CHR2=0x80000000, CHR3=0x000005F6, CHR4=0x00000000
CHR5=0x00000000, CHR6=0x00000000, CHR7=0x00000000, CHR8=0x00000000
CHR9=0x00000000, CHR10=0x00002000
```

```
SDMA Registers:
SDC=0x00002201, SDCM=0x00000080, SGC=0x0000C000
CRDP=0x0EDCA600, CTDP=0x0EDCA850, FTDB=0x0EDCA850
Main Routing Register=0x0003FFF8 BRG Conf Register=0x00490013
Rx Clk Routing Register=0x76543218 Tx Clk Routing Register=0x76543219
GPP Registers:
Conf=0x30002   , Io=0x64000   , Data=0x7F1BBFFB, Level=0x180000
Conf0=0x30002   , Io0=0x64000   , Data0=0x7F1BBFFB, Level0=0x180000
TDM FPGA Registers:
TDM FPGA Version: 23.0
```

9. Which of the following commands was used to generate the preceding output?

Quick Answer: **122**
Detailed Answer: **124**

- ❍ **A. show interfaces**
- ❍ **B. show controllers**
- ❍ **C. show hardware**
- ❍ **D. show rx ring**

10. Based on the preceding output, which of the following cable types is connected to the Serial0/1/0 interface?

Quick Answer: **122**
Detailed Answer: **124**

- ❍ **A.** Level 0
- ❍ **B.** SDMA male interface
- ❍ **C.** SDMA female interface
- ❍ **D.** DTE
- ❍ **E.** DCE

11. The preceding output indicates a problem with the connection. What can be done to resolve this problem?

Quick Answer: **122**
Detailed Answer: **125**

- ❍ **A.** Issue the **clock rate** command on the opposite end of the connection.
- ❍ **B.** Replace the cable connecting the two routers.
- ❍ **C.** Disconnect the third and fourth pins of the serial link.
- ❍ **D.** Use a straight-through instead of a crossover serial cable.

Quick Check

12. What is the difference between the **clock rate** command and the **bandwidth** command? (Choose four.)

Quick Answer: **122**
Detailed Answer: **125**

- ❍ **A.** The **clock rate** command determines the actual speed of the connection.
- ❍ **B.** The **bandwidth** command determines the actual speed of the connection.
- ❍ **C.** The **clock rate** command determines the logical speed of the connection.
- ❍ **D.** The **bandwidth** command determines the logical speed of the connection.
- ❍ **E.** The **clock rate** command is entered in Kbps.
- ❍ **F.** The **bandwidth** command is entered in Kbps.
- ❍ **G.** The **clock rate** command is entered in bps.
- ❍ **H.** The **bandwidth** command is entered in bps.

13. Your organization is having difficulty choosing the type of WAN connection to use between offices. Which of the following are advantages of a leased line connection? (Choose three.)

Quick Answer: **122**
Detailed Answer: **125**

- ❍ **A.** Typically lower cost when compared to other WAN connections
- ❍ **B.** The most simplistic WAN connection to configure
- ❍ **C.** Flexibility to connect to multiple sites through a single interface
- ❍ **D.** An always available, reliable connection
- ❍ **E.** Typically provides higher quality of service compared to other WAN connections

14. When Cisco implemented the HDLC data link protocol in its equipment, they made a modification that caused Cisco's version of HDLC to become proprietary. What did the modification accomplish?

Quick Answer: **122**
Detailed Answer: **125**

- ❍ **A.** Cisco's version of HDLC provides plain-text authentication.
- ❍ **B.** Cisco's version of HDLC provides encrypted authentication.
- ❍ **C.** Cisco's version of HDLC allows the use of multiple network layer protocols.
- ❍ **D.** Cisco's version of HDLC implements multilink capabilities.
- ❍ **E.** Cisco's version of HDLC implements data compression.

Quick Check

15. You are the network administrator of ACME Corp. You have received a number of tickets from your San Diego office complaining about server connectivity issues. You verify the WAN interface connecting the corporate office to the San Diego office:

Quick Answer: **122**
Detailed Answer: **125**

```
Router# show interfaces serial
Serial 0 is administratively down, line protocol is down
   Hardware is MCI Serial
   Internet address is 150.136.190.203, subnet mask is 255.255.255.0
   MTU 1500 bytes, BW 1544 Kbit, DLY 20000 usec, rely 255/255, load
➥1/255
   Encapsulation HDLC, loopback not set, keepalive set (10 sec)
   Last input 0:00:07, output 0:00:00, output hang never
   Output queue 0/40, 0 drops; input queue 0/75, 0 drops
   Five minute input rate 0 bits/sec, 0 packets/sec
   Five minute output rate 0 bits/sec, 0 packets/sec
       16263 packets input, 1347238 bytes, 0 no buffer
       Received 13983 broadcasts, 0 runts, 0 giants
       2 input errors, 0 CRC, 0 frame, 0 overrun, 0 ignored, 2 abort
1 carrier transitions
     22146 packets output, 2383680 bytes, 0 underruns
     0 output errors, 0 collisions, 2 interface resets, 0 restarts
```

What is the most likely cause of the problem?

- ❍ **A.** The line protocol is down due to an HDLC encapsulation mismatch. HDLC is Cisco proprietary and should be changed to PPP.
- ❍ **B.** The interface is experiencing input errors.
- ❍ **C.** The keepalive value is set too low.
- ❍ **D.** The interface is in a shutdown state.

16. Which of the following are components of the PPP protocol? (Choose two.)

Quick Answer: **122**
Detailed Answer: **125**

- ❍ **A.** Synchronous
- ❍ **B.** Asynchronous
- ❍ **C.** NCP
- ❍ **D.** LCP
- ❍ **E.** HSSI
- ❍ **F.** LSSI

Quick Check

Use the following output to answer the following two questions:

```
Serial0/1/0 is up, line protocol is up
  Hardware is GT96K Serial
  Internet address is 192.168.2.1/24
  MTU 1350 bytes, BW 128 Kbit, DLY 20000 usec,
     reliability 255/255, txload 1/255, rxload 1/255
  Encapsulation HDLC, loopback not set
  Keepalive set (10 sec)
  CRC checking enabled
  Last input 00:00:01, output 00:00:03, output hang never
  Last clearing of "show interface" counters never
  Input queue: 0/75/0/0 (size/max/drops/flushes); Total output
➥drops: 0
  Queueing strategy: fifo
  Output queue: 0/40 (size/max)
  5 minute input rate 0 bits/sec, 0 packets/sec
  5 minute output rate 0 bits/sec, 0 packets/sec
     138 packets input, 9604 bytes, 0 no buffer
     Received 105 broadcasts, 0 runts, 0 giants, 0 throttles
     0 input errors, 0 CRC, 0 frame, 0 overrun, 0 ignored, 0 abort
     139 packets output, 10742 bytes, 0 underruns
     0 output errors, 0 collisions, 11 interface resets
     0 output buffer failures, 0 output buffers swapped out
     5 carrier transitions
     DCD=up  DSR=up  DTR=up  RTS=up  CTS=up
```

17. Which of the following commands could be used to generate the output shown?

Quick Answer: **122**
Detailed Answer: **125**

- ❍ **A. show ip interface brief**
- ❍ **B. show ip interface**
- ❍ **C. show interface**
- ❍ **D. show controllers**
- ❍ **E. show interface stats**

18. Based on the output shown, what is the currently configured clock rate on the Serial0/1/0 interface?

Quick Answer: **122**
Detailed Answer: **126**

- ❍ **A.** 1/255
- ❍ **B.** 128Kbps
- ❍ **C.** 1350Kbps
- ❍ **D.** You cannot determine the clock rate using this command.

Quick Check

19. Identify two advantages of circuit switched connections. (Choose two.)

Quick Answer: **122**
Detailed Answer: **126**

- ❍ **A.** High-speed data rates
- ❍ **B.** Widely available
- ❍ **C.** Inexpensive
- ❍ **D.** Fast connect times
- ❍ **E.** Low cost international connectivity

20. In which configuration mode do you specify PPP authentication parameters?

Quick Answer: **122**
Detailed Answer: **126**

- ❍ **A.** User mode
- ❍ **B.** Privileged mode
- ❍ **C.** Global configuration mode
- ❍ **D.** Interface configuration mode
- ❍ **E.** Sub-interface configuration mode

21. Which of the following statements are true regarding leased lines connections? (Choose two.)

Quick Answer: **122**
Detailed Answer: **126**

- ❍ **A.** The most fundamental building block of leased line connections is a DS1, which can be incrementally added to achieve a higher speed connection.
- ❍ **B.** In the United States, a T1 speed can be achieved by bundling 12 DS0s into a single connection.
- ❍ **C.** To achieve higher speed connectivity in the United States, 28 DS0s can be bundled together to create a T3 connection.
- ❍ **D.** In Europe, an E1 connection uses standards similar to a T1 connection, but possesses different bandwidth and frame structures.
- ❍ **E.** A single DS0 represents the amount of bandwidth necessary to complete an uncompressed, digitized phone call.

Quick Check

22. Examine the following configuration. Will the PPP link successfully establish between RouterA and RouterB?

Quick Answer: **122**
Detailed Answer: **126**

```
RouterA(config)#username RouterB password ppplink
RouterA(config)#interface serial0/0
RouterA(config-if)#encapsulation ppp
RouterA(config-if)#ppp authentication chap

RouterB(config)#username RouterA password cisco
RouterB(config)#interface serial0/0
RouterB(config-if)#encapsulation ppp
RouterB(config-if)#ppp authentication chap
```

❍ **A.** Yes, assuming all physical connectivity is working correctly.

❍ **B.** Yes, provided the enable secret on RouterA is configured as “cisco”, and the enable secret on RouterB is configured as “ppplink”.

❍ **C.** No, to support authentication you must use HDLC encapsulation.

❍ **D.** No, PPP CHAP authentication requires that both routers be configured with the same password.

23. When using Frame Relay connections, your end router is considered which of the following?

Quick Answer: **122**
Detailed Answer: **126**

❍ **A.** A Frame Relay switch

❍ **B.** A DTE

❍ **C.** A DLCI

❍ **D.** LMI-based

24. Which of the following represent the Layer 2 addressing used in a Frame Relay environment?

Quick Answer: **122**
Detailed Answer: **126**

❍ **A.** DLCI

❍ **B.** MAC

❍ **C.** VPI/VCI

❍ **D.** LMI

25. Frame Relay falls into which category of WAN connections?

Quick Answer: **122**
Detailed Answer: **126**

❍ **A.** Leased line

❍ **B.** Circuit switched

❍ **C.** Packet switched

❍ **D.** Cell switched

Quick Check

Quick Answer: **122**
Detailed Answer: **126**

26. ATM WAN connections transmit cells that are fixed at a _____ byte length.

- ❍ **A.** 48
- ❍ **B.** 53
- ❍ **C.** 192
- ❍ **D.** 1024

Quick Check Answer Key

1. D
2. See detailed answer
3. B
4. B, C, G
5. D
6. C
7. D
8. B, E, F
9. B
10. D
11. A
12. A, D, F, G
13. B, D, E
14. C
15. D
16. C, D
17. C
18. D
19. B, C
20. D
21. D, E
22. D
23. B
24. A
25. C
26. B

Answers and Explanations

1. **D.** Cisco serial ports connect to a CSU/DSU unit using a proprietary DB-60 connector. Newer serial ports that are able to fit two serial interfaces per WIC card use "smart serial" connector types. Answers A, B, and C are industry standard CSU/DSU connectors. A Cisco serial cable will have a DB-60 connection on one end of the cable (which connects to the router) and an industry standard connector on the other end of the cable (which connects to the CSU/DSU).

2.

FIGURE 6.3 Network diagram.

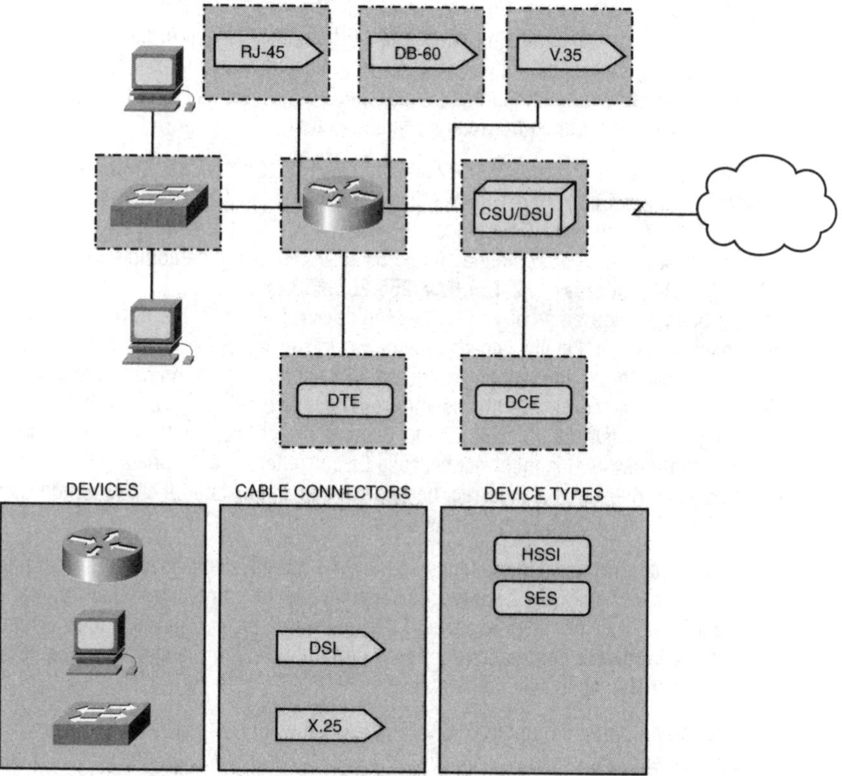

3. **B.** Frame Relay (and all other WAN technologies) represents a data link layer technology, just as Ethernet represents a data link layer technology for the LAN. Answers A and C are incorrect because these are incorrect layers. Answer D is incorrect because the OSI model applies to all network types.

4. **B, C, G.** ATM, HDLC, and PPP all represent data link layer WAN protocols. Answers E and F are incorrect because leased line and packet switched are WAN link options rather than WAN protocols. Answer A is incorrect because fiber optic is a cable type rather than a WAN protocol. Finally, answer D is incorrect because T1 is a measure of speed rather than a WAN protocol.

5. **D.** Each DS0 provides 64kbps of bandwidth. If you have ordered a connection providing 6 DS0s, your total speed will be (6 * 64kbps) = 384kbps. All other answers are incorrect.

6. **C.** A T1 connection is composed of 24 DS0s while a T3 connection is composed of 672 DS0s. It is a common mistake to believe a T3 is simply three T1 lines bundled together! All other answers have incorrect values.

7. **D.** When configuring back-to-back serial crossover connections in a lab environment, the router with the DCE end of the cable connection must set the speed of the connection using the **clock rate** *rate_in_bps* command. Answers A and B are incorrect because the bandwidth command is used to set the logical speed of the interface for use with routing protocols. Answer C is incorrect because the unit of measure for use with the **clock rate** command is bits per second (bps). Answers E and F are incorrect because a space is required between clock and rate.

8. **B, E, F.** Because the IP address of R2 is stated as 192.168.6.37/30, reverse-engineering the original subnet reveals the subnet range as 192.168.6.36 to 192.168.6.39. Because the first and last IP address of the range are unusable, R2's IP address must be 192.168.6.38 and should be assigned using the command **R2(config-if)#ip address 192.168.6.38 255.255.255.252**. Because the serial interface has not been configured as of yet, we need to power it on using the **R2(config-if)#no shutdown** command. Finally, because the network diagram shows R2 is a non-Cisco router, we need to use the industry standard PPP encapsulation. Answer A is incorrect because the enable command moves you from user to privileged mode rather than powering on an interface. Answers C and D are incorrect because these IP addresses are not valid. Answer G is incorrect because Cisco routers use proprietary HDLC encapsulation. Answer H is incorrect because the question stated the connection was a leased line rather than a Frame Relay circuit.

9. **B.** The **show controllers** command is used to view the physical aspects of router interfaces. Answer A is incorrect because the **show interfaces** command focuses primarily on data link and network layer aspects of the router interfaces. Answer C is incorrect as the **show hardware** command produces output identical to the **show version** command. Answer D is an invalid command.

10. **D.** By taking note of the output "DTE V.35 clocks stopped," you are able to determine that the DTE end of the serial connection is plugged into the router. Answers A, B, and C are invalid cable types. Answer E would be the opposite side of the DTE cable connection.

11. **A.** By again taking note of the output "DTE V.35 clocks stopped," you are able to see that the DTE interface is not receiving a clocking signal from the opposite end of the connection (the DCE side). To correct this issue, you can enter the **clock rate** *rate* command on the DCE end of the connection to set accurate clocking on the line. Answer B could be correct, but it is not the most likely cause of the DTE clock stoppage. The cable should be replaced only after testing the effects of the **clock rate** command. Answer C is incorrect because the third and fourth pins of the serial cable have nothing to do with this problem. Answer D is incorrect because straight-through and crossover are terms that apply to Ethernet connectivity rather than serial.

12. **A, D, F, G.** The **clock rate** command is entered on the DCE end of the connection and controls the actual speed of the connection. It is entered in units of bits per second (bps). The **bandwidth** command determines the logical speed of the connection and is entered in terms of kilobits per second (kbps). All other answers do not apply.

13. **B, D, E.** Leased line WAN connections are typically the simplest WAN link to configure that offers consistent availability and quality of service. Answer A is incorrect because leased lines typically cost more than other WAN connection types. Answer C is incorrect because leased lines are always point-to-point connections and do not offer the flexibility of other WAN connection types such as Frame Relay.

14. **C.** Cisco's version of HDLC provided support for multiple network layer protocols (such as IP, IPX, AppleTalk, and so on) before PPP had been fully developed. Answers A, B, D, and E are all benefits of PPP rather than Cisco HDLC.

15. **D.** Any interface that has a state of **administratively down** is in a shutdown state. This can be reversed by typing the **no shutdown** command under interface configuration mode. If the cause of failure were an encapsulation mismatch (as stated in answer A), the interface status would be **up** with a line protocol status of **down**, indicating a data link layer mismatch. A low number of input errors (answer B) could be normal for an interface running for an extended amount of time, and a keepalive value of 10 seconds (answer C) is a standard value.

16. **C, D.** The Link Control Protocol (LCP) is used to establish, configure, and test data link connectivity with PPP. The Network Control Programs (NCPs) are used to establish and configure different network layer protocols, which allow you to use more than one network layer protocol over the PPP WAN link at a time. Answers A and B are categories of WAN connections rather than PPP-focused technology. Answers E and F do not apply to this question.

17. **C.** The **show interface** command allows you to see general interface configuration information and packet statistics. Answer A is incorrect because the **show ip interface brief** command shows a columnized output of all interfaces on your router along with a brief view of physical, data link, and network layer status. Answer B is incorrect as the **show ip interface** output focuses on IP addressing information. Answer D is incorrect because the **show controllers** command focuses solely on physical layer information. Answer E is incorrect because the **show interface stats** gives a brief view of packet statistics passing through the router.

18. **D.** While the **show interface** command can display the configured logical bandwidth value (which is 128kbps in this instance), it cannot display the configured clock rate. This can only be shown using the **show controllers** command. All other answers do not apply.

19. **B, C.** Circuit switched connections are WAN links that use the Public Switched Telephone Network (PSTN) to communicate. The most common circuit switched connection type is a modem. The three advantages of circuit switched connections are that they are simple, widely available, and have a relatively low cost. Answer A is incorrect because circuit switched connections are low-speed in nature. Answer D is incorrect because circuit switched connections have long setup (dialing) times. Answer E is incorrect because dialing internationally using a modem can be costly.

20. **D.** All PPP parameters, including authentication, are configured under the specific Serial interface to which they apply. All other answers do not apply.

21. **D, E.** The two statements listed for these answers are true. Answer A is incorrect because the most fundamental building block is a DS0 rather than a DS1. Answer B is incorrect because a T1 speed is achieved by bundling 24 DS0s rather than 12. Answer C is incorrect because T3 connections are a bundle of 28 DS1s rather than 28 DS0s.

22. **D.** PPP CHAP authentication requires that both routers be configured with the same password. This is because CHAP uses a hashing system in which the actual password is never sent over the WAN link. This immediately makes answers A and B incorrect. Answer C is incorrect because HDLC does not support authentication options.

23. **B.** Regardless of the type of WAN connection you install, your router equipment will be the DTE end of the connection (unless you are operating in a lab environment). Answer A is incorrect because the service provider hosts Frame Relay switching equipment. Answer C is incorrect because DLCIs define the addressing used in Frame Relay. Answer D is incorrect because LMI is the signaling protocol used between your router and the Frame Relay service provider.

24. **A.** The Data Link Connection Identifier (DLCI) is used for Layer 2 communication over a Frame Relay network. Answer B is incorrect because MAC addresses are used in Ethernet networks. Answer C is incorrect because VPI/VCI pairs are used in ATM networks. Answer D is incorrect because LMI is a signaling protocol and does not deal with addressing.

25. **C.** Frame Relay falls into the Packet Switched category of network connections. Based on this, all other answers are incorrect.

26. **B.** ATM connections use fixed 53-byte packet sizes. 48-bytes of this is the actual data being carried, and 5 bytes is dedicated to header information. Based on this, all other answers are incorrect.

PART II

ICND2

Chapter 7 Advanced Switching Concepts

Chapter 8 Subnetting, VLSM, and IPv6

Chapter 9 Advanced Routing Configuration

Chapter 10 Access Lists and Network Address Translation

Chapter 11 Frame Relay, PPP, and VPN Connectivity

Appendix What's on the CD-ROM

7

CHAPTER SEVEN

Advanced Switching Concepts

This chapter covers the following ICND2 objectives that fall under the content areas, **Configure, verify, and troubleshoot a switch with VLANs and interswitch communications:**

- Describe enhanced switching technologies (including VTP, RSTP, VLAN, PVSTP, and 802.1q).
- Describe how VLANs create logically separate networks and the need for routing between them.
- Configure, verify, and troubleshoot VLANs.
- Configure, verify, and troubleshoot trunking on Cisco switches.
- Configure, verify, and troubleshoot inter-VLAN routing.
- Configure, verify, and troubleshoot VTP.
- Configure, verify, and troubleshoot RSTP operation.
- Interpret the output of various **SHOW** and **DEBUG** commands to verify the operational status of a Cisco switched network.
- Implement basic switch security (including port security, unassigned ports, trunk access, and so on).

Quick Check

1. Refer to Figure 7.1. Which of the following are true regarding the logical configuration shown? (Choose three.)

Quick Answer: **150**
Detailed Answer: **151**

FIGURE 7.1 Network diagram.

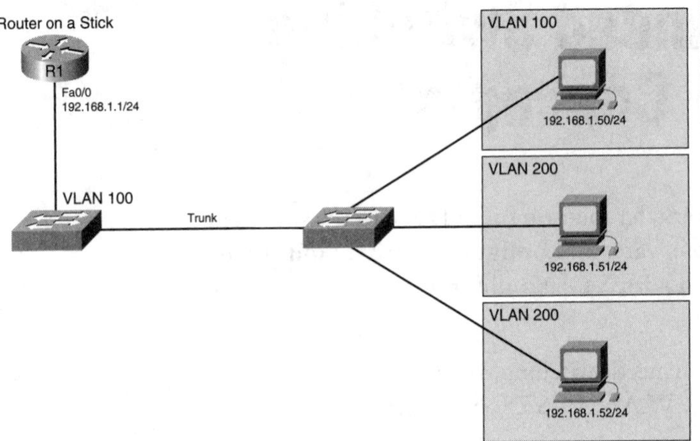

- ❍ **A.** The R1 should be connected to VLAN 200.
- ❍ **B.** The link between R1 and the switch should be configured as a trunk link.
- ❍ **C.** The Ethernet interface on R1 should be 1000Mbps or faster to support multi-VLAN routing.
- ❍ **D.** The clients should be configured on separate subnets.
- ❍ **E.** The link between switches should not be configured as a trunk link.
- ❍ **F.** The hosts in VLAN 200 will be able to communicate with each other and the host in VLAN 100, but not R1.
- ❍ **G.** The host in VLAN 100 will be able to communicate with R1.

2. Which of the following statements regarding VLANs is true?

Quick Answer: **150**
Detailed Answer: **151**

- ❍ **A.** A VLAN is a physical broadcast domain spanning multiple logical subnets.
- ❍ **B.** A VLAN is a logical broadcast domain spanning multiple physical segments.
- ❍ **C.** A VLAN is a logical broadcast domain spanning multiple logical subnets.
- ❍ **D.** A VLAN is a physical broadcast domain spanning multiple physical subnets.

Quick Check

3. In 802.1q trunking, what is the default native VLAN ID?

Quick Answer: **150**
Detailed Answer: **151**

- ❍ **A.** VLAN 0
- ❍ **B.** VLAN 1
- ❍ **C.** VLAN A
- ❍ **D.** There is no default VLAN ID.

4. The network shown in Figure 7.2 has just been configured. HostA is able to access the Internet, but is unable to reach HostB. What is the most likely problem with this configuration?

Quick Answer: **150**
Detailed Answer: **151**

FIGURE 7.2 Network diagram.

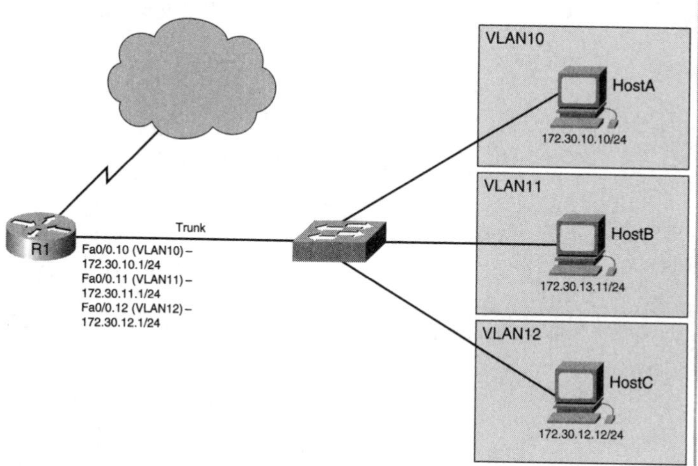

- ❍ **A.** The port connecting the router to the switch is incorrectly configured as a trunk port.
- ❍ **B.** HostB is assigned to the incorrect VLAN.
- ❍ **C.** The gateway for HostB is on a different subnet than HostB.
- ❍ **D.** The FastEthernet subinterface on the router is shut down.
- ❍ **E.** The IP address of HostA is incorrect.

Quick Check

5. Which of the following statements about 802.1q frame tagging are correct? (Choose three.)

   ❍ **A.** The 802.1q protocol tags frames for the native VLAN.
   ❍ **B.** The 802.1q protocol does not tag frames for the native VLAN.
   ❍ **C.** Tagged frames can be read by ordinary stations.
   ❍ **D.** Tagged frames cannot be read by ordinary stations.
   ❍ **E.** 802.1q uses a tagging mechanism proprietary to Cisco.
   ❍ **F.** 802.1q uses a tagging mechanism that is used in multivendor switch implementations.

Quick Answer: **150**
Detailed Answer: **151**

6. Which of the following are modes under which VTP operates? (Choose three.)

   ❍ **A.** Server
   ❍ **B.** Client
   ❍ **C.** Peer
   ❍ **D.** Transparent
   ❍ **E.** Static
   ❍ **F.** Dynamic

Quick Answer: **150**
Detailed Answer: **151**

Quick Check

Quick Answer: **150**
Detailed Answer: **152**

7. How would the Rapid Spanning Tree Protocol (RSTP) prevent loops in the network shown in Figure 7.3?

FIGURE 7.3 Network diagram.

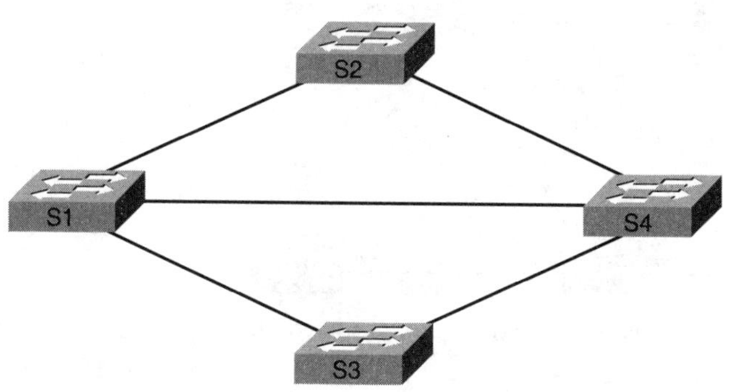

- ❍ **A.** RSTP would shut down S3 to eliminate redundant connections.
- ❍ **B.** RSTP would enable load balancing on the redundant links to more equally spread the traffic across the network.
- ❍ **C.** RSTP turns the LED amber on links that should be disconnected by an administrator.
- ❍ **D.** RSTP places redundant paths into a blocking (disabled) state.
- ❍ **E.** RSTP enables the L3 engine of the switches to make intelligent routing decisions for the redundant links.

Quick Check

Use Figure 7.4 to answer the next three questions.

FIGURE 7.4 Network diagram.

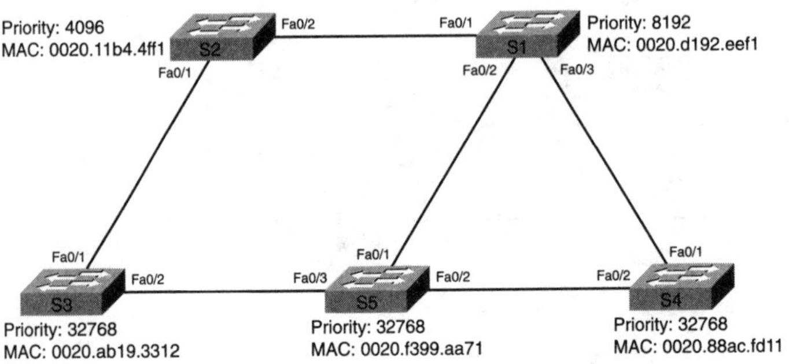

8. Based on Figure 7.4, which of the following switches will assume the RSTP role of root bridge?

Quick Answer: **150**
Detailed Answer: **152**

- ❍ **A.** S1
- ❍ **B.** S2
- ❍ **C.** S3
- ❍ **D.** S4
- ❍ **E.** S5

9. Based on Figure 7.4, which of the following ports will be considered root ports? (Choose four.)

Quick Answer: **150**
Detailed Answer: **152**

- ❍ **A.** S1, Fa0/1
- ❍ **B.** S1, Fa0/2
- ❍ **C.** S1, Fa0/3
- ❍ **D.** S2, Fa0/1
- ❍ **E.** S2, Fa0/2
- ❍ **F.** S3, Fa0/1
- ❍ **G.** S3, Fa0/2
- ❍ **H.** S4, Fa0/1
- ❍ **I.** S4, Fa0/2
- ❍ **J.** S5, Fa0/1
- ❍ **K.** S5, Fa0/2
- ❍ **L.** S5, Fa0/3

Quick Check

10. Based on Figure 7.4, which of the following ports will be blocked? (Choose two.)

Quick Answer: **150**
Detailed Answer: **153**

- ❍ **A.** S1, Fa0/1
- ❍ **B.** S1, Fa0/2
- ❍ **C.** S1, Fa0/3
- ❍ **D.** S2, Fa0/1
- ❍ **E.** S2, Fa0/2
- ❍ **F.** S3, Fa0/1
- ❍ **G.** S3, Fa0/2
- ❍ **H.** S4, Fa0/1
- ❍ **I.** S4, Fa0/2
- ❍ **J.** S5, Fa0/1
- ❍ **K.** S5, Fa0/2
- ❍ **L.** S5, Fa0/3

11. Which of the following protocols is responsible for replicating VLAN information between switches?

Quick Answer: **150**
Detailed Answer: **153**

- ❍ **A.** ISL
- ❍ **B.** VTP
- ❍ **C.** 802.1q
- ❍ **D.** STP
- ❍ **E.** RSTP

12. Which of the following **show** commands will display the currently created VLANs on the switch?

Quick Answer: **150**
Detailed Answer: **153**

- ❍ **A. show running-config**
- ❍ **B. show 802.1q**
- ❍ **C. show vlan**
- ❍ **D. show 802.1q vlan**
- ❍ **E. show isl vlan**

Quick Check

13. Your organization enforces strict port security settings in its LAN environment. Every port is limited to a single MAC address and uses the sticky MAC learning feature. After the network has been in operation for some time, management reports that the switchport security settings are not functioning. Based on the following output, what is the most likely cause of this problem?

Quick Answer: **150**
Detailed Answer: **153**

```
CAT3550#sh run int fa0/15
Building configuration...

Current configuration : 148 bytes
!
interface FastEthernet0/15
 switchport access vlan 200
 switchport mode access
 spanning-tree portfast
 switchport port-security maximum 1
 switchport port-security violation shutdown
 switchport port-security mac-address sticky
end
```

- ❍ **A.** Port security features need to be enabled on a per-interface basis by typing the command **switchport port-security**.
- ❍ **B.** Port security features are incompatible with VLAN assignments.
- ❍ **C.** Port security features are incompatible with STP portfast features.
- ❍ **D.** Port security features must be enabled on the entire switch from global configuration mode by typing the command **switchport port-security**.

14. Which of the following are reasons for implementing VLANs in an organization? (Choose three.)

Quick Answer: **150**
Detailed Answer: **153**

- ❍ **A.** To reduce the size of a network
- ❍ **B.** To implement security boundaries
- ❍ **C.** To reduce the size of the collision domain
- ❍ **D.** To control broadcast traffic
- ❍ **E.** To group together departments or resources

Quick Check

Quick Answer: **150**
Detailed Answer: **153**

15. Given the topology shown in Figure 7.5, which of the following ports would be placed in the blocking state?

FIGURE 7.5 Network diagram.

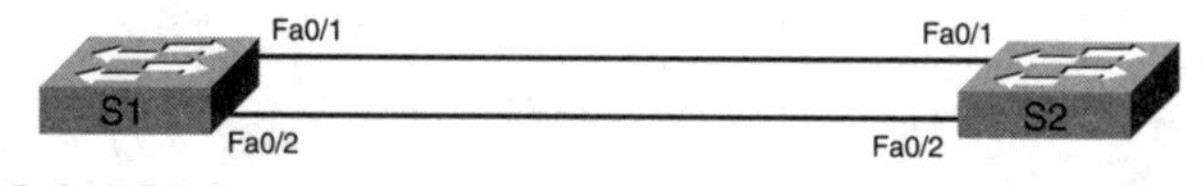

- ❍ **A.** S1, Fa0/1
- ❍ **B.** S1, Fa0/2
- ❍ **C.** S2, Fa0/1
- ❍ **D.** S2, Fa0/2

Quick Check

Quick Answer: **150**
Detailed Answer: **153**

16. Based on the following output, what is the current state of FastEthernet 0/18?

```
CAT3550#show interface fastethernet 0/4 switchport
Name: Fa0/4
Switchport: Enabled
Administrative Mode: dynamic desirable
Operational Mode: static access
Administrative Trunking Encapsulation: negotiate
Operational Trunking Encapsulation: native
Negotiation of Trunking: On
Access Mode VLAN: 300 (WIRELESS)
Trunking Native Mode VLAN: 1 (default)
Administrative Native VLAN tagging: enabled
Voice VLAN: none
Administrative private-vlan host-association: none
Administrative private-vlan mapping: none
Administrative private-vlan trunk native VLAN: none
Administrative private-vlan trunk Native VLAN tagging: enabled
Administrative private-vlan trunk encapsulation: dot1q
Administrative private-vlan trunk normal VLANs: none
Administrative private-vlan trunk private VLANs: none
Operational private-vlan: none
Trunking VLANs Enabled: ALL
Pruning VLANs Enabled: 2-1001
Capture Mode Disabled
Capture VLANs Allowed: ALL

Protected: false
Unknown unicast blocked: disabled
Unknown multicast blocked: disabled
Appliance trust: none
```

- ❍ **A.** The port is currently operating as an access port.
- ❍ **B.** The port is currently trunking using the ISL protocol.
- ❍ **C.** The port is currently trunking using the 802.1q protocol.
- ❍ **D.** The port is currently disabled.

Quick Check

17. HostA in Figure 7.6 would like to send a broadcast to all the hosts in its same VLAN. To what IP address should HostA send the broadcast message?

Quick Answer: **150**
Detailed Answer: **154**

FIGURE 7.6 Network diagram.

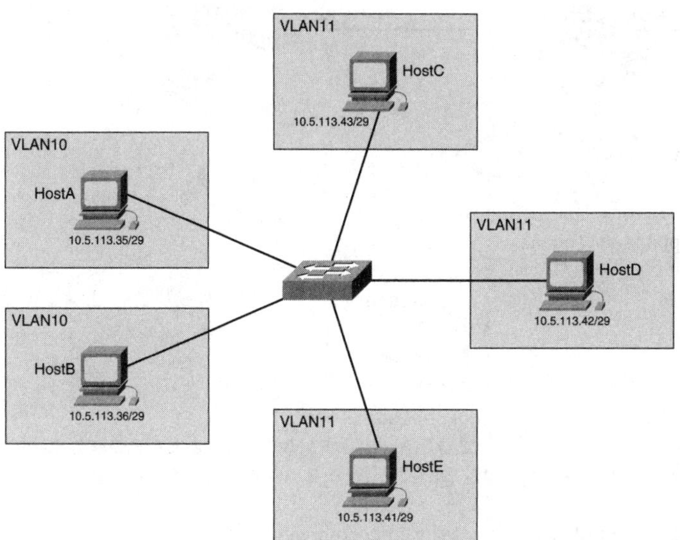

- ❍ **A.** 10.5.113.39
- ❍ **B.** 10.5.113.40
- ❍ **C.** 10.5.113.248
- ❍ **D.** 10.5.113.255
- ❍ **E.** HostA will not be able to send a broadcast because it is assigned to a VLAN.

Quick Check

18. Use Figure 7.7 and the following output to answer the following question.

Quick Answer: **150**
Detailed Answer: **154**

FIGURE 7.7 Network diagram.

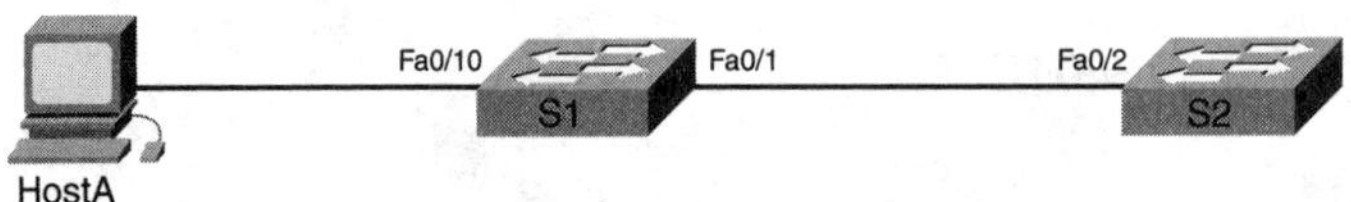


```
S1#show vtp status
VTP Version                     : 2
Configuration Revision          : 0
Maximum VLANs supported locally : 1005
Number of existing VLANs        : 12
VTP Operating Mode              : Transparent
VTP Domain Name                 : ADTEC
VTP Pruning Mode                : Disabled
VTP V2 Mode                     : Disabled
VTP Traps Generation            : Disabled
MD5 digest                      : 0xAA 0xFB 0xB4 0x2C 0x10 0x18 0x62 0xD9
Configuration last modified by 172.30.1.1 at 0-0-00 00:00:00
```

What will be the result of issuing the following commands?

```
S1(config)#vlan 50
S1(config-vlan)#name Sales
S1(config)#interface fa0/10
S1(config-if)#switchport mode access
S1(config-if)#switchport access vlan 50
```

- ❍ **A.** VLAN 50 will be created on S1 and replicate to S2.
- ❍ **B.** VLAN 50 will be created on S1 and will not replicate to S2.
- ❍ **C.** VLAN 50 will not be created on S1 but will replicate to S2.
- ❍ **D.** VLAN 50 will not be created on S1 and will not replicate to S2.

Quick Check

19. Based on Cisco's best practice security recommendations, how should you configure ports that are not currently connected to a device?

Quick Answer: **150**
Detailed Answer: **154**

- ❍ **A.** They should be hard-coded as access ports to prevent trunk negotiation.
- ❍ **B.** They should be assigned to a nonrouted VLAN to prevent access to other areas of the network.
- ❍ **C.** They should be assigned to an Internet-only VLAN.
- ❍ **D.** They should be placed in the shutdown state.

20. You are returning one of your company lab switches to the production network. Because the lab network had many VLANs you do not want to propagate to the corporate network, you remove the switch from the lab network, erase the switch configuration using the **erase startup-config** command, and reboot. After rebooting, you find the VLANs used in the lab environment still exist. What is the most likely cause of this problem?

Quick Answer: **150**
Detailed Answer: **154**

- ❍ **A.** The **erase startup-config** command should also be followed with the **erase running-config** command.
- ❍ **B.** In addition to the **erase startup-config** command, you also need to execute the **erase vlan** command to remove the VLAN information.
- ❍ **C.** The lab switch needs to be disconnected from the lab network or it will receive updates via VTP with the old VLAN database.
- ❍ **D.** In addition to the **erase startup-config** command, you also need to execute the **delete flash:vlan.dat** command before rebooting the switch.

21. You are managing the network shown in Figure 7.8.

Quick Answer: **150**
Detailed Answer: **154**

FIGURE 7.8 Network diagram.

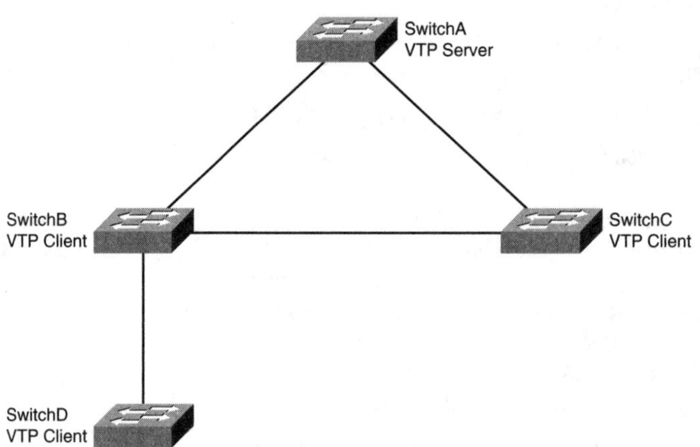

You are currently connected to SwitchD and want to add VLAN 500 to your VTP domain. Upon issuing the command **vlan 500** from global configuration mode, the switch gives you an error message. How can you resolve the problem and add the VLAN?

- ❍ **A.** The command **vlan 500** cannot be entered from global configuration mode. You must exit to privileged mode before issuing this command.
- ❍ **B.** You cannot have multiple VTP clients connected together. Connect SwitchD directly to SwitchA and then issue the command.
- ❍ **C.** You must first issue the command **vtp server** on SwitchD; then issue the command **vlan 500** from global configuration mode.
- ❍ **D.** Because VTP only supports a single server environment, you must issue the command **vlan 500** from SwitchA and allow it to replicate to the VTP clients.
- ❍ **E.** Because SwitchA, SwitchB, and SwitchC are connected with redundant links, STP will disable the link to SwitchD. Correct the cabling and then reissue the command.

Quick Check

22. Your corporate network is configured as shown in Figure 7.9.

Quick Answer: **150**
Detailed Answer: **154**

FIGURE 7.9 Network diagram.

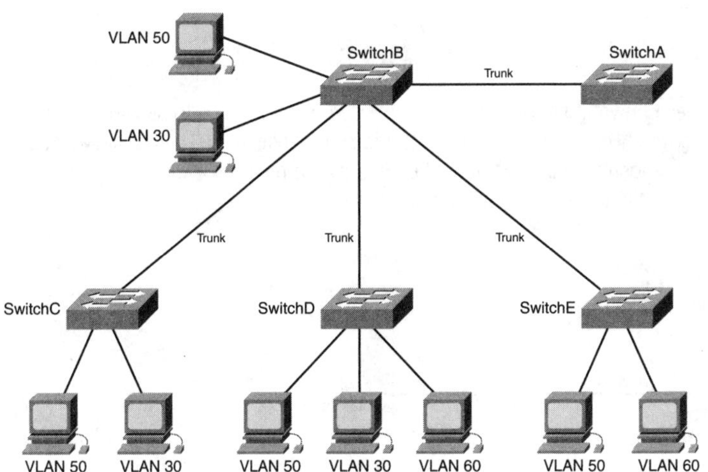

Upon extensive monitoring, you find that SwitchE is receiving excessive broadcast traffic for VLAN 30. What can you do to eliminate this traffic?

- ❍ **A.** Disable the trunk link between SwitchB and SwitchE, configure the port as an access port, and use the command **switchport access vlan 50 60** to add only VLAN 50 and VLAN 60 on the link between SwitchB and SwitchE.
- ❍ **B.** Disable trunk links on all switches. Trunk links are not required for this network.
- ❍ **C.** Enable VTP pruning features throughout the entire network.
- ❍ **D.** Add VLAN 30 to SwitchE using the command **vlan 30** from global configuration mode. The addition of this VLAN will minimize the broadcast traffic.

Quick Check

23. All Cisco switches, by default, are configured in VTP __________ mode.

Quick Answer: **150**
Detailed Answer: **155**

- ❍ **A.** Server
- ❍ **B.** Client
- ❍ **C.** Transparent
- ❍ **D.** Compatibility

24. The two switches shown in Figure 7.10 are connected using a manually configured 802.1q trunk; all VLAN traffic sent between the switches are tagged with a VLAN identifier. If a switch receives untagged traffic on the trunk link, how is it handled?

Quick Answer: **150**
Detailed Answer: **155**

FIGURE 7.10 Network diagram.

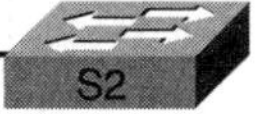

- ❍ **A.** The switch reports a tagging error and drops the untagged frame.
- ❍ **B.** It is considered a port-security violation, and the interface is immediately placed in the err-disable state.
- ❍ **C.** It is placed into the Native VLAN.
- ❍ **D.** The port reconfigures itself as an access port because end-user devices are still connected.

25. You are required to create a new VLAN for your organization's marketing department. You want to use VLAN 48 for this group. Enter the commands necessary to accomplish the following objectives:

Quick Answer: **150**
Detailed Answer: **155**

- Create VLAN 48.
- Assign the name "Marketing" to this VLAN.
- Assign ports 1–10 of SwitchA to this VLAN.
- Verify the assignment.
- Save your configuration.

The necessary prompts and switch output have been provided:

Switch#______________________

Switch(config)# ______________________

Switch(config-vlan)# ______________________

Switch(config-vlan)# ______________________

Switch(config)# ______________________

Switch(config-if-range)# ______________________

Switch(config-if-range)# ______________________

Switch#______________________

```
VLAN Name                             Status    Ports
---------------------------------- -------   ----------------
1    default                          active    Fa0/11, Fa0/12, Fa0/13,
                                                Fa0/14, Fa0/15, Fa0/16,
                                                Fa0/17, Fa0/18, Fa0/19,
                                                Fa0/20, Fa0/21, Fa0/22,
                                                Fa0/23, Fa0/24, Gi0/1,
                                                Gi0/2
48   Marketing                        active    Fa0/1, Fa0/2, Fa0/3, Fa0/4,
                                                Fa0/5, Fa0/6, Fa0/7, Fa0/8,
                                                Fa0/9, Fa0/10,
1002 fddi-default                     act/unsup
1003 token-ring-default               act/unsup
1004 fddinet-default                  act/unsup
1005 trnet-default                    act/unsup
```

Switch#______________________

```
Destination filename [startup-config]?
Building configuration...
[OK]
```

Quick Check

Quick Answer: **150**
Detailed Answer: **156**

26. Ports FastEthernet 0/1 through FastEthernet 0/20 are assigned to VLAN 550. Your corporation has decided to merge VLAN 550 back into the default VLAN 1. You enter global configuration mode on the switch and enter the command **no VLAN 550**. What happens to ports FastEthernet 0/1 through FastEthernet 0/20?

❍ **A.** They are automatically moved back to VLAN 1.

❍ **B.** The ports FastEthernet 0/1 through FastEthernet 0/20 lose all network connectivity.

❍ **C.** They remain in VLAN 550; VLAN 550 will be automatically re-created on the switch as soon as one of the devices on ports FastEthernet 0/1 through FastEthernet 0/20 send some traffic.

❍ **D.** They remain in VLAN 550; the switch will return an error message "VLAN 550 still in use" after issuing the **no VLAN 550** command.

Quick Check
Quick Answer: **150**
Detailed Answer: **156**

27. Your organization has a campus network design as shown in Figure 7.11. On close inspection, it is discovered that many of the links the organization connected to to provide more bandwidth between switches have been disabled by STP. How can this issue be resolved?

FIGURE 7.11 Network diagram.

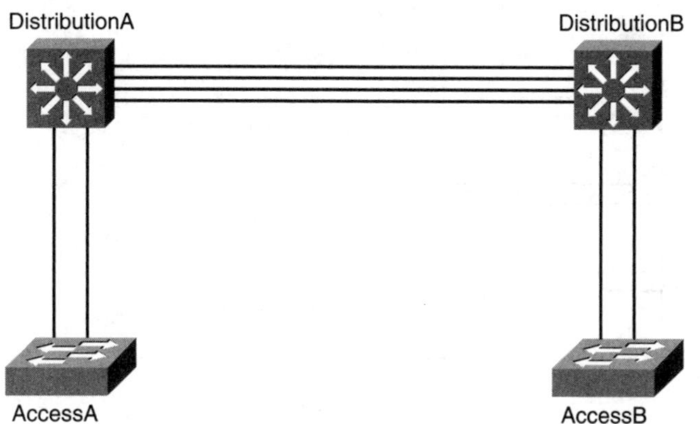

- ❍ **A.** To use all the bandwidth on the redundant links, STP must be disabled on DistributionA and DistributionB.
- ❍ **B.** Because the redundant links cause loops in the network, they must remain disabled unless the primary links have been removed.
- ❍ **C.** You can enable the EtherChannel feature on all switches in the diagram to bundle the physical links into a single, logical bundle.
- ❍ **D.** You can enable the EtherChannel feature on only the links between DistributionA and DistributionB switches to bundle the physical links into a single, logical bundle.
- ❍ **E.** You can enable LAPD on the Distribution switches and LAPB on the access layer switches to bundle the physical links into a single, logical bundle.

Quick Check

28. Industry standard 802.1D STP identifies three states through which a port must transition before it reaches the Forwarding state. In Figure 7.12, match the correct port state and timer in the proper order. Not all answers will be used, and some answers may be used more than once. Note: The first port state does not require a timer.

Quick Answer: **150**
Detailed Answer: **156**

FIGURE 7.12 STP timers.

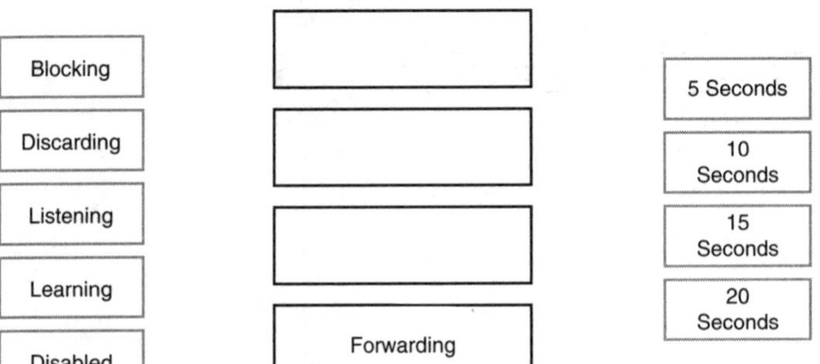

29. Users in your company network have been complaining that they are unable to initially connect to the network after resuming their computers from sleep mode. On further inspection, it appears as though the PC is initially assigned an IP address from the range 169.254.X.X, and later obtains one of your corporate IP addresses somewhere between 30 and 60 seconds after the PC resumes. What is the most likely solution to this problem?

Quick Answer: **150**
Detailed Answer: **156**

- ❍ **A.** You should disable STP on the ports connecting to the PCs by using the PortFast feature.
- ❍ **B.** You should convert all STP switches to RSTP.
- ❍ **C.** Ports should all be configured with the command **switchport mode access** to eliminate the trunk detection algorithm.
- ❍ **D.** The DHCP server should be located closer to the clients on the LAN to eliminate the DHCP request delays.

Quick Check

Quick Answer: **150**
Detailed Answer: **157**

30. Figure 7.13 depicts which of the following forms of STP?

FIGURE 7.13 Network diagram.

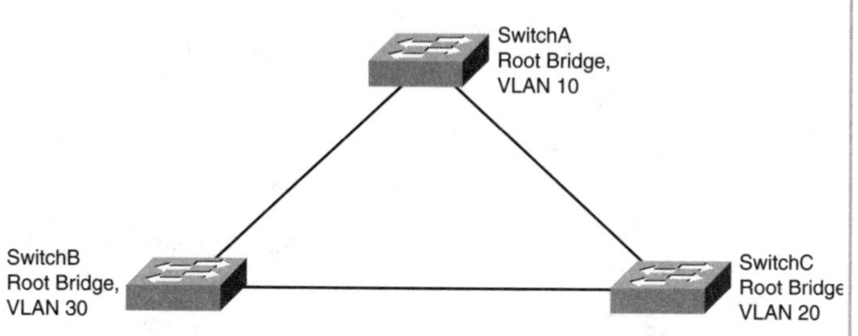

- ❍ **A.** 802.1D
- ❍ **B.** PVSTP+
- ❍ **C.** CSTP
- ❍ **D.** RSTP

Quick Check Answer Key

1. B, D, G
2. B
3. B
4. C
5. B, D, F
6. A, B, D
7. D
8. B
9. A, F, H, J
10. K, L
11. B
12. C
13. A
14. B, D, E
15. D
16. A
17. A
18. B
19. D
20. D
21. C
22. C
23. A
24. C
25. See detailed answer
26. B
27. C
28. See detailed answer
29. A
30. B

Answers and Explanations

1. **B, D, G.** To properly configure a Router on a Stick, the link to the switch should be configured as a trunk. As it stands right now, only VLAN 100 reaches the router, which allows it to communicate with the hosts in VLAN 100 but not the hosts in VLAN 200. Anytime you have separate VLANs, your network should include separate subnets (one subnet per VLAN). Answer A is incorrect because R1 should be connected to both VLAN 100 and 200 via a trunk link. Answer C is incorrect because multi-VLAN routing (Router on a Stick configurations) only requires a FastEthernet interface. Answer E is incorrect because this scenario requires the interswitch link to be configured as a trunk. Answer F is incorrect because the hosts in VLAN 200 can communicate, but they will not be able to communicate with the host in VLAN 100 without a proper routing configuration.

2. **B.** VLANs are logical broadcast domains, defined by the administrator, and can span multiple physical segments. Answer A is incorrect because VLANs are logical broadcast domains, not physical. Answer C is incorrect because VLANs span multiple physical subnets, not logical subnets. Answer D is incorrect because VLANs create logical broadcast domains, not physical domains.

3. **B**. In 802.1q trunking, the default identifier value of the native VLAN is VLAN 1. Answer A is incorrect because VLAN 1 is the default VLAN, not VLAN 0. Answer C is incorrect because the default VLAN identifier is numerical. Answer D is incorrect, as there is a default VLAN ID (VLAN 1).

4. **C.** In this case, HostB has been assigned to VLAN 11. The Fa0/0.11 subinterface of the router, which is responding to requests for this VLAN, is assigned to the 172.30.11.0/24 subnet. HostB is assigned to the 172.30.13.0/24 subnet, which places it on a different subnet than the router subinterface. HostB will be unable to communicate outside its VLAN. Answer A is incorrect because a Router on a Stick configuration uses a trunk port connection to a switch. Answer B is incorrect because the problem is not related to a VLAN assignment but rather a subnet assignment. Answer D is incorrect because there is nothing to indicate the subinterface is shut down. Answer E is incorrect because HostA is assigned to the correct subnet.

5. **B, D, F.** The 802.1q protocol does not tag native VLAN frames, and tagged frames cannot be read by ordinary stations. Answer A is incorrect because native VLAN frames are not tagged. Answer C is incorrect because the information added when a frame is tagged renders it unreadable by ordinary stations. Answer E is incorrect because ISL tagging is proprietary to Cisco, while 802.1Q is an open, industry standard.

6. **A, B, D.** Server mode is one of three VTP modes of operation; Client mode is a VTP mode of operation that does not allow creation, modification, or deletion of VLANs; and although Transparent mode acts much like Server mode, it does not synchronize information. Answers C, E, and F are incorrect because Peer, Static, and Dynamic are not VTP modes.

7. **D**. The goal of RSTP is to disable any redundant links in the network to prevent switch loops, which can result in a variety of network problems. Answer A is incorrect because RSTP does not shut down any switches in the network. Answer B is incorrect because RSTP does not do load balancing. This is the job of a tool such as EtherChannel. Answer C is incorrect because RSTP does not require any physical changes by an administrator. Answer E is incorrect because RSTP is a Layer 2 function.

Figure 7.14 provides a visual representation of the next three answer explanations.

FIGURE 7.14 Network diagram.

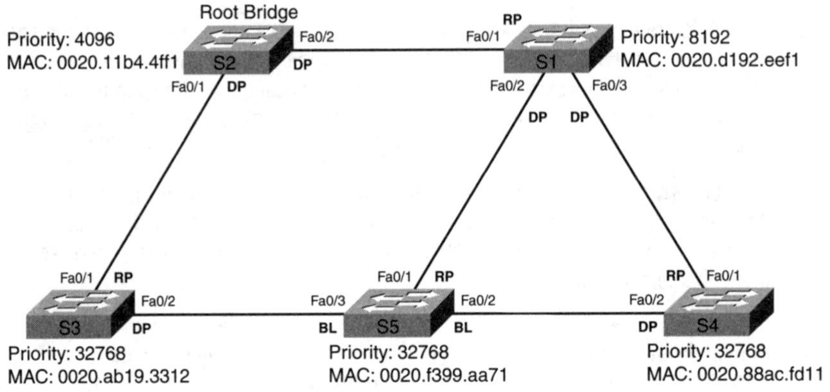

8. **B.** S2 becomes the root bridge of the network. The root bridge is elected based on the switch with the lowest Bridge ID. The Bridge ID is the combination of the Bridge Priority and MAC address in the format 4096.0020.11b4.4ff1. S1 would become the backup bridge in this network. All other answers do not apply.

9. **A, F, H, J.** The root port is chosen based on the following ordered criteria:

   1. Lowest cost to the root bridge is preferred.
   2. (if tied) Lowest neighbor Bridge ID is preferred.
   3. (if tied) Lower port number is preferred.

   Because all interfaces are 100Mbps, they will assume an equal STP cost of 19. Answer A is correct because Fa0/1 represents the lowest cost path from S1 to the root bridge. Answer F is correct because Fa0/1 represents the lowest cost path from S3 to the root bridge. Answer H is correct because Fa0/1 represents the lowest cost path from S4 to the root bridge. S5 has two equal cost paths to the root bridge, one through S3 and the other through S1. S5 uses the Fa0/1 interface because S1 has a lower Bridge ID than S3 (the second tie breaker in the preceding path criteria), making answer J correct. All other answers do not apply.

10. **K, L.** After the switches have labeled the root port, they use the same decision criteria to determine which ports should be designated ports and which should be blocked ports. S4 and S5 both have equal cost paths to the root bridge, but S5 blocks its Fa0/2 interface because it has a higher Bridge ID than S4, making answer K correct. Answer L is correct because S3 has a better path cost to the root bridge than S5, causing its Fa0/2 interface to be the designated port, and S5's Fa0/3 port becomes blocked. All other answers do not apply.

11. **B.** The VLAN Trunking Protocol (VTP) is responsible for replicating VLANs between switches over trunk links. Answers A and C are incorrect because these are two trunking protocols. Answers D and E are incorrect because STP and RSTP are designed to prevent loops in the network rather than replicate VLANs.

12. **C.** The **show vlan** command will display all of the current VLANs on the switch along with the ports that are assigned to each VLAN. Answer A is incorrect because VLAN information is stored in a file called vlan.dat in the Flash memory of the switch rather than existing in the running configuration. Answers B, D, and E are incorrect because these commands produce invalid syntax messages.

13. **A.** Switchport port security features must be enabled on each interface by typing the **switchport port-security** command. Unfortunately, switchport port security cannot be enabled on a global basis, making answer D incorrect. Answers B and C are incorrect because port security features work just fine with VLAN and STP features.

14. **B, D, E.** VLANs are logical separations in the Layer 3 domain. A VLAN = a subnet = a broadcast domain. Each time you create a VLAN, you separate broadcasts from other VLANs, implement a logical security boundary, and group departments or resources. Answer A is incorrect because a VLAN does not reduce your network size. Answer C is incorrect because each port on a switch represents its own collision domain.

15. **D.** Because both switches have been assigned the default STP priority (32768), the switch with the lowest MAC address will become the root bridge. All the ports of S1 will be considered designated ports, so S2 must block one of its own. It goes through the following decision criteria:

    1. Lowest cost to the root bridge is preferred.
    2. (if tied) Lowest neighbor Bridge ID is preferred.
    3. (if tied) Lower port number is preferred.

    Because both ports have the same cost, and S2 is connected to the same neighbor on both Fa0/1 and Fa0/2, the lower port number is preferred. In this case Fa0/1 will forward, and Fa0/2 will be blocked. All other answers do not apply.

16. **A.** If you look at the Operational Mode portion of the **show interface** output, you can see that the port is currently operating as an access port. Administratively, the port is configured in a state of "dynamic desirable," which means it will dynamically change between an access port or a trunk port based on the type of device being connected. Answers B and C are incorrect because the port is currently not operating as a trunk. Answer D is incorrect because the port is not disabled.

17. **A.** By reverse-engineering the subnet mask assigned to the hosts in VLAN 10, you can find the broadcast address as 10.5.113.39. Answers B and C are incorrect because these are separate subnets from the hosts in VLAN 10. Answer D is incorrect because this would be the broadcast address if we were using a /24 subnet mask. Answer E is incorrect because VLANs allow broadcasts to hosts within the same VLAN but not between VLANs.

18. **B.** Based on the output, we can see that S1 is set to Transparent mode. In this mode, S1 will not pass any VTP updates to other switches nor apply incoming VTP updates to itself. This causes VLAN 50 to create locally but not replicate to S2. All other answers do not apply.

19. **D.** Ports that are not currently in use should be shut down. This will prevent unauthorized devices from connecting to the network. Answer A is incorrect because hard-coding access port status for active hosts is an excellent security practice, but nonconnected ports should be shut down. Answers B and C are incorrect because a nonrouted or Internet VLAN would still provide minimal Layer 2 connectivity to your network where an attacker could begin wedging his way into your network.

20. **D.** The VLAN and VTP information for the switch is stored in a flash file named vlan.dat rather than in the running or startup configuration files. To remove the VLAN information from a switch, this file must be deleted. Answer A is incorrect because there is no **erase running-config** command. The running-config can only be removed through a reboot. Answer B is incorrect because there is no **erase vlan** command; rather the VLAN database is removed using the **delete flash:vlan.dat** command. Answer C is incorrect because the question stated that the switch was removed from the lab network. However, if the switch was not removed from the lab network, it may receive VTP information with the old VLAN database upon reboot.

21. **C.** VTP clients are not able to modify the VLAN database. Before you can add the VLAN from SwitchD, you must convert it to a VTP server. Answer A is incorrect because the **vlan** command is performed from global configuration mode. Answer B is incorrect because you can have multiple VTP clients connected together. The first VTP client to receive the update from the server will pass it to the other VTP clients. Answer D is incorrect because VTP does support a multiple server environment. It uses the VTP Rev number to determine the server with the most recent copy of the database. Answer E is incorrect because STP will disable a redundant link, depending on the placement of the STP root bridge; however, this will not affect connectivity to SwitchD.

22. **C.** VTP pruning allows the switches to dynamically remove unnecessary VLAN traffic from trunk links. In this case, VTP pruning would discover that no clients in VLAN 30 existed on SwitchE and would remove all VLAN 30 traffic between SwitchB and SwitchE. Answer A is incorrect because you cannot assign multiple VLANs to an access port. Answer B is incorrect because trunk links are absolutely required for a multiple VLAN configuration. Answer D is incorrect because adding the VLAN will accomplish nothing toward minimizing broadcast traffic.

23. **A.** By default, all Cisco switches are VTP servers, which give them the capability to add, remove, and change VLANs in the VTP domain and replicate those changes to other switches. Answers B and C are incorrect because these modes require an administrator to change the default Cisco switch functionality. Answer D is an invalid VTP mode.

24. **C.** When configuring an 802.1q trunk link, the Native VLAN is used to handle any traffic received on the trunk without a VLAN tag. The Native VLAN should always match between two trunked switches; by default, the Native VLAN is VLAN 1. Answer A is incorrect because the frame will be assigned to the Native VLAN rather than be dropped. Answer B is incorrect because an untagged frame does not cause a security violation. Answer D is incorrect because a trunk will remain a trunk unless manually reconfigured by the administrator.

25. The VLAN configuration is as follows:

```
Switch#configure terminal
Switch(config)#vlan 48
Switch(config-vlan)#name Marketing
Switch(config-vlan)#exit
Switch(config)#interface range fastethernet 0/1 - 10
Switch(config-if-range)#switchport access vlan 48
Switch(config-if-range)#end
Switch#show vlan
VLAN Name                             Status    Ports
---- -------------------------------- ------    -------------------------
1    default                          active    Fa0/11, Fa0/12, Fa0/13,
                                                Fa0/14, Fa0/15, Fa0/16,
                                                Fa0/17, Fa0/18, Fa0/19,
                                                Fa0/20, Fa0/21, Fa0/22,
                                                Fa0/23, Fa0/24, Gi0/1,
                                                Gi0/2
48   Marketing                        active    Fa0/1, Fa0/2, Fa0/3,
                                                Fa0/4, Fa0/5, Fa0/6,
                                                Fa0/7, Fa0/8, Fa0/9,
                                                Fa0/10,
1002 fddi-default                     act/unsup
1003 token-ring-default               act/unsup
1004 fddinet-default                  act/unsup
1005 trnet-default                    act/unsup
Switch#copy running-config startup-config
Destination filename [startup-config]?
Building configuration...
[OK]
```

26. **B.** If a port is assigned to a VLAN and the VLAN is deleted, the port loses all network connectivity. The port LED on the switch will also turn amber. To resolve this issue, move under the "lost port" and use the command **switchport access vlan <vlan #>** to reassign the port to a new VLAN. Answer A is incorrect because the port remains assigned to the now deleted VLAN. Answer C is incorrect because the port is assigned to VLAN 550, but the VLAN is not automatically re-created. Answer D is incorrect because the switch does not return an error message when the VLAN is deleted.

27. **C.** EtherChannel allows you to bundle the physical links into a single, logical bundle. It can be enabled on any modern, managed Cisco switch. Answers A and B are incorrect because STP does not need to be disabled to support this environment. After EtherChannel is enabled, STP sees all the physical links as a single connection. Answer D is incorrect because EtherChannel would be necessary on all switches to complete this configuration. Answer E is incorrect because LAPD and LAPB are old ISDN standards and have nothing to do with this configuration.

28. The port states and associated timers are shown in Figure 7.15. Keep in mind that the Blocking port state has a variable time that can be as long as 20 seconds (known as the max-age timer).

FIGURE 7.15 STP timers.

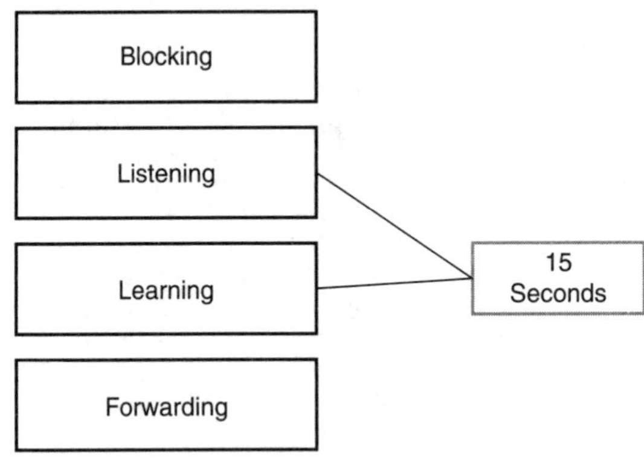

29. **A.** By default, 802.1d STP is operational on all ports of a Cisco switch. This causes a 30-second delay when connecting any network device. The PC will attempt to receive a new DHCP address and fail upon initially resuming. This causes a temporary state of being unable to access network resources. The PortFast STP feature disables STP timers on ports connecting to nonswitched devices. Answer B is incorrect because RSTP still depends on the PortFast feature. Answer C is incorrect because configuring ports as access ports does not affect the STP state. Answer D is incorrect because the DHCP server can be located anywhere on the network and still allow the clients to receive IP addresses.

30. **B.** The Per-VLAN Spanning Tree Protocol (PVSTP+) allows a separate instance of STP for each VLAN that exists on your switch. Because Figure 7.13 shows multiple root bridges (one on each VLAN), it can be assumed that the PVSTP protocol is running. PVSTP+ is Cisco proprietary and was eventually standardized by the IEEE in Multiple STP (MSTP, or 802.1s). Answers A and C are incorrect because Common STP (also known as 802.1D, or the original STP standard) only runs one instance of STP on the entire switch regardless of the number of VLANs. Answer D is incorrect because Rapid STP (RSTP) was initially released to run only one instance of RSTP per switch. Cisco added the multiple VLAN capability in PVRSTP+.

CHAPTER EIGHT

Subnetting, VLSM, and IPv6

This chapter covers the following ICND2 objectives that fall under the content areas, **Implement an IP addressing scheme and IP Services to meet network requirements in a medium-size Enterprise branch office network:**

- Calculate and apply a VLSM IP addressing design to a network.
- Determine the appropriate classless addressing scheme using VLSM and summarization to satisfy addressing requirements in a LAN/WAN environment.
- Describe the technological requirements for running IPv6 (including protocols, dual stack, tunneling, and so on).
- Describe IPv6 addresses.
- Identify and correct common problems associated with IP addressing and host configurations.

Quick Check

1. Refer to Figure 8.1. The administrator wants to reduce the size of the Central router routing table. Which of the following summary routes would represent all the LANs in Tempe, with no additional subnets?

Quick Answer: **175**
Detailed Answer: **176**

FIGURE 8.1 Network diagram.

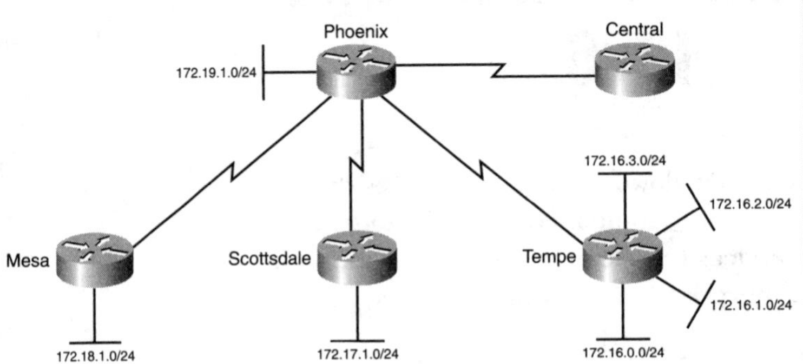

- ❍ **A.** 172.16.0.0/24
- ❍ **B.** 172.16.0.0/23
- ❍ **C.** 172.16.0.0/22
- ❍ **D.** 172.16.1.0/24
- ❍ **E.** 172.16.1.0/23
- ❍ **F.** 172.16.1.0/22

2. An Ethernet port on a router in your organization is assigned the IP address 10.65.64.1/21. What is the maximum number of hosts allowed on this subnet?

Quick Answer: **175**
Detailed Answer: **176**

- ❍ **A.** 254
- ❍ **B.** 510
- ❍ **C.** 1022
- ❍ **D.** 2046
- ❍ **E.** 4094
- ❍ **F.** 4096

Quick Check

3. Refer to Figure 8.2. All routers in the network have been configured with the **ip subnet-zero** command. Which subnet addresses should be used for Network A and Network B? (Choose two.)

Quick Answer: **175**
Detailed Answer: **176**

FIGURE 8.2 Network diagram.

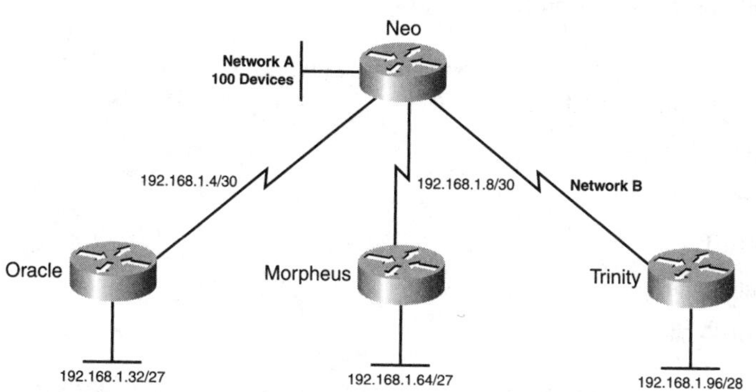

- ❍ **A.** Network A – 192.168.1.112/25
- ❍ **B.** Network A – 192.168.1.112/26
- ❍ **C.** Network A – 192.168.1.128/25
- ❍ **D.** Network B – 192.168.1.10/30
- ❍ **E.** Network B – 192.168.1.70/30
- ❍ **F.** Network B – 192.168.1.0/30

4. Which of the following are invalid IPv6 communication types? (Choose two.)

Quick Answer: **175**
Detailed Answer: **176**

- ❍ **A.** Unicast
- ❍ **B.** Multicast
- ❍ **C.** Broadcast
- ❍ **D.** Anycast
- ❍ **E.** Cryptocast

Quick Check

5. Which of the following are valid IPv6 addresses? (Choose three.)

Quick Answer: **175**
Detailed Answer: **176**

- ❍ **A.** 2001:0db8:0000:0000:0000:0000:1428:57ab
- ❍ **B.** 2001:0db8::1428:57ab
- ❍ **C.** 2001::1685:2123::1428:57ab
- ❍ **D.** 2001:99:ab:1:99:2:1:9
- ❍ **E.** 2001:1428:57ab:1685:2123:1428:57ab

6. A router that is running both IPv4 and IPv6 addressing on the same interface is known as what type of router?

Quick Answer: **175**
Detailed Answer: **177**

- ❍ **A.** 6to4
- ❍ **B.** 4to6
- ❍ **C.** NAT-PT
- ❍ **D.** 4to6 tunneling
- ❍ **E.** Dual-stack

7. RouterA is acting as an OSPF ABR between Area 1 and Area 0 as shown in Figure 8.3. Your organization wants to implement route summarization capabilities between these two areas. Which of the following describe the most efficient route summarization possibilities? (Choose two.)

Quick Answer: **175**
Detailed Answer: **177**

FIGURE 8.3 Network diagram.

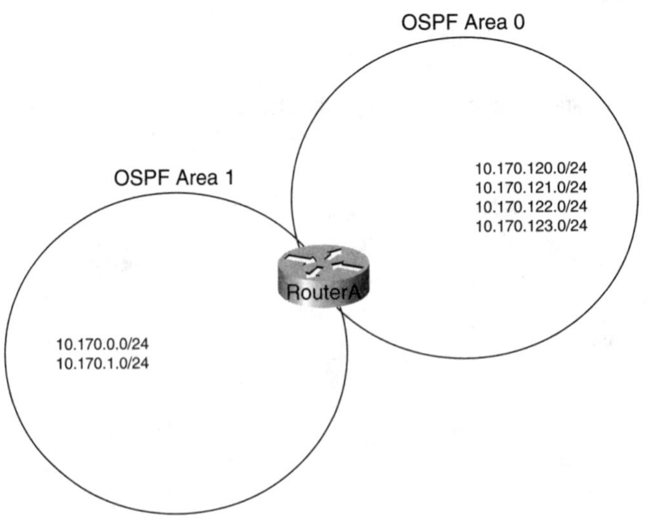

Quick Check

- ❍ **A.** OSPF Area 0 – 10.170.0.0/16
- ❍ **B.** OSPF Area 0 – 10.170.112.0/21
- ❍ **C.** OSPF Area 0 – 10.170.112.0/20
- ❍ **D.** OSPF Area 0 – 10.170.112.0/22
- ❍ **E.** OSPF Area 0 – 10.170.120.0/22
- ❍ **F.** OSPF Area 1 – 10.170.0.0/16
- ❍ **G.** OSPF Area 1 – 10.170.0.0/21
- ❍ **H.** OSPF Area 1 – 10.170.0.0/22
- ❍ **I.** OSPF Area 1 – 10.170.0.0/23

Quick Answer: **175**
Detailed Answer: **177**

8. You are designing an IP address scheme for your new remote office. The vice president of IT calls to tell you that you will be in charge of the 192.168.1.64/26 subnetwork. This supplies you with a single subnetwork with 62 hosts. You need to have at least four subnets with 14 hosts in each subnet. What custom subnet mask should you use?

- ❍ **A.** 255.255.255.128
- ❍ **B.** 255.255.255.192
- ❍ **C.** 255.255.255.224
- ❍ **D.** 255.255.255.240
- ❍ **E.** 255.255.255.248

Quick Answer: **175**
Detailed Answer: **177**

9. Identify three valid host addresses in any subnet of the 201.168.27.0 network, assuming a fixed subnet mask of 255.255.255.240. (Choose three.)

- ❍ **A.** 201.168.27.33
- ❍ **B.** 201.168.27.112
- ❍ **C.** 201.168.27.119
- ❍ **D.** 201.168.27.126
- ❍ **E.** 201.168.27.175
- ❍ **F.** 201.168.27.208

Quick Answer: **175**
Detailed Answer: **177**

Quick Check

10. A new network is being designed for your company, Acme, Inc. If you use a Class C IP network, which subnet masks will provide one usable subnet per department while allowing enough usable host addresses for each department specified in the table? (Choose three.)

Quick Answer: **175**
Detailed Answer: **178**

Department	Number of Users
Corporate	117
Customer Support	15
Financial	25
HR	5
Engineering	5

- ❍ **A.** 255.255.255.0
- ❍ **B.** 255.255.255.128
- ❍ **C.** 255.255.255.192
- ❍ **D.** 255.255.255.224
- ❍ **E.** 255.255.255.240
- ❍ **F.** 255.255.255.248
- ❍ **G.** 255.255.255.252

11. You are troubleshooting your router's interfaces. For some reason, the Ethernet interface will not accept the IP address of 192.168.5.95/27 that you've assigned. Which of the following explains the router's refusal to take the IP address?

Quick Answer: **175**
Detailed Answer: **178**

- ❍ **A.** Class C addresses cannot be assigned to Ethernet interfaces.
- ❍ **B.** The /27 is an invalid mask.
- ❍ **C.** It is a broadcast address.
- ❍ **D.** It is a network address.
- ❍ **E.** It is a public address.
- ❍ **F.** It is a private address.

Quick Check

12. Your organization has moved to IPv6 addressing. The corporate office is connected to the two branch offices through the Internet, as shown in Figure 8.4. What tunneling type is this organization using?

Quick Answer: **175**
Detailed Answer: **178**

FIGURE 8.4 Network diagram.

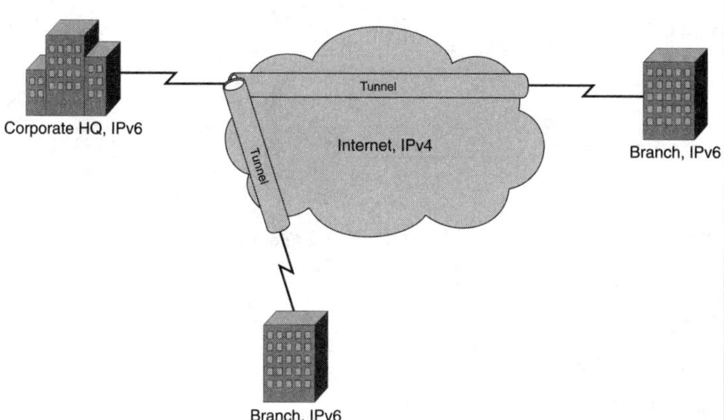

- ❍ **A.** IPv6 VPN
- ❍ **B.** 6to4 tunneling
- ❍ **C.** 4to6 tunneling
- ❍ **D.** NAT-PT, VPN based

Quick Check
Quick Answer: **175**
Detailed Answer: **178**

13. Your organization has opened a new branch office, as shown in Figure 8.5. The corporation uses 10.0.0.0/8 addressing and wants to use 172.16.X.X/24 address blocks for the branch offices. The new branch office will be large enough to require two of these blocks. Which two blocks will be easily summarizable to a single routing table entry? (Choose two.)

FIGURE 8.5 Network diagram.

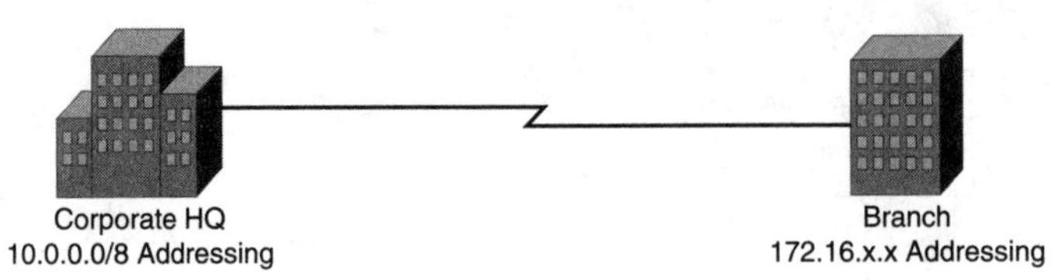

- ❍ **A.** 172.16.111.0/24
- ❍ **B.** 172.16.112.0/24
- ❍ **C.** 172.16.113.0/24
- ❍ **D.** 172.16.165.0/24
- ❍ **E.** 172.16.166.0/24

Quick Check

14. Widget, Inc., uses the Class B address 172.30.0.0/16 to address its organization. The western region of the organization (shown in Figure 8.6) has been allocated the 172.30.32.0/20 block. As the administrator of the Phoenix office, you are required to allocate valid subnets to the HQ and three branch offices shown in Figure 8.6. Draw lines showing the subnet that should be assigned to each office. All answers will not be used.

Quick Answer: **175**
Detailed Answer: **179**

FIGURE 8.6 Network diagram.

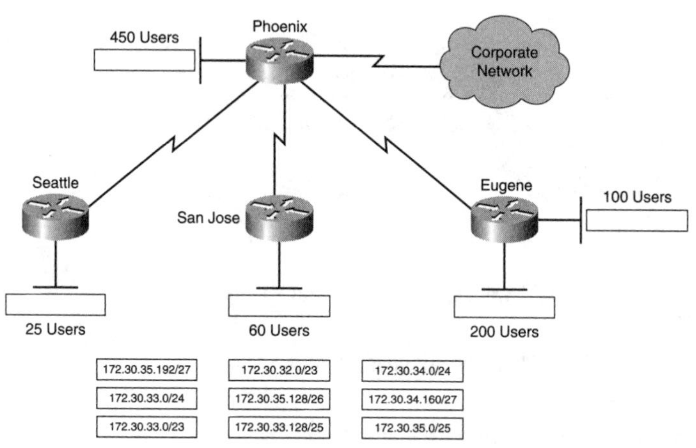

15. Which of the following routing protocols support VLSM capabilities? (Choose three.)

Quick Answer: **175**
Detailed Answer: **179**

- ❍ **A.** RIP
- ❍ **B.** RIPv2
- ❍ **C.** EIGRP
- ❍ **D.** IGRP
- ❍ **E.** OSPF

Quick Check

Quick Answer: **175**
Detailed Answer: **179**

16. XYZ Company has constructed the network shown in Figure 8.7. The company currently is using EIGRP with auto-summarization features enabled. How will routers in the corporate network see the 172.16.x.x networks behind R1?

FIGURE 8.7 Network diagram.

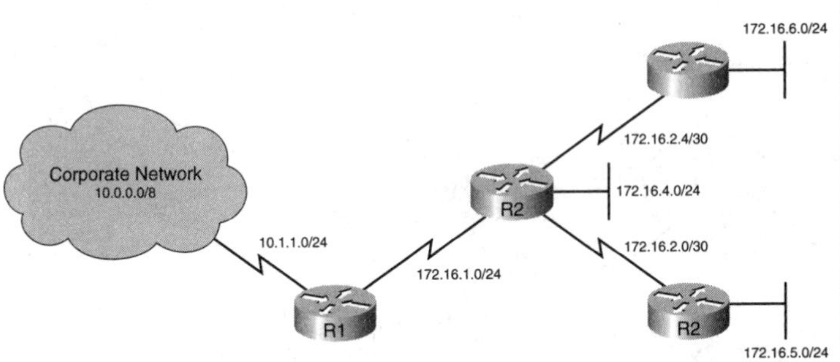

- ❍ **A.** Networks behind R1 will be summarized into a single 172.16.0.0/16 entry.
- ❍ **B.** Networks behind R1 will be summarized into a single 172.16.0.0/21 entry.
- ❍ **C.** The /24 networks behind R1 will be auto-summarized into a single 172.16.0.0/16 entry. The /30 WAN link networks will be auto-summarized into a single 172.16.2.0/24 entry.
- ❍ **D.** The /24 networks behind R1 will be auto-summarized into a single 172.16.0.0/21 entry. The /30 WAN link networks will be auto-summarized into a single 172.16.2.0/24 entry.
- ❍ **E.** EIGRP cannot handle VLSM configurations with auto-summarization enabled. This network will experience connectivity issues.

Quick Check

17. An IPv6 address is a _____-bit address.

Quick Answer: **175**
Detailed Answer: **179**

- ❍ **A.** 16
- ❍ **B.** 32
- ❍ **C.** 64
- ❍ **D.** 128
- ❍ **E.** 256

18. In IPv6, Internet-valid addresses are known by what name?

Quick Answer: **175**
Detailed Answer: **179**

- ❍ **A.** Private
- ❍ **B.** Public
- ❍ **C.** Unique
- ❍ **D.** Unspecified
- ❍ **E.** Global

19. In IPv6, a __________ address is used to communicate with hosts on the directly attached network and will never forward beyond the first router hop.

Quick Answer: **175**
Detailed Answer: **180**

- ❍ **A.** Global
- ❍ **B.** Private
- ❍ **C.** Link local
- ❍ **D.** Private restricted
- ❍ **E.** Auto-generated

20. Which of the following commands could you use to assign an IPv6 address to your router?

Quick Answer: **175**
Detailed Answer: **180**

- ❍ **A.** Router(config-if)#**ip address fe01:3112:abcd::0001 255.255.255.0**
- ❍ **B.** Router(config-if)#**ip address fe01:3112:abcd::0001/48**
- ❍ **C.** Router(config-if)#**ip address 6 fe01:3112:abcd::0001 255.255.255.0**
- ❍ **D.** Router(config-if)#**ip address 6 fe01:3112:abcd::0001/48**
- ❍ **E.** Router(config-if)#**ipv6 address fe01:3112:abcd::0001 255.255.255.0**
- ❍ **F.** Router(config-if)#**ipv6 address fe01:3112:abcd::0001/48**

Quick Check

21. Which of the following commands could you use to start a RIPng process on your router?

Quick Answer: **175**
Detailed Answer: **180**

- ❍ **A.** Router(config)#**router RIPng**
- ❍ **B.** Router(config)#**ipv6 router rip RIPng**
- ❍ **C.** Router(config)#**routerv6 RIP**
- ❍ **D.** Router(config)#**ripv6**

22. TooCow University has acquired the 150.60.130.0/24 public address from the local ISP to use in its campus network. Each building has a specific number of devices that are required to be publicly accessible, as shown in Figure 8.8. Which of the following subnets would accommodate the network shown? (Choose four.)

Quick Answer: **175**
Detailed Answer: **180**

FIGURE 8.8 Network diagram.

- ❍ **A.** 150.60.130.128/26
- ❍ **B.** 150.60.130.128/27
- ❍ **C.** 150.60.130.96/27
- ❍ **D.** 150.60.130.192/28
- ❍ **E.** 150.60.130.32/27
- ❍ **F.** 150.60.130.160/27
- ❍ **G.** 150.60.130.16/28
- ❍ **H.** 150.60.130.0/25

Quick Check

23. Choose the most efficient summary address to encompass the following subnets:

Quick Answer: **175**
Detailed Answer: **180**

192.168.112.0/24

192.168.113.0/24

192.168.114.0/24

192.168.115.0/24

192.168.116.0/24

192.168.117.0/24

192.168.118.0/24

192.168.119.0/24

❍ **A.** 192.168.110.0/20
❍ **B.** 192.168.110.0/21
❍ **C.** 192.168.110.0/22
❍ **D.** 192.168.112.0/20
❍ **E.** 192.168.112.0/21
❍ **F.** 192.168.112.0/22

24. Choose the most efficient summary address to encompass the following subnets:

Quick Answer: **175**
Detailed Answer: **181**

172.16.4.0/24

172.16.5.0/24

172.16.6.0/24

172.16.128.0/24

❍ **A.** 172.16.0.0/21
❍ **B.** 172.16.4.0/21
❍ **C.** 172.16.4.0/22
❍ **D.** 172.16.0.0/16

25. Is 172.20.2.255/23 a valid IP address?

Quick Answer: **175**
Detailed Answer: **181**

❍ **A.** No, it is the broadcast address for the 172.16.2.0/24 subnet.
❍ **B.** No, it is the broadcast address for the 172.16.2.0/23 subnet.
❍ **C.** Yes, but you cannot assign the IP address to a host.
❍ **D.** Yes, and you can assign the IP address to a host.

Quick Check

26. Given the subnet 10.5.12.0/22, which of the following IP addresses are valid host addresses residing within the network? (Choose three.)

❍ **A.** 10.5.14.253

❍ **B.** 10.5.14.255

❍ **C.** 10.5.13.0

❍ **D.** 10.5.16.1

❍ **E.** 10.5.16.2

Quick Answer: **175**
Detailed Answer: **181**

27. Which of the following is a valid equivalent of the IPv6 address 2001:0ab9:0000:0000:0003:0000:59ff:1ac5?

❍ **A.** 2001:0ab9::3::59ff:1ac5

❍ **B.** 2001:ab9:0:0:3::59ff:1ac5

❍ **C.** 2001:ab9::359ff:1ac5

❍ **D.** 2001:0ab9:__:3:_:59ff:1ac5

Quick Answer: **175**
Detailed Answer: **181**

Quick Check

28. Your organization has decided to move forward with a complete readdressing of the entire network. Using Figure 8.9 as a guide, break the 172.18.0.0/16 network into initial allocations for the regions. Draw lines connecting the correct allocations to the regions.

Quick Answer: 175
Detailed Answer: 182

FIGURE 8.9 Network diagram.

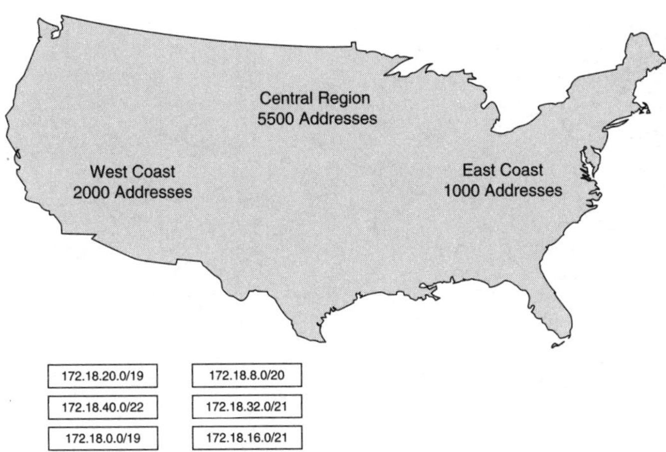

29. Observe the following output from the **show run** command:

Quick Answer: 175
Detailed Answer: 182

```
Current configuration : 104 bytes
!
interface FastEthernet0/0
 ip address 172.30.2.1 255.255.252.0
 no ip route-cache
 no ip mroute-cache
end
```

How many host IP addresses are able to be used from the network to which this FastEthernet interface is connected?

- ❍ **A.** 255
- ❍ **B.** 1022
- ❍ **C.** 1024
- ❍ **D.** 2046
- ❍ **E.** 2048

Quick Check

30. Which of the following commands enables the IPv6 protocol on a router?

   - ❍ **A.** Router(config)#**ipv6 unicast-routing**
   - ❍ **B.** Router(config)#**ipv6 enable**
   - ❍ **C.** Router(config)#**enable ipv6**
   - ❍ **D.** Router(config)#**ipv6**
   - ❍ **E.** Router(config)#**router ipv6**

Quick Answer: **175**
Detailed Answer: **182**

Quick Check Answer Key

1. C
2. D
3. C, F
4. C, E
5. A, B, D
6. E
7. E, I
8. D
9. A, C, D
10. B, D, F
11. C
12. B
13. B, C
14. See detailed answer
15. B, C, E
16. A
17. D
18. E
19. C
20. F
21. B
22. B, D, F, H
23. E
24. D
25. D
26. A, B, C
27. B
28. See detailed answer
29. B
30. A

Answers and Explanations

1. **C.** 172.16.0-3.0/22 breaks down into the following binary equivalents:

   172.16.0.0 = 10101100.00010000.00000000.00000000

   172.16.1.0 = 10101100.00010000.00000001.00000000

   172.16.2.0 = 10101100.00010000.00000010.00000000

   172.16.3.0 = 10101100.00010000.00000011.00000000

   Based on these binary values, you can see that the first 22 bits on each one of these IP addresses are the same. This makes the accurate summary address 172.16.0.0/22. All other answers are not valid.

2. **D.** To find the valid number of hosts on a subnet, use the formula $(2^{x}) - 2$, where "x" is the number of host bits in the subnet mask. A /21 (255.255.248.0) subnet mask has 11 host bits. $(2^{11}) - 2 = 2046$. All other answers are not valid.

3. **C, F.** These styles of VLSM are common on the ICND2/CCNA exam. It's usually best to reverse-engineer the given subnets to see what ranges are in use and then compare the answers to fill in what's left over. In this case, the given ranges are:

   192.168.1.32-63/27 (Behind the Oracle router)

   192.168.1.64-95/27 (Behind the Morpheus router)

   192.168.1.96-111/28 (Behind the Trinity router)

   192.168.1.4-7/30 (Neo-Oracle WAN link)

   192.168.1.8-11/30 (Neo-Morpheus WAN link)

   With that given information, answer C (192.168.1.128-255/25) and answer F (192.168.1.0-3/30) best fit the scenario. Answers A, D, and E are incorrect because these are invalid subnet addresses. Answer B is incorrect because the /26 mask will only provide 64 IP addresses, which is not sufficient for the size of Network A. These addresses also overlap with the other office subnets.

4. **C, E.** IPv6 uses three types of communication: Unicast (one-to-one), Multicast (one-to-many), and Anycast (one-to-closest). Answer C is incorrect because the concept of Broadcast messaging is tied with the IPv4 protocol and is no longer valid in IPv6. Answer E is incorrect because there is no such thing as Cryptocast messaging.

5. **A, B, D.** An IPv6 address consists of eight sets that can be four hexadecimal characters each. Consecutive sets of zeros can be abbreviated with a double colon (::), but this can only be used once in each IP address. Leading zeros can also be dropped. Based on these rules, addresses from the question can be described as:

   2001:0db8:0000:0000:0000:0000:1428:57ab (Valid, eight sets)

   2001:0db8::1428:57ab (Valid, same address as above with abbreviation)

   2001::1685:2123::1428:57ab (Invalid use of double colon)

   2001:99:ab:1:99:2:1:9 (Valid, dropped leading zeros)

   2001:1428:57ab:1685:2123: 1428:57ab (Invalid, only seven sets)

6. **E.** A dual-stack router can receive requests from both IPv4 and IPv6 clients on the same interface. This provides a smoother transition between the two protocols. Answers A, B, and D are incorrect because these all describe tunneling methods (IPv4 tunneled through an IPv6 network = 4to6). Answer C is incorrect because this describes a newer form of NAT that is able to translate between IPv4 and IPv6 addressing.

7. **E, I.** 10.170.120-123.0/24 breaks into the following binary equivalents:

    10.170.120.0 = 00001010.10101010.01111000.00000000

    10.170.121.0 = 00001010.10101010.01111001.00000000

    10.170.122.0 = 00001010.10101010.01111010.00000000

    10.170.123.0 = 00001010.10101010.01111011.00000000

   Based on this, we can see that the first 22 bits of each subnet are the same, thus the summary address is 10.170.120.0/22 for Area 0 (answer E). 10.170.0-1.0/24 breaks into the following binary equivalents:

    10.170.0.0 = 00001010.10101010. 00000000.00000000

    10.170.1.0 = 00001010.10101010. 00000001.00000000

   Based on this, we can see that the first 23 bits of each subnet are the same, thus the summary address is 10.170.0.0/23 (answer I). All other answers are not valid.

8. **D.** This subnet mask gives you four additional subnets using VLSM, with up to 14 hosts per subnetwork. Answer A is incorrect, as it is a higher subnet mask than your original /26, which is actually called *supernetting*. Answer B is incorrect because it is your original subnet mask. Answer C is incorrect, as it does not give you enough subnets. Answer E is incorrect, as it gives you enough subnets (six), but you would have only six hosts.

9. **A, C,** and **D.** A subnet mask of 255.255.255.240 divides the fourth octet into subnet parts: the highest four bits and a host part (the lowest four bits). You simply check the fourth octet to ensure that all subnet and host parts are okay. The host bit portion cannot be 0000 or 1111. Answers A, C, and D are correct because 33 in decimal is 00100001, 119 in decimal is 01110111, and 126 in decimal is 01111110. Answer B is incorrect, as 112 in decimal is 01110000 in binary. This is not a valid host address in this network. All its host bits are zero. Answer E is incorrect, as 175 in decimal is 10101111 in binary. All host bits are ones. This is the local broadcast address and cannot be used as a host address. Answer F is incorrect, as 208 in decimal is 11010000 in binary. This is not a valid host address in this network, and all its host bits are zero.

10. **B, D, F.** The departments will use the following subnet masks:

Department	Number of Users	Subnet Mask
Corporate	117	255.255.255.128 (126 hosts)
Customer Support	15	255.255.255.224 (30 hosts)
Financial	25	255.255.255.224 (30 hosts)
HR	5	255.255.255.248 (6 hosts)
Engineering	5	255.255.255.248 (6 hosts)

All other answers are invalid.

11. **C.** It is not a valid host address; 192.168.5.95/27 is a directed broadcast address for the 192.168.5.64 network. Answer A is incorrect, as you can certainly assign Class C addresses to any type of interface. Answer B is incorrect, as the /27 mask is the 255.255.255.224 subnet mask, which is perfectly valid. Answer D is incorrect because 192.168.5.95/27 represents a broadcast address rather than a network address. Answer E is incorrect because it is a private IP address. Answer F is incorrect, as the fact that it is a private IP address will not cause it to be refused by an interface.

12. **B.** One of the IPv6 transition schemes includes an IPv6 to IPv4 (6to4) tunneling method. This allows you to tunnel your IPv6 networks through an IPv4 network. Answer A is incorrect because the VPN is actually using the IPv4 Internet as its connection point. Answer C is incorrect because 4to6 tunnels involve IPv4 networks tunneling through an IPv6 network. Answer D is incorrect because NAT-PT is a form of NAT that can handle translations between protocol suites. It is not related to VPN technology.

13. **B, C.** 172.16.112.0/24 and 172.16.113.0/24 can be summarized into the single entry 172.16.112.0/23. Answers A, D, and E represent addresses that cannot be summarized into a single routing entry that only encompasses two of the /24 network ranges.

14.

FIGURE 8.10 Network diagram.

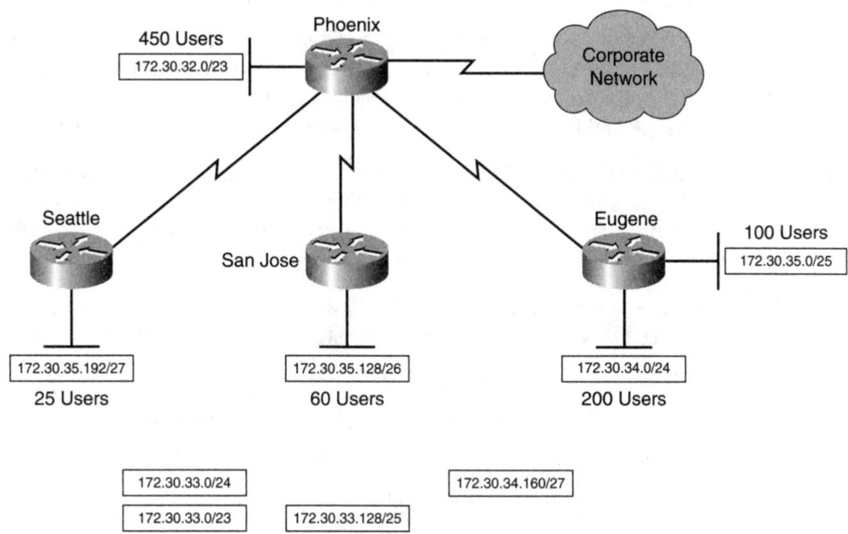

15. **B, C, E.** RIPv2, EIGRP, and OSPF all support Variable Length Subnet Mask (VLSM) capabilities. Answers A and D are incorrect because RIPv1 and IGRP are classful routing protocols and do not support VLSM.

16. **A.** When auto-summarization is enabled, EIGRP will summarize networks back to their classful boundary anytime a discontiguous network is reached (such as the transition from 10.0.0.0/8 networks to 172.16.0.0/16 networks). In this case, R1 will summarize the corporate network back to 10.0.0.0/8 as it passes the routing update to R2. It will also summarize all the 172.16.x.x networks back to 172.16.0.0/16 as it passes the routing update into the corporate network. Answers B, C, and D are incorrect because auto-summarization only summarizes back to a classful boundary rather than to more specific subnet masks. Answer E is incorrect because EIGRP can handle VLSM with auto-summarization enabled.

17. **D.** IPv6 addresses have been expanded to 128-bit addressing from the 32-bit addressing of IPv4. This provides a virtually inexhaustible number of addresses (although, I'm sure many thought the same of the IPv4 address space). All other answers do not apply.

18. **E.** The Internet-valid addresses are considered "global" addresses in IPv6. They are specified to begin with 2000::/3. Answer A is incorrect because private addresses are for use in a private network, as it currently happens in IPv4 addressing. Answer B is incorrect because global addresses have replaced public addresses. Answers C and D do not apply directly to IPv6 addressing.

19. **C.** Link-local addressing is a new concept when moving from IPv4 to IPv6. Link-local addresses are used to communicate directly on a link. This is used for communication such as establishing OSPF neighbor relationships or sending RIP routes. Answer A is incorrect because global addresses can access the Internet directly. Answer B is incorrect because private IPv6 addresses can route through an organization. The addresses shown in answers D and E do not exist in the IPv6 environment.

20. **F.** IPv6 addresses are assigned using the **ipv6 address** command. In IPv6, there is no decimal version of the subnet mask; all subnet masks are written in bit-notation. Answers A, C, and E are incorrect because they use the decimal version of the subnet mask. Answers B and D are incorrect because they use the incorrect command.

21. **B.** The exact syntax to enable the RIPng (RIP for IPv6) routing protocol is **ipv6 router rip** <*tag*>. The tag can be anything from a number to a name; in this question, the tag was "RIPng". This tag must be used when enabling RIP on an interface-by-interface basis. Answers A, C, and D will produce invalid syntax messages.

22. **B, D, F, H.** To perform the most efficient VLSM, always begin with the biggest subnet first. The ranges that will properly address the network in Figure 8.8 are as follows:

    - Server Farm: 150.60.130.0-127/25 (answer H)
    - College of Education: 150.60.130.128-159/27 (answer B)
    - College of Business: 150.60.130.160-191/27 (answer F)
    - Administration: 150.60.130.192-207/28 (answer D)

    Answers A, C, E, and G are incorrect because they would each address a portion of the network but would not function correctly with the other given subnets.

23. The binary equivalents of the shown addresses are as follows, reflected in answer E:

    192.168.112.0 = <u>11000000.10101000.01110000.00000000</u>

    192.168.113.0 = <u>11000000.10101000.01110001.00000000</u>

    192.168.114.0 = <u>11000000.10101000.01110010.00000000</u>

    192.168.115.0 = <u>11000000.10101000.01110011.00000000</u>

    192.168.116.0 = <u>11000000.10101000.01110100.00000000</u>

    192.168.117.0 = <u>11000000.10101000.01110101.00000000</u>

    192.168.118.0 = <u>11000000.10101000.01110110.00000000</u>

    192.168.119.0 = <u>11000000.10101000.01110111.00000000</u>

    This shows that the first 21 bits of all these addresses are the same making the summary address 192.168.112.0/21. Answers A, B, and C are incorrect because 192.168.110.0 is an inaccurate starting point for the subnets. Answers D and F assume the wrong subnet mask.

24. The binary equivalents of the shown addresses are as follows, reflected in answer D:

172.16.4.0 = 10101100.00010000.00000100.00000000

172.16.5.0 = 10101100.00010000.00000101.00000000

172.16.6.0 = 10101100.00010000.00000110.00000000

172.16.128.0 = 10101100.00010000.10000000.00000000

Because of the last subnet (172.16.128.0/24), a good summarization is not possible with these subnets. We must drop back to the classful summarization of 172.16.0.0/16. This helps demonstrate why discontiguous network addressing can destroy your network summarization efficiency. Answers A, B, and C are incorrect because the summarization addresses fail to encompass the 172.16.128.0/24 subnet.

25. **D.** The IP address 172.20.2.255/23 comes from the range of 172.20.2.0 through 172.30.3.255. The network ID 172.20.2.0 cannot be assigned to a host. The broadcast ID 172.20.3.255 cannot be assigned to a host. Everything in the middle of the range will function just fine. The other answers do not apply.

26. **A, B, C.** Given the 10.5.12.0/22 subnet, we can find the range of addresses to be 10.5.12.0 to 10.5.15.255. This makes Answers A, B, and C correct. Answers D and E are incorrect because they belong to the next subnet.

27. **B.** There are two ways of shortening an IPv6 address: removing a single group of consecutive zeros by using the double colon (::) and removing leading zeros from a set. Answer B (2001:ab9:0:0:3::59ff:1ac5) shortens the sets by removing leading zeros and abbreviates the second group of consecutive zeros by using the ::. Answer A incorrectly uses a :: twice in the IPv6 address. Answer C has too many characters in one of the sets. Answer D uses the underscore character, which is invalid.

28.

FIGURE 8.11 Network diagram.

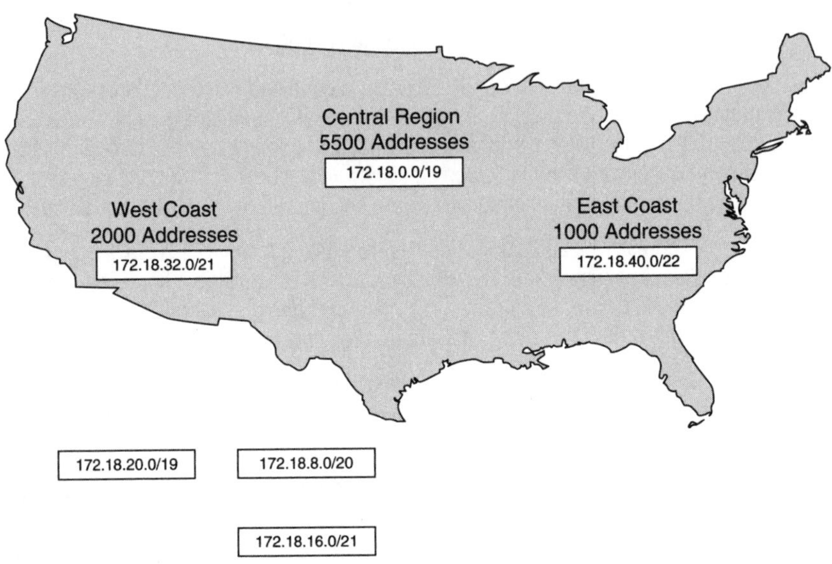

29. **B.** To find the number of valid host IP addresses, use the formula $(2^x) - 2$, where "x" represents the number of host bits. In this case, the FastEthernet interface has the subnet mask 255.255.252.0, which uses 10 hosts bits. $(2^{10}) - 2 = 1022$. The other answers are not valid.

30. **A.** To enable the IPv6 protocol, use the command **ipv6 unicast-routing** from global configuration mode. All other answers produce an invalid syntax or incomplete command message.

CHAPTER NINE

Advanced Routing Configuration

This chapter covers the following ICND2 objectives that fall under the content areas, **Configure and troubleshoot basic operation and routing on Cisco devices:**

- ▶ Compare and contrast methods of routing and routing protocols.
- ▶ Configure, verify, and troubleshoot OSPF.
- ▶ Configure, verify, and troubleshoot EIGRP.
- ▶ Verify configuration and connectivity using ping, traceroute, and Telnet or SSH.
- ▶ Troubleshoot routing implementation issues.
- ▶ Verify router hardware and software operation using **SHOW** and **DEBUG** commands.
- ▶ Implement basic router security.

Quick Check

1. You are configuring the router shown in Figure 9.1 for OSPF. Which of the following network commands will add all shown interfaces on R1 to the OSPF process? (Choose two.)

Quick Answer: **202**
Detailed Answer: **203**

FIGURE 9.1 Network diagram.

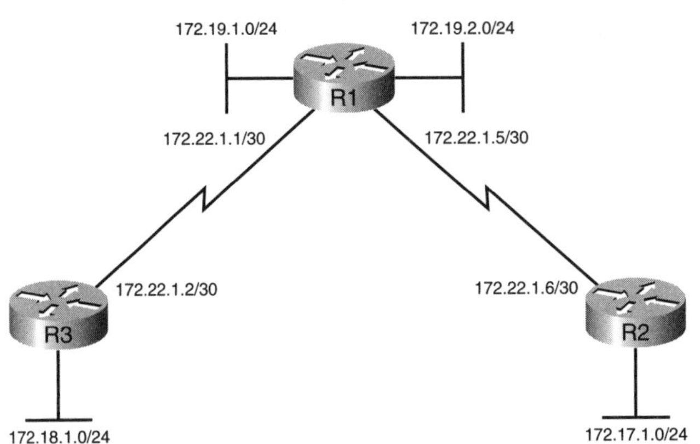

- ❍ **A.** R1(config-router)#**network 172.0.0.0 255.0.0.0 area 0**
- ❍ **B.** R1(config-router)#**network 172.19-22.0.0 255.255.0.0 area 0**
- ❍ **C.** R1(config-router)#**network 172.0.0.0 0.255.255.255 area 0**
- ❍ **D.** R1(config-router)#**network 172.19-22.0.0 0.0.255.255 area 0**
- ❍ **E.** R1(config-router)#**network 0.0.0.0 255.255.255.255 area 0**

Quick Check

Quick Answer: **202**
Detailed Answer: **203**

2. You issue the following command:

```
RouterA#show ip route

Codes: C - connected, S - static, I - IGRP, R - RIP, M - mobile,
A B – BGP D - EIGRP, EX - EIGRP external, O - OSPF, IA – OSPF
A inter area N1 - OSPF NSSA external type 1, N2 - OSPF NSSA
A external type 2 E1 - OSPF external type 1, E2 - OSPF external
A type 2, E - EGP i - IS-IS, L1 - IS-IS level-1, L2 - IS-IS
A level-2, * - candidate default U - per-user static route, o -
A ODR
Gateway of last resort is 172.31.0.1 to network 0.0.0.0
D 192.168.15.0/24 [90/2681856] via 10.0.0.2, 3w2d, Serial0/1
R 172.16.0.0/16 [120/1] via 172.31.0.1, 00:00:05, Serial0/0
 172.31.0.0/16 is variably subnetted, 2 subnets, 2 masks
D 172.31.0.0/16 is a summary, 3w2d, Null0
C 172.31.0.0/24 is directly connected, Serial0/0
C 192.168.250.0/24 is directly connected, Serial0/1.1
C 10.0.0.0/8 is directly connected, Serial0/1
 150.1.0.0/16 is variably subnetted, 2 subnets, 2 masks
C 150.1.3.0/24 is directly connected, Ethernet0/0
D 150.1.0.0/16 is a summary, 3w2d, Null0
S* 0.0.0.0/0 [1/0] via 172.31.0.1
```

What is the meaning of the [90/2681856] in the output following the command?

❍ **A.** It's the port number and hop count of the RIP routing protocol.

❍ **B.** It's the administrative distance and hop count of the EIGRP routing protocol.

❍ **C.** It's the port number and metric of the EIGRP routing protocol.

❍ **D.** It's the administrative distance and metric of the route learned through EIGRP.

Quick Check

3. When dealing with distance-vector routing protocols, you encounter the term *split-horizon*. Which of the following statements describes this feature?

Quick Answer: **202**
Detailed Answer: **203**

- ❍ **A.** It allows routers to split up networks.
- ❍ **B.** All distance-vector protocols require fallback routers that might cause momentary loops as the topology changes.
- ❍ **C.** Convergence is achieved if all information about routers is sent out on all active interfaces.
- ❍ **D.** Information about a router should not be sent back in the direction from which the original update came.

4. You type **show ip route** on RouterA to find out what entries are in your RIP routing table. Which of the following routes would not be found on a separate router receiving an RIP update from RouterA?

Quick Answer: **202**
Detailed Answer: **203**

- ❍ **A. R 172.16.0.0/16 [120/4]**
- ❍ **B. R 192.168.9.0/24 [120/2]**
- ❍ **C. C 192.168.4.0/24**
- ❍ **D. R 192.168.7.0/24 [120/15]**
- ❍ **E. R 192.168.8.0/24 [120/8]**

5. Refer to the network diagram shown in Figure 9.2.

Quick Answer: **202**
Detailed Answer: **203**

FIGURE 9.2 Network diagram.

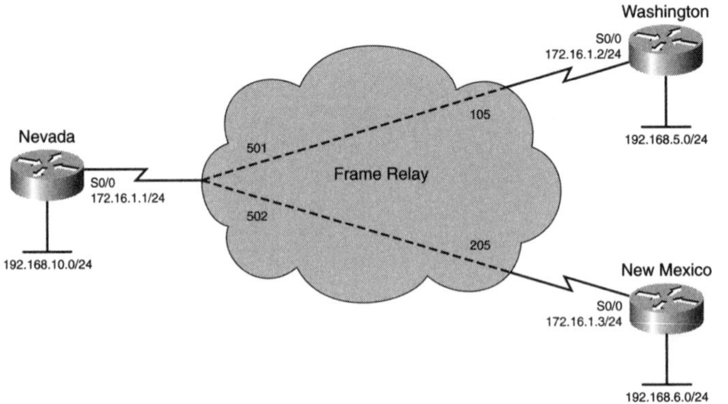

Quick Check

You have configured the routers shown using the EIGRP protocol. The relevant configuration is as follows:

Washington router:

```
Wash(config)#router eigrp 100
Wash(config-router)#network 172.16.0.0
Wash(config-router)#network 192.168.5.0
Wash(config-router)#no auto-summary
```

Nevada router:

```
Nev(config)#router eigrp 100
Nev(config-router)#network 172.16.0.0
Nev(config-router)#network 192.168.10.0
Nev(config-router)#no auto-summary
```

New Mexico router:

```
NewM(config)#router eigrp 100
NewM(config-router)#network 172.16.0.0
NewM(config-router)#network 192.168.6.0
NewM(config-router)#no auto-summary
```

Users in Washington and New Mexico are complaining about connectivity issues; however, users in Nevada seem to be working just fine. What is the most likely cause of the problem?

- ❍ **A.** The EIGRP protocol is not to be used on Frame Relay networks. Cisco recommends using either OSPF or RIP industry standard protocols in this style of configuration.
- ❍ **B.** Because EIGRP is technically categorized as a distance-vector routing protocol, split-horizon causes problems in this configuration.
- ❍ **C.** The EIGRP autonomous system 100 is reserved for loopback routing protocol communication.
- ❍ **D.** The **no auto-summary** command causes routing issues in this environment because the configuration is using class C subnet masks for the 172.16.0.0 network.

Quick Check

6. Which statements are true regarding the command sequence shown here? (Choose three.)

Quick Answer: **202**
Detailed Answer: **203**

```
RouterA(config)# interface loopback 0
RouterA(config-if)# ip address 192.168.31.33 255.255.255.255
```

- ❍ **A.** It creates a virtual interface.
- ❍ **B.** It uses a subnet mask.
- ❍ **C.** It ensures that an interface is always active, even if a router is shut off.
- ❍ **D.** It provides an easier way to identify OSPF routing updates.
- ❍ **E.** The mask of 255.255.255.255 is called a wildcard mask.

7. Which of the following distance vector loop prevention algorithms prevent flapping router interfaces from causing a major network disruption?

Quick Answer: **202**
Detailed Answer: **204**

- ❍ **A.** Split-horizon
- ❍ **B.** Route poisoning
- ❍ **C.** Hold-down timers
- ❍ **D.** Poison reverse
- ❍ **E.** Triggered updates

8. Your organization is considering breaking their single area OSPF network into multiple areas. What are valid reasons to make this change? (Choose two.)

Quick Answer: **202**
Detailed Answer: **204**

- ❍ **A.** Implementation of OSPF route summarization
- ❍ **B.** Reducing the number of times the SPF algorithm runs on routers
- ❍ **C.** To provide interoperability with other routing protocols
- ❍ **D.** To implement security boundaries between networks
- ❍ **E.** To limit the number of OSPF neighbor relationships

Quick Check

9. Using Figure 9.3, draw lines connecting the type of router to the router's position on the network diagram. Some answers may be used more than once, and others will not be used at all.

Quick Answer: **202**
Detailed Answer: **204**

FIGURE 9.3 Network diagram.

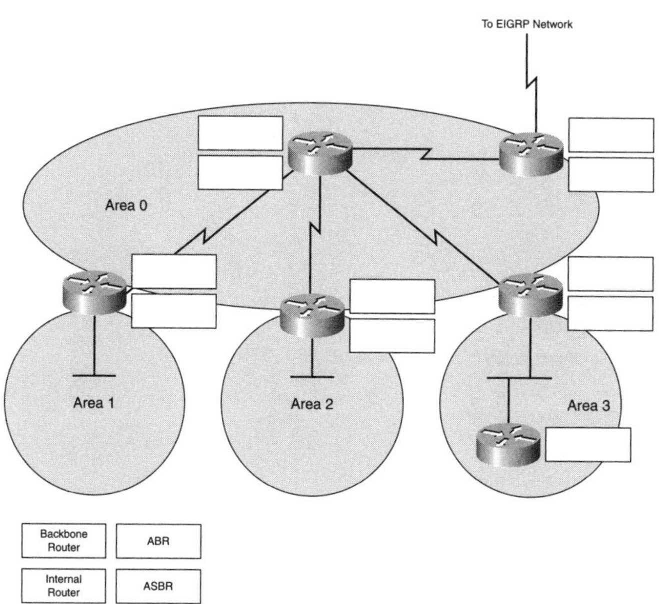

10. How are OSPF Hello messages sent to an attached network?

Quick Answer: **202**
Detailed Answer: **205**

- ❍ **A.** Unicast messages to each neighbor
- ❍ **B.** Multicast to the group IP 224.0.0.5
- ❍ **C.** Multicast to the group IP 224.0.0.10
- ❍ **D.** Broadcast

Quick Check

Quick Answer: **202**
Detailed Answer: **205**

11. Refer to Figure 9.4. Which of the following OSPF configurations will enable OSPF on only the Serial 0/0 and FastEthernet 0/0 interfaces of R3? (Choose two.)

FIGURE 9.4 Network diagram.

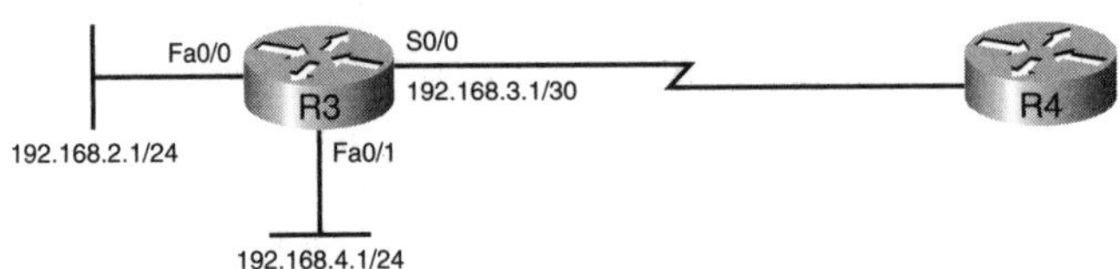

❍ **A.**

```
Router(config)#router ospf 1
Router(config-router)#router-id 3.3.3.3
Router(config-router)#network 192.168.0.0 0.0.255.255 area 0
```

❍ **B.**

```
Router(config)#router ospf 1
Router(config-router)#router-id 3.3.3.3
Router(config-router)#network 192.168.0.0 0.0.3.255 area 0
```

❍ **C.**

```
Router(config)#router ospf 1
Router(config-router)#router-id 3.3.3.3
Router(config-router)#network 192.168.2.1 0.0.0.0 area 0
Router(config-router)#network 192.168.3.1 0.0.0.0 area 0
```

❍ **D.**

```
Router(config)#router ospf 1
Router(config-router)#router-id 3.3.3.3
Router(config-router)#network 192.168.2.0 255.255.255.0 area 0
Router(config-router)#network 192.168.3.0 255.255.255.0 area 0
```

❍ **E.**

```
Router(config)#router ospf 1
Router(config-router)#router-id 3.3.3.3
Router(config-router)#network 192.168.2.0 area 0
Router(config-router)#network 192.168.3.0 area 0
```

Quick Check

12. After configuring OSPF on a router, you decide to verify the interface status by using the **show ip interface brief** command.

Quick Answer: **202**
Detailed Answer: **205**

```
Router#show ip interface brief
Interface            IP-Address     OK?    Method    Status     Protocol
FastEthernet0/0      192.168.10.1   YES    manual    up         up
FastEthernet0/1      192.168.11.1   YES    unset     up         up
Serial0/0/0          200.1.5.9      YES    unset     up         up
Loopback3            10.1.1.25      YES    unset     up         up
```

Based on this output, what is the OSPF router-id? (Note: The **router-id** command was not used in the OSPF configuration.)

- ❍ **A.** 192.168.10.1
- ❍ **B.** 192.168.11.1
- ❍ **C.** 200.1.5.9
- ❍ **D.** 10.1.1.25

Quick Check

13. As shown in Figure 9.5, your organization has decided to run OSPF between the internal routers R2 and R3. Because of this, R3 can currently reach any OSPF network in Area 0. Many of the transactions your company performs are saved to database servers behind R4, which is controlled by a third party. Because of the large number of 192.168.x.x networks available behind R4, you decide to configure connectivity via a static route using the following syntax:

Quick Answer: 202
Detailed Answer: 205

```
R3(config)#ip route 192.168.0.0 255.255.0.0 192.168.3.2
```

After configuring this static route, your router receives traffic destined for the 192.168.1.0/24 subnet. How does your router handle this traffic?

FIGURE 9.5 Network diagram.

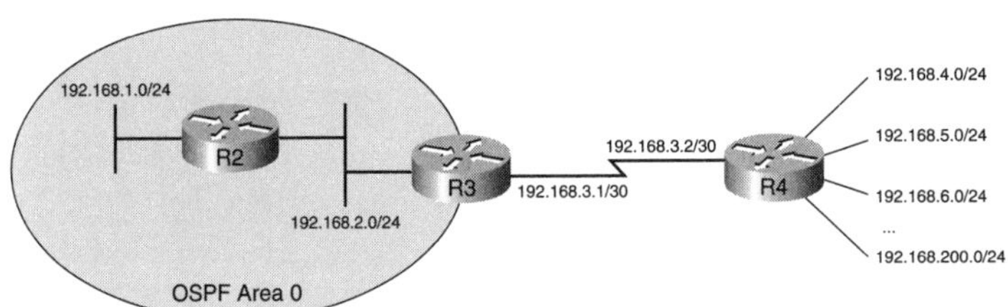

- ❍ **A.** R3 forwards the traffic to R4 because the administrative distance of the static route is better than the administrative distance of the OSPF route.
- ❍ **B.** R3 forwards the traffic to R4 because the subnet mask on the static route shows a greater number of networks than the subnet mask on the OSPF routes.
- ❍ **C.** R3 forwards the traffic to R2 because OSPF routes are preferred to static routes.
- ❍ **D.** R3 forwards the traffic to R2 because the OSPF routes received have a more specific subnet mask than the static route.

Quick Check

Use the following output to answer the next four questions:

```
Neighbor ID     Pri   State      Dead Time   Address    Interface
192.168.45.1    1     FULL/DR    00:00:36    10.0.0.1   Ethernet0
```

14. Based on the command output, when was the last OSPF Hello message received? (Note: The default OSPF timer configuration has not been modified.)

   ❍ **A.** 1 second ago
   ❍ **B.** 4 seconds ago
   ❍ **C.** 24 seconds ago
   ❍ **D.** 36 seconds ago

Quick Answer: **202**
Detailed Answer: **206**

15. Based on the command output, what is the IP address of the remote neighbor?

   ❍ **A.** 192.168.45.1
   ❍ **B.** 10.0.0.1
   ❍ **C.** 192.168.45.2
   ❍ **D.** 10.0.0.2

Quick Answer: **202**
Detailed Answer: **206**

16. Assuming this is a complete OSPF neighbor table, what can we assume about the OSPF state of THIS OSPF router? (Note: The default OSPF timer and priority configuration have not been modified. Assume the output shows a complete table.)

   ❍ **A.** It is a backbone router.
   ❍ **B.** It is a backup designated router.
   ❍ **C.** It is an internal router.
   ❍ **D.** It has missed at least two hello messages.
   ❍ **E.** It has missed at least three hello messages.

Quick Answer: **202**
Detailed Answer: **206**

17. What command was used to generate the shown OSPF output?

   ❍ **A.** **show ip ospf neighbor**
   ❍ **B.** **show ip ospf interface**
   ❍ **C.** **show ip ospf**
   ❍ **D.** **show ip ospf database**

Quick Answer: **202**
Detailed Answer: **206**

Quick Check

18. You are managing the network shown in Figure 9.6. Users in Arizona are complaining about connectivity issues to the New York and Florida offices. While performing some basic connectivity tests, you receive the following output from the Arizona router:

Quick Answer: 202
Detailed Answer: 206

```
Arizona#ping 172.17.2.1
Type escape sequence to abort.
Sending 5, 100-byte ICMP Echos to 172.17.2.1, timeout is 2
seconds:
!.!.!
Success rate is 60 percent (3/5), round-trip min/avg/max =
4/6/8 ms
```

FIGURE 9.6 Network diagram.

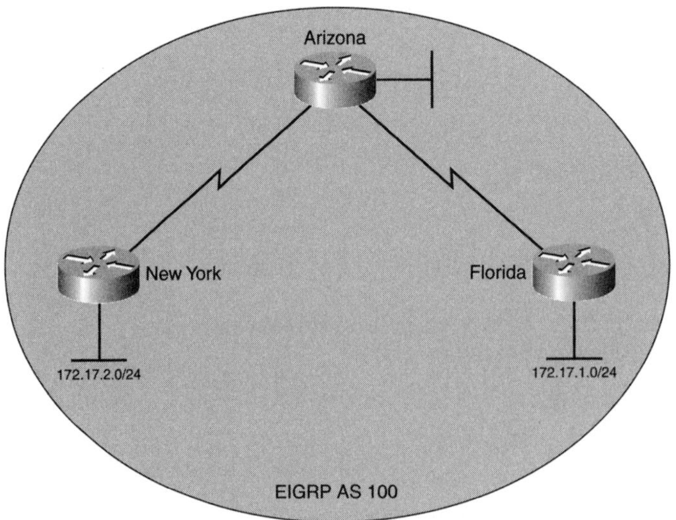

What is the most likely cause of this issue?

- ❍ **A.** EIGRP does not support VLSM by default. The Arizona router must be using different subnet masks than the New York and Florida offices.
- ❍ **B.** The New York and Florida offices are using discontiguous subnets.
- ❍ **C.** The Arizona router must be configured in a separate EIGRP AS than the New York and Florida routers.
- ❍ **D.** EIGRP auto-summarization is causing inappropriate load-balancing issues.

Quick Check

19. Which of the following EIGRP metric criteria make a difference in routing decisions, by default? (Choose two.)

Quick Answer: **202**
Detailed Answer: **206**

- ❍ **A.** Bandwidth
- ❍ **B.** Load
- ❍ **C.** Delay
- ❍ **D.** Reliability

20. Refer to Figure 9.7. Based on the shown EIGRP configuration, which of the following paths to Network A will appear in the R1 routing table? (Note: The numbers shown in the network diagram represent the EIGRP metric; all interfaces are subnets of the 172.16.x.x network.) (Choose two.)

Quick Answer: **202**
Detailed Answer: **206**

```
R1(config)#router eigrp 200
R1(config-router)#network 172.16.0.0 0.0.255.255
R1(config-router)#variance 2
```

FIGURE 9.7 Network diagram.

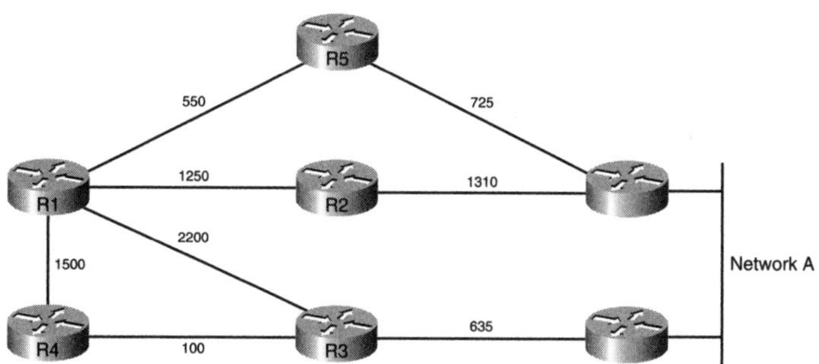

- ❍ **A.** R1 -- R5
- ❍ **B.** R1 -- R2
- ❍ **C.** R1 -- R3
- ❍ **D.** R1 -- R4

Quick Check

21. Refer to Figure 9.8. Based on the network diagram, which of the following configurations will enable EIGRP on all interfaces of R3? (Choose two.)

Quick Answer: **202**
Detailed Answer: **207**

FIGURE 9.8 Network diagram.

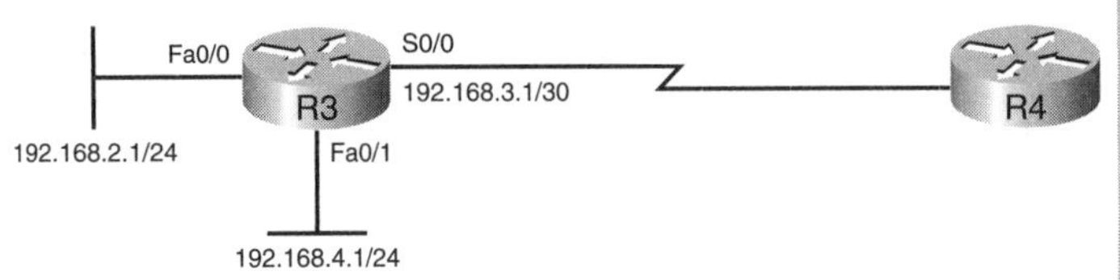

❍ **A.**

```
R3(config)#router eigrp 250
R3(config-router)#network 192.168.0.0
```

❍ **B.**

```
R3(config)#router eigrp 250
R3(config-router)#network 192.168.2.0
R3(config-router)#network 192.168.3.0
R3(config-router)#network 192.168.4.0
```

❍ **C.**

```
R3(config)#router eigrp 250
R3(config-router)#network 192.168.2.0 0.0.255.255
```

❍ **D.**

```
R3(config)#router eigrp 250
R3(config-router)#network 192.168.0.0 0.0.0.255
```

Quick Check

Quick Answer: **202**
Detailed Answer: **207**

22. Based on the network shown in Figure 9.9, enter an OSPF configuration that meets the following criteria:

- ▶ OSPF must advertise all interfaces attached to R4 except the Fa0/0 network.
- ▶ You must use exactly two network statements.
- ▶ You cannot use a wildcard mask of 0.0.0.0 or 255.255.255.255.
- ▶ All interfaces must be placed in OSPF area 0.
- ▶ OSPF should use a process ID of 100.

The necessary prompts have been provided for you.

FIGURE 9.9 Network diagram.

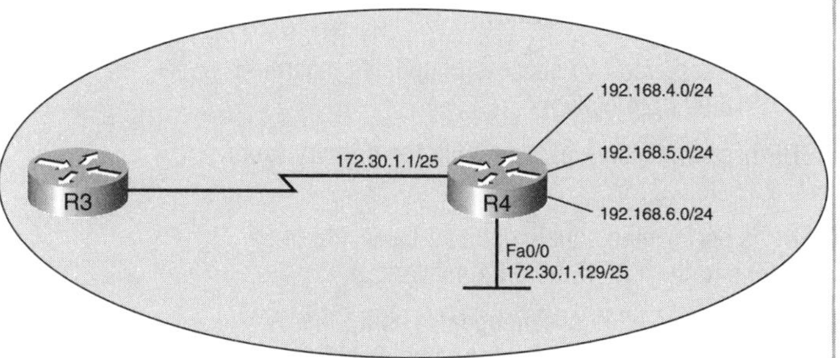

R4(config)#____________________________________

R4(config-router)#____________________________________

R4(config-router)#____________________________________

Quick Check

Use the following output to answer the next three questions:

```
Router#show ip eigrp topology

IP-EIGRP Topology Table for process 77

       Codes: P - Passive, A - Active, U - Update, Q - Query, R - Reply,
       r - Reply status

P 172.16.90.0 255.255.255.0, 2 successors, FD is 46251776
          via 172.16.80.28 (46251776/46226176), Ethernet0
          via 172.16.81.28 (46251776/46226176), Ethernet1
          via 172.16.80.31 (46277376/46251776), Serial0
P 172.16.81.0 255.255.255.0, 1 successors, FD is 307200
          via 172.16.81.28 (307200/281600), Ethernet1
          via 172.16.80.31 (332800/307200), Serial0
```

23. Based on the EIGRP topology table, the 172.16.90.0/24 network has two successors. What does this mean?

Quick Answer: **202**
Detailed Answer: **207**

- ❍ **A.** EIGRP has received two successful updates regarding the 172.16.90.0/24 network.
- ❍ **B.** EIGRP has two backup paths should the primary route to 172.16.90.0/24 fail.
- ❍ **C.** EIGRP is performing equal-cost load-balancing over two paths to the 172.16.90.0/24 network.
- ❍ **D.** EIGRP has received duplicate updates about the 172.16.90.0/24 network from the same neighbor.

24. Based on the EIGRP topology table, the 172.16.90.0/24 and 172.16.81.0/24 routes are marked as Passive. What does this mean?

Quick Answer: **202**
Detailed Answer: **207**

- ❍ **A.** The two routes are currently not in use.
- ❍ **B.** The two routes are currently in active use.
- ❍ **C.** The EIGRP process has at least one backup route for each active path.
- ❍ **D.** These networks have been advertised but not used.

25. Based on the EIGRP topology table, what is the best advertised distance (AD) for the 172.16.81.0/24 network?

Quick Answer: **202**
Detailed Answer: **207**

- ❍ **A.** 307200
- ❍ **B.** 281600
- ❍ **C.** 332800
- ❍ **D.** 307200

Quick Check

26. What is the primary difference between classful and classless routing protocols?

Quick Answer: **202**
Detailed Answer: **207**

❍ **A.** Classful protocols can handle only small networks, whereas classless protocols can support large networks.

❍ **B.** Classful protocols do not send subnet mask information with route advertisements, whereas classless protocols do send subnet mask information.

❍ **C.** Classful protocols have more implementation complexity than classless protocols.

❍ **D.** Classful protocols send route updates on specific time intervals, whereas classless protocols send updates only when necessary.

27. What routing algorithm is used for OSPF and EIGRP, respectively?

Quick Answer: **202**
Detailed Answer: **207**

❍ **A.** Cost/Composite

❍ **B.** Bandwidth/Composite

❍ **C.** Link-State/Hybrid

❍ **D.** SPF/Dual

28. You are attempting to telnet to a router named AZCentral as shown in the following code:

Quick Answer: **202**
Detailed Answer: **208**

```
Router-1#telnet AZCentral
Trying AZCentral (10.3.3.1) ... Open
Password required, but none set
[Connection to AZCentral closed by foreign host]
```

Which of the following are true?

❍ **A.** Your router does not currently have a Telnet password set.

❍ **B.** The AZCentral router does not currently have a Telnet password set.

❍ **C.** Your router does not currently have an enable secret password set.

❍ **D.** The AZCentral router does not currently have an enable secret password set.

Quick Check

Quick Answer: **202**
Detailed Answer: **208**

29. Enter a router configuration that meets the following criteria:

- Configures the password CiscoTelnet on VTY ports 0 through 4.
- Configures the password CiscoLocal on CON and AUX ports and requires logins to these ports.
- Configures the password CiscoEncrypt as the password to enter privileged mode. Make sure that this password is protected with the strongest possible encryption.
- Encrypts all passwords on your router that are typically stored in clear text.
- Save the configuration.

The necessary prompts have been provided for you.

Router(config)#______________________________

Router(config-line)#______________________________

Router(config-line)#______________________________

Router(config)#______________________________

Router(config-line)#______________________________

Router(config-line)#______________________________

Router(config-line)#______________________________

Router(config)#______________________________

Router(config-line)#______________________________

Router(config-line)#______________________________

Router(config-line)#______________________________

Router(config)#______________________________

Router(config)#______________________________

Router(config)#______________________________

Router#______________________________

Quick Check

30. Which protocol should you use to establish secure terminal connectivity to a remote device?

Quick Answer: **202**
Detailed Answer: **208**

- ❍ **A.** SNMPv1
- ❍ **B.** SNMPv2
- ❍ **C.** SNMPv3
- ❍ **D.** Telnet
- ❍ **E.** WPA
- ❍ **F.** WEP
- ❍ **G.** SSH

Quick Check Answer Key

1. C, E
2. D
3. D
4. D
5. B
6. A, B, D
7. C
8. A, B
9. See detailed answer
10. B
11. B, C
12. D
13. D
14. B
15. B
16. B
17. A
18. D
19. A, C
20. A, D
21. B, C
22. See detailed answer
23. C
24. B
25. B
26. B
27. D
28. B
29. See detailed answer
30. G

Answers and Explanations

1. **C, E.** Using the command **network 172.0.0.0 0.255.255.255** will activate the OSPF process on any interface that begins with 172. Because all interfaces on R1 begin with 172, the objective is accomplished. Using the command **network 0.0.0.0 255.255.255.255** will activate OSPF on all interfaces regardless of their IP address. Answers A and B are incorrect because OSPF uses the wildcard mask with the network statement rather than the subnet mask. Answer D is incorrect because you cannot use a "range" style command with OSPF.

2. **D.** The **show ip route** command shows what routes are available for the router. In this case, the information in the brackets is the administrative distance and metric (bandwidth and delay) of the EIGRP route. Answer A is incorrect, as it is not the port number, but the administrative distance. Answer B is incorrect, as EIGRP does not use hops as its metric. Answer C is incorrect, as the first number is the Advertised Distance (AD) of EIGRP, not the port number.

3. **D.** With all distance-vector routing protocols, split-horizon states that it is not useful to send information back the way it came. Answer A is incorrect, as routers themselves are the devices that split networks, not split-horizon. Answer B is incorrect, as split-horizon is used to solve routing loop issues. Answer C is incorrect because distance-vector routing protocols are notoriously slow in updating, as a result of their periodic nature. This can cause convergence issues.

4. **D.** The metric shown on this route is 15. If it is passed to a neighboring router, it increments by one, equaling 16, which is unreachable. Answer A is incorrect, as this route could be passed to neighbors. Answer B is incorrect, as this route could be passed to a neighboring router. Answer C is incorrect, as a directly connected network could be advertised to a neighboring router. Answer E is incorrect, as this route is also within the 15-hop limit.

5. **B.** EIGRP is called many names. Some call it a hybrid routing protocol (primarily Cisco); others call it an advanced distance-vector protocol. However, technically, it falls under the distance-vector category of protocols, which causes all the distance-vector loop prevention mechanisms to apply. One of these mechanisms is split-horizon, which prevents a router from sending an update back in the same direction from which it was received. By looking at the diagram, the Nevada router receives updates on its Serial 0/0 interface from both Washington and New Mexico. It does not send those updates back out, keeping the Washington and New Mexico routers from learning about each other. Answer A is incorrect because EIGRP works just fine on Frame Relay networks. Answer C is incorrect because there are no reserved EIGRP AS numbers. Answer D is incorrect because the **no auto-summary** command simply disables classful summarization features in EIGRP.

6. **A, B, and D.** The command creates a virtual loopback interface with a particular IP address using the 255.255.255.255 subnet mask. This subnet mask is typically called a "host mask" because it only includes a single IP address. When an OSPF router sends a routing update, it includes the router ID to identify itself. In OSPF, the router ID is the highest IP address of a loopback interface. Answer C is incorrect, as a router that is not powered up does not have any active interfaces. Answer E is incorrect, as 255.255.255.255 is typically called a host mask.

7. **C.** Hold-down timers are your best friend and worst enemy when it comes to route updates. When a route update is received, the distance-vector router will immediately set a hold-down timer and refuse any updates about the route until the hold-down timer expires. This prevents a flapping interface from causing networkwide triggered updates. Answer A is incorrect because split-horizon prevents updates from being sent back in the same direction they were received. Answers B and E are incorrect because triggered updates and route poisoning work together to mark a route as unreachable and send an update as soon as the network outage occurs. Answer D is incorrect because poison reverse is used to confirm a failed route.

8. **A, B.** Implementing multiple OSPF areas allows you to add route summarization to your network on the Area Border Routers (ABRs—routers connecting two or more areas). Because summarization hides the specifics of routes, the SPF algorithm does not receive as many network changes for specific networks in other areas. This minimizes the number of times the SPF algorithm runs, freeing more resources on your routers. Answer C is incorrect because multiple OSPF areas do not provide interoperability with other routing protocols. This is the job of the Autonomous System Boundary Router (ASBR) OSPF device. Answer D is incorrect because security boundaries are implemented through access lists rather than OSPF areas. Answer E is incorrect because your routers will usually have the same number of neighbor relationships in a multiarea OSPF environment as they do in a single area.

9.

FIGURE 9.10 Network diagram.

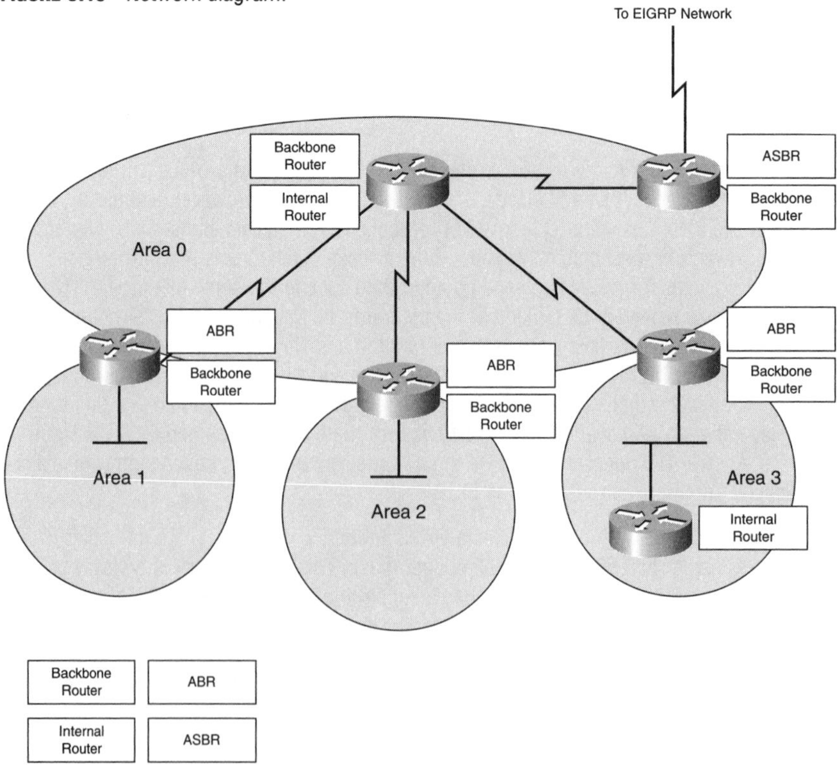

10. **B.** OSPF Hello messages are sent to the group IP address 224.0.0.5. All OSPF routers listen to this multicast address. Answer A is incorrect because OSPF messages use multicast rather than unicast (unless specifically configured to do so—this is discussed in CCNP studies). Answer C is incorrect because 224.0.0.10 is the EIGRP multicast address. Answer D is incorrect because OSPF uses multicast rather than broadcast.

11. **B, C.** Answer B gets a little tricky—remember that the wildcard mask is the opposite of the subnet mask. The subnet mask 255.255.252.0 applied to the 192.168.0.0 address would encompass the range from 192.168.0.0 to 192.168.3.255. Thus, when we use a wildcard mask of 0.0.3.255, we are encompassing that same range for the OSPF network statement, which meets the requirements of only enabling OSPF on the Fa0/0 and S0/0 interfaces. Answer C is a common method to enable OSPF on specific interfaces by using a wildcard mask of 0.0.0.0. Answer A is incorrect because this will enable OSPF on more interfaces than is necessary. Answer D is incorrect because you cannot use a subnet mask with the OSPF network statement. Answer E is incorrect because the wildcard mask is missing (the Cisco IOS will generate an invalid input error message).

12. **D.** When choosing the OSPF router-id, the following rules are used:

    - Prefer the IP address entered using the **router-id** command.
    - (if **router-id** command not present) Prefer the highest loopback interface IP address.
    - (if loopback interface not present) Prefer the highest physical interface IP address.

    The question stated that the **router-id** command was not used, so we need to check whether the router has a loopback interface. In this case, the IP address of Loopback 3 (10.1.1.25) becomes the OSPF router-id. If the loopback interface had not been present, the IP address of Serial 0/0/0 would have become the router-id.

13. **D.** Routers make best-path determinations based on the following criteria:

    - Prefer the route with the most specific subnet mask.
    - (if subnet mask is equal) Prefer the route with the lower administrative distance.
    - (if administrative distance is equal) Prefer the route with the lower metric.

    In this case, the initial criteria breaks the tie. The static route has a subnet mask of 255.255.0.0 (less specific), while the route learned via OSPF has a subnet mask of 255.255.255.0 (more specific). If the subnet masks would have been equal, the static route would be preferred because of its lower administrative distance. Answer A is incorrect because the administrative distance is used only if the route specificity is tied. Answer B is incorrect because the routing decision process is exactly the opposite: The more specific the route, the better it is. Answer C is incorrect because static routes are typically preferred to OSPF routes if the subnet mask is equal.

14. **B.** The default OSPF hold-down timer (dead timer) and hello timer for high-speed networks (such as Ethernet) is 40 seconds and 10 seconds, respectively. Based on the **show ip ospf neighbor** output, we can see that the Dead Time is currently shown as 36 seconds. Based on this, we can derive the last Hello message as being sent 4 seconds ago. All other answers do not apply.

15. **B.** The output from this command shows the neighboring router's router-id as 192.168.45.1. The router-id represents the "name" of the OSPF router and may not be the actual IP address used in communication (making answer A incorrect). The address field shows the physical interface IP address as 10.0.0.1. This is the actual IP address used for communication. Answers C and D are incorrect because these IP addresses are shown nowhere in the neighbor table.

16. **B.** This router must be a Backup Designated Router (BDR). On Ethernet networks, one router will always be set as the Designated Router (DR), and one of the other routers will be the BDR. Because the DR is shown in the neighbor and we are told this is a complete neighbor table, THIS router (the router on which the command was executed) must be the BDR. Answers A and C are OSPF router types and cannot be determined from this output. Answers D and E are incorrect because the output shows that no hello messages have been missed.

17. **A.** The command **show ip ospf neighbor** was used to generate this output. Answer B is incorrect because the **show ip ospf interface** will show the interfaces on the router that is running OSPF. Answer C is incorrect, as the **show ip ospf** command will show general OSPF status and statistics. Answer D is incorrect because the **show ip ospf database** command will show the current link state database (topology table) for the network.

18. **D.** The ping output is typical of an EIGRP auto-summarization issue. If the Arizona-New York and the Arizona-Florida WAN links are using a subnet other than 172.17.x.x addressing, the New York and Florida routers will auto-summarize the 172.17.1.0/24 and 172.17.2.0/24 networks back to the 172.17.0.0/16 classful boundaries. The Arizona router will receive two equal cost paths to this summarized network and will attempt to load balance between them. Answer A is incorrect because EIGRP does support VLSM by default. Answer B is incorrect because the New York and Florida offices are using contiguous (172.17.X.X) addressing. Answer C is incorrect because the routers must be in the same AS number to communicate.

19. **A, C.** By default, EIGRP uses the Bandwidth and Delay in its metric decision criteria. Answers B and D are incorrect because the Load and Reliability can be added to the calculation in rare instances but are not factored in by default.

20. **A, D.** The **variance 2** command causes EIGRP to logically load balance across networks that have a metric twice as bad as the successor (primary) route. In this case, the best route is through R5, which has a metric of 1275 (550 + 725). The path from R1 — R4 ends up with a metric of 2235 (1500 + 100 + 635), which is under the maximum of 2550 (1275 * 2 variance). Answer B is incorrect because the cumulative metric through R2 is 2560 (1250 + 1310), exceeding the maximum of 2550 allowed by the variance. Answer C is incorrect because the cost from R1 -- R3 is 2835 (2200 + 635), exceeding the 2550 maximum the variance allows.

21. **B, C.** EIGRP allows you to enter network statements with or without the wildcard mask. If you do not use a wildcard mask, the default class is assumed on the network. Because 192.168.x.x is a Class C network, entering the specific network statements **network 192.168.2.0**, **network 192.168.3.0**, and **network 192.168.4.0** will cause EIGRP to operate on all interfaces. Answer C is also correct. Even though the network statement was entered incorrectly (**network 192.168.2.0 0.0.255.255**), the stated wildcard mask will not pay attention to the third octet and will cause EIGRP to route for any interface beginning with 192.168.x.x. Answer A is incorrect because entering the **network 192.168.0.0** command without a wildcard mask will only route for the specific Class C network. Answer D is incorrect because the wildcard mask is too specific to include any of the shown interfaces.

22. The configuration of OSPF should be as follows:

```
R4(config)#router ospf 100
R4(config-router)#network 192.168.0.0 0.0.255.255 area 0
R4(config-router)#network 172.30.1.0 0.0.0.127 area 0
```

23. **C.** In EIGRP terminology, a *successor* is a primary route, whereas a *feasible successor* is a backup route. Because the topology table shows two successors for the 172.16.90.0/24 network, we can assume these successors are used in the routing tables for load balancing. Answer A is incorrect because the successor status does not reflect the number of updates. Answer B is incorrect because the feasible successor represents backup paths rather than the successor. Answer D is incorrect because this is not related to the topology table.

24. **B.** Continuing with the strange EIGRP terminology, a *passive* route is a route that is currently in use (and is stable), whereas an *active* route is experiencing a connectivity failure (and is actively trying to find a replacement). Answer A is incorrect because passive routes are actively used in the routing table. Answer C is incorrect because backup paths are seen as feasible successors rather than passive or active. Answer D is incorrect because passive routes are advertised and used.

25. **B.** When reading the EIGRP topology table, the routes are listed followed by the next-hop IP address, the Feasible Distance (FD), and the Advertised Distance (AD). The FD and AD are represented by the numbers in parentheses, such as (307200/281600). The first number represents the FD, (how far the network is from THIS router); the second number represents the AD (how far the network is from the NEIGHBORING router). In this case, the lowest AD is 281600. All other answers do not apply.

26. **B.** Classful protocols (which only include RIPv1 and IGRP) do not send subnet mask information in route updates, preventing them from supporting VLSM environments. Answer A is incorrect because classful routing protocols can support larger networks if a consistent subnet mask is used. Answer C is incorrect because classful protocols are usually easier to implement than classless. Answer D is incorrect because this describes the difference between distance vector and link state routing protocols.

27. **D.** The OSPF protocol uses the Shortest Path First (SPF) routing algorithm, whereas the EIGRP protocol uses the Diffused Update Algorithm (DUAL). Answers A and B and are incorrect because these represent metrics rather than routing algorithms. Answer C is incorrect because these represent classes of routing protocols rather than algorithms.

28. **B.** By default, Cisco routers do not have a password set under the VTY ports. To prevent users from reaching the unconfigured router, the IOS will display the **Password required, but none set** message to any host attempting to connect remotely through Telnet or SSH. If a router does not have an enable secret password set but has a password set under the VTY ports, a remote user will be able to telnet into user mode but will not be able to enter privileged mode.

29. The router password configuration should be as follows:

```
Router(config)#line vty 0 4
Router(config-line)#password CiscoTelnet
Router(config-line)#exit
Router(config)#line con 0
Router(config-line)#password CiscoLocal
Router(config-line)#login
Router(config-line)#exit
Router(config)#line aux 0
Router(config-line)#password CiscoLocal
Router(config-line)#login
Router(config-line)#exit
Router(config)#enable secret CiscoEncrypt
Router(config)#service password-encryption
Router(config)#exit
Router#copy running-config startup-config
```

30. **G.** The Secure Shell (SSH) uses data encryption when transferring data between devices and is considered the best way to establish terminal connectivity remotely. Answers A, B, and C are incorrect. Although SNMP does allow for secure remote management, it does not provide terminal connectivity. Answer D is incorrect because Telnet is a very unsecure (clear text) protocol. Answers E and F are incorrect because these represent wireless security standards rather than secure management standards.

CHAPTER 10

Access Lists and Network Address Translation

This chapter covers the following ICND2 objectives that fall under the content areas, **Implement, verify, and troubleshoot NAT and ACLs in a medium-size Enterprise branch office network:**

- Describe the purpose and types of access control lists.
- Configure and apply access control lists based on network filtering requirements.
- Configure and apply an access control list to limit Telnet and SSH access to the router.
- Verify and monitor ACLs in a network environment.
- Troubleshoot ACL implementation issues.
- Explain the basic operation of NAT.
- Configure Network Address Translation for given network requirements using CLI.
- Troubleshoot NAT implementation issues.

Quick Check

Quick Answer: **230**
Detailed Answer: **231**

1. You have been assigned to create an ACL that restricts HostA and HostB (shown in Figure 10.1) from reaching ServerA. You have constructed the following syntax:

```
access-list 101 deny ip host 192.168.42.101 host 192.168.100.100
access-list 101 deny ip host 192.168.50.63 host 192.168.100.100
access-list 101 permit ip any any
```

Where should you assign this access list to provide the most efficient filtering?

FIGURE 10.1 Network diagram.

- ❍ **A.** R1, S0/0 *in*

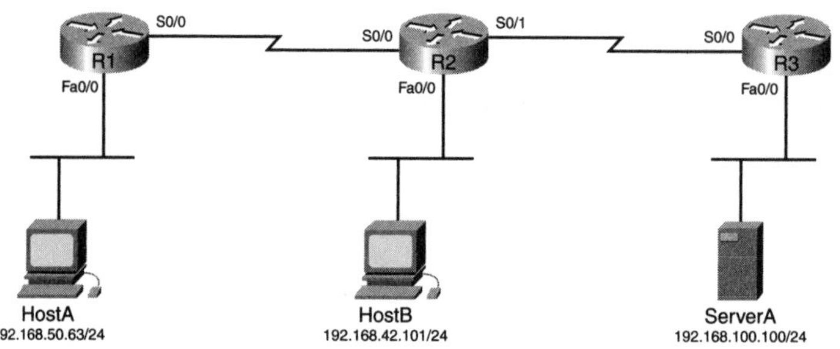

- ❍ **B.** R1, S0/0 *out*
- ❍ **C.** R2, S0/0 *in*
- ❍ **D.** R2, S0/0 *out*
- ❍ **E.** R2, S0/1 *in*
- ❍ **F.** R2, S0/1 *out*
- ❍ **G.** R3, S0/0 *in*
- ❍ **H.** R3, S0/0 *out*
- ❍ **I.** R3, Fa0/0 *in*
- ❍ **J.** R3, Fa0/0 *out*

Quick Check

2. While reviewing a router's configuration, you see that access list 99 is currently in use. What type of access list is this?

Quick Answer: **230**
Detailed Answer: **231**

- ❍ **A.** Standard
- ❍ **B.** Extended
- ❍ **C.** Expanded
- ❍ **D.** Dynamic
- ❍ **E.** Basic

3. You notice in a recently submitted network trouble ticket that one of the servers on a remote network can no longer be accessed by users. You test the connection by using a ping from the router:

Quick Answer: **230**
Detailed Answer: **231**

```
Neo#ping 172.17.2.138
Type escape sequence to abort.
Sending 5, 100-byte ICMP Echos to 172.17.2.138, timeout is 2 seconds:
U.U.U
Success rate is 0 percent (0/5), round-trip min/avg/max = 4/6/8 ms
```

Based on this output, what is the most likely cause of the problem?

- ❍ **A.** The server's IP address has recently changed; the old IP address is currently unassigned.
- ❍ **B.** An access list is blocking access from the Neo router to the server's IP address.
- ❍ **C.** The traffic is incorrectly load balancing between the source and destination server.
- ❍ **D.** The server's network card has been unplugged from the local switch.
- ❍ **E.** A static NAT translation has been misconfigured on the router in front of the server.

Quick Check

Quick Answer: **230**
Detailed Answer: **231**

4. Based on the network shown in Figure 10.2 and the Jerusalem and Nazareth partial router configurations, what will occur when HostA attempts to communicate with ServerA?

```
Jerusalem#show run
!<output omitted>
access-list 5 permit host 172.30.5.50
interface Serial 0/0
 ip access-group 5 in
interface FastEthernet 0/0
 ip access-group 5 in

Nazareth#show run
!<output omitted>
access-list 5 permit host 172.30.5.50
interface Serial 0/0
 ip access-group 5 in
interface FastEthernet 0/0
 ip access-group 5 out
```

FIGURE 10.2 Network diagram.

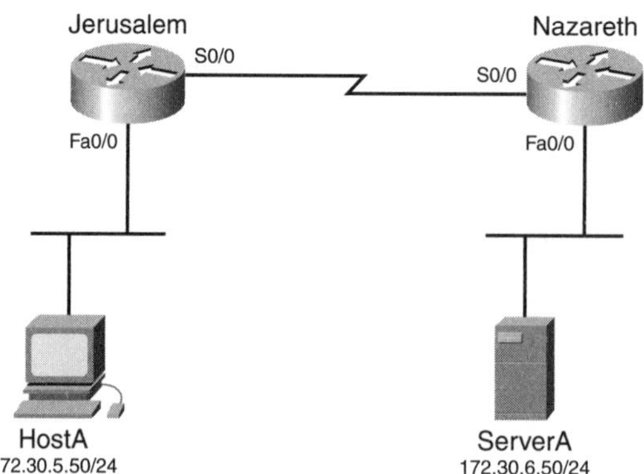

❍ **A.** Communication between HostA and ServerA will be successful.

❍ **B.** HostA will be denied from passing through Jerusalem's Fa0/0 interface.

❍ **C.** HostA will be denied from passing through Jerusalem's S0/0 interface.

❍ **D.** ServerA will be denied from passing through Nazareth's Fa0/0 interface.

❍ **E.** ServerA will be denied from passing through Jerusalem's S0/0 interface.

Quick Check

5. What are other ways of writing the following access list? (Choose two.)

Quick Answer: **230**
Detailed Answer: **231**

```
Router(config)#access-list 1 permit any
```

- ❍ **A. access-list 1 permit 0.0.0.0 0.0.0.0**
- ❍ **B. access-list 1 permit 0.0.0.0 255.255.255.255**
- ❍ **C. access-list 1 permit 255.255.255.255 0.0.0.0**
- ❍ **D. access-list 1 permit 255.255.255.255 255.255.255.255**

6. Which IP addresses would match the shown access list? (Choose two.)

Quick Answer: **230**
Detailed Answer: **231**

```
Router(config)#access-list 1 permit 10.53.210.5 255.255.0.0
```

- ❍ **A.** 10.53.100.100
- ❍ **B.** 162.1.210.5
- ❍ **C.** 10.5.53.210
- ❍ **D.** 10.53.0.1
- ❍ **E.** 192.168.210.5

7. You have an internal web server that must be accessed from the corporate Internet connection. This internal web server has the IP address 172.16.55.10. The router accesses the Internet through the FastEthernet0/1 interface. What NAT syntax is necessary to forward HTTP requests to the internal web server?

Quick Answer: **230**
Detailed Answer: **231**

- ❍ **A. ip nat outside destination tcp 80 fastEthernet0/1 172.16.55.10 80**
- ❍ **B. ip nat inside source static tcp 172.16.55.10 80 interface fastEthernet 0/1 80**
- ❍ **C. ip nat outside source tcp 80 172.16.55.10 80 interface fastEthernet0/1 80**
- ❍ **D. ip nat inside destination static tcp 172.16.55.10 80 interface fastEthernet 0/1 80**

Quick Check
Quick Answer: **230**
Detailed Answer: **232**

8. You want to configure NAT for the small office network shown in Figure 10.3. Users on the network should share the IP address assigned to the Internet facing Serial link when accessing the Internet. The company has also purchased an additional public IP address (210.51.95.56/28), which should be dedicated to the FTP server and is not assigned to the Internet facing Serial link. Which of the following configurations accomplishes these objectives?

FIGURE 10.3 Network diagram.

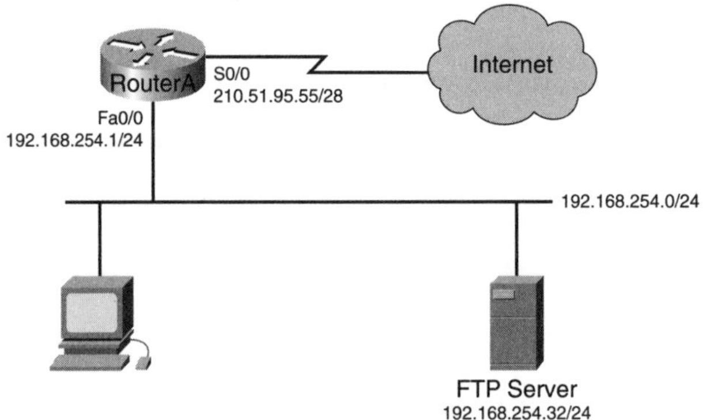

❍ **A.**

```
interface fastethernet 0/0
 ip nat inside
interface serial 0/0
 ip nat outside
ip nat inside source static 192.168.254.32 210.51.95.56
ip nat inside source interface fastethernet 0/0 interface
➥serial 0/0 overload
```

❍ **B.**

```
interface fastethernet 0/0
 ip nat inside
interface serial 0/0
 ip address 210.51.95.56 255.255.255.240 secondary
 ip nat outside
ip nat inside source static 192.168.254.32 interface
➥serial 0/0 secondary
ip nat inside source interface fastethernet 0/0 interface
➥serial 0/0 overload
```

Quick Check

❍ **C.**

```
interface fastethernet 0/0
 ip nat inside
interface serial 0/0
 ip nat outside
ip access-list standard INSIDE_ADDRESSES
 permit 192.168.254.0 0.0.0.255
ip nat inside source static 192.168.254.32 210.51.95.56
ip nat inside source list INSIDE_ADDRESSES interface
➥serial 0/0 overload
```

❍ **D.**

```
interface fastethernet 0/0
 ip nat inside
interface serial 0/0
 ip address 210.51.95.56 255.255.255.240 secondary
 ip nat outside
access-list 50 permit 192.168.254.0 0.0.0.255
ip nat inside source static 192.168.254.32 interface
➥serial 0/0 secondary
ip nat inside source list 50 interface serial 0/0 overload
```

9. You are troubleshooting a NAT configuration on your router. It seems that all the syntax is in place, but users are not able to access the Internet. You are able to ping Internet websites from your router successfully. What is the most likely cause of the problem?

Quick Answer: **230**
Detailed Answer: **232**

Relevant router configuration:

```
interface fastethernet 0/0
  ip address 192.168.1.1 255.255.255.0
interface fastethernet 0/1
  ip address dhcp
  ip nat outside
ip route 0.0.0.0 0.0.0.0 fastethernet 0/1
access-list 50 permit 192.168.1.0 0.0.0.255
ip nat inside source static tcp 192.168.1.50 80 interface
➥fastethernet 0/1 80
ip nat inside source list 50 interface fastethernet 0/1
➥overload
```

❍ **A.** The static route is incorrect. It needs to be pointed to the ISP next-hop address rather than the router's local interface.

❍ **B.** The NAT configuration is incomplete.

❍ **C.** Static NAT features cannot be combined with the NAT Overload features.

❍ **D.** You cannot use NAT Overload with a DHCP-assigned outside IP address.

Quick Check
Quick Answer: **230**
Detailed Answer: **232**

10. You are the administrator of the Frodo router, shown in Figure 10.4. You need to prevent outside users from telnetting to the router. Only the 10.1.5.0/24 subnet should have Telnet access to the router.

FIGURE 10.4 Network diagram.

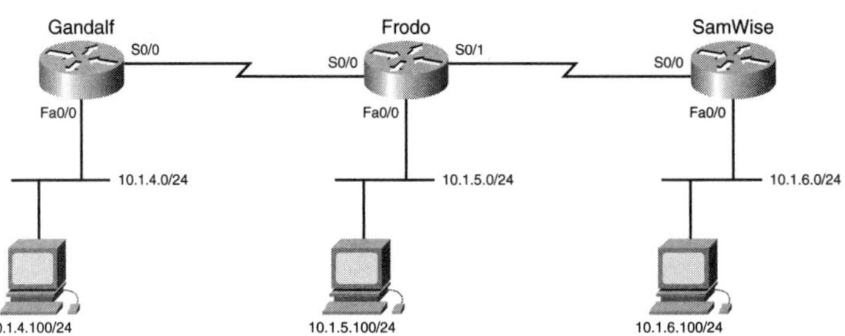

Create and apply an access list that meets the following requirements:

- Blocks users outside the 10.1.5.0/24 subnet from telnetting to the router.
- The access list can be no longer than three lines.
- The access list can only be assigned in one place.

Write the syntax to create and apply the access list on the following lines; begin from global configuration mode:

Router(config)#____

____

____

____

____

____

____

____

Quick Check

11. Your organization has decided to limit Internet access to only HTTP and HTTPS protocols. After applying the following configuration, all Internet access is lost (including HTTP and HTTPS). What is the most likely cause of the problem?

Quick Answer: 230
Detailed Answer: 232

Relevant router configuration:

```
interface fastethernet 0/0
 ip address 192.168.1.1 255.255.255.0
 ip nat inside
interface serial 0/1
 ip address 183.15.190.21 255.255.255.224
 ip nat outside
 ip access-group 150 out
ip route 0.0.0.0 0.0.0.0 183.15.190.1
access-list 50 permit 192.168.1.0 0.0.0.255
access-list 150 permit tcp 192.168.1.0 0.0.0.255 80 any
access-list 150 permit tcp 192.168.1.0 0.0.0.255 443 any
ip nat inside source list 50 interface serial 0/1 overload
```

- ❍ **A.** Access list 150 should permit the IP protocol rather than TCP.
- ❍ **B.** The NAT Overload configuration is incorrect.
- ❍ **C.** Access list 150 is applied to the wrong interface and in the wrong direction.
- ❍ **D.** Access list 150 is blocking source port information rather than destination port information.

12. Which of the following statements are correct regarding the placement of access lists? (Choose two.)

Quick Answer: 230
Detailed Answer: 233

- ❍ **A.** Place extended access lists close to the source.
- ❍ **B.** Place extended access lists close to the destination.
- ❍ **C.** Place standard access lists close to the source.
- ❍ **D.** Place standard access lists close to the destination.

Quick Check

Quick Answer: **230**
Detailed Answer: **233**

13. You are managing the router shown in Figure 10.5. Based on this diagram and the following output, which access list is preventing outside users from reaching the internal network?

FIGURE 10.5 Network diagram.

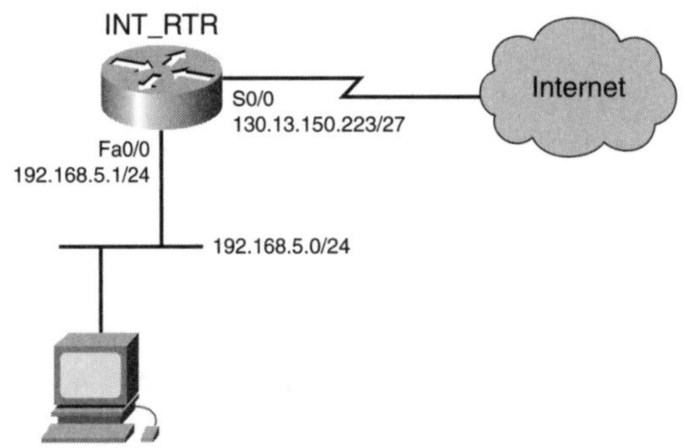


```
INT_RTR#show ip interface
FastEthernet0/0 is up, line protocol is up
  Internet address is 192.168.5.1/24
  Broadcast address is 255.255.255.255
  Address determined by non-volatile memory
  MTU is 1500 bytes
  Helper address is not set
  Directed broadcast forwarding is disabled
  Multicast reserved groups joined: 224.0.0.10
  Outgoing access list is not set
  Inbound  access list is 181
  Proxy ARP is enabled
  Local Proxy ARP is disabled
  Security level is default
  Split horizon is enabled
  ICMP redirects are always sent
  ICMP unreachables are always sent
  ICMP mask replies are never sent
  IP fast switching is enabled
  IP fast switching on the same interface is disabled
  IP Flow switching is disabled
  IP CEF switching is enabled
  IP CEF Feature Fast switching turbo vector
  IP multicast fast switching is enabled
  IP multicast distributed fast switching is disabled
  IP route-cache flags are Fast, CEF
  Router Discovery is disabled
  IP output packet accounting is disabled
  IP access violation accounting is disabled
  TCP/IP header compression is disabled
  RTP/IP header compression is disabled
```

Quick Check

```
  Policy routing is disabled
  Network address translation is enabled, interface in
➥domain inside
  WCCP Redirect outbound is disabled
  WCCP Redirect inbound is disabled
  WCCP Redirect exclude is disabled
  BGP Policy Mapping is disabled
Serial0/0 is up, line protocol is up
  Internet address is 130.13.150.223/27
  Broadcast address is 255.255.255.255
  Address determined by non-volatile memory
  MTU is 1500 bytes
  Helper address is not set
  Directed broadcast forwarding is disabled
  Outgoing access list is 130
  Inbound  access list is 131
  Proxy ARP is enabled
  Local Proxy ARP is disabled
  Security level is default
  Split horizon is enabled
  ICMP redirects are always sent
  ICMP unreachables are always sent
  ICMP mask replies are never sent
  IP fast switching is enabled
  IP fast switching on the same interface is disabled
  IP Flow switching is disabled
  IP CEF switching is enabled
  IP CEF Feature Fast switching turbo vector
  IP multicast fast switching is enabled
  IP multicast distributed fast switching is disabled
  IP route-cache flags are Fast, CEF
  Router Discovery is disabled
  IP output packet accounting is disabled
  IP access violation accounting is disabled
  TCP/IP header compression is disabled
  RTP/IP header compression is disabled
  Policy routing is disabled
  Network address translation is enabled, interface in
➥domain inside
  WCCP Redirect outbound is disabled
  WCCP Redirect inbound is disabled
  WCCP Redirect exclude is disabled
  BGP Policy Mapping is disabled
```

❍ **A.** Access list 130

❍ **B.** Access list 131

❍ **C.** Access list 180

❍ **D.** You cannot determine the access list assignment based on this output.

Quick Check

14. Which type of access list dynamically opens ports on the outside interface for traffic responding to internal requests?

Quick Answer: **230**
Detailed Answer: **233**

- ❍ **A.** Extended
- ❍ **B.** Expanded
- ❍ **C.** Reflexive
- ❍ **D.** Dynamic
- ❍ **E.** Inspection

15. Which **show** command will allow you to see the access lists you have created on your router along with the number of packets that have matched the access list entries?

Quick Answer: **230**
Detailed Answer: **233**

- ❍ **A. show access-list**
- ❍ **B. show interface**
- ❍ **C. show ip interface**
- ❍ **D. show running-config**
- ❍ **E. show interface access-list**

Quick Check

Quick Answer: **230**
Detailed Answer: **234**

16. Draw lines in Figure 10.6 connecting the protocol names to the well-known port numbers. Each protocol will only connect to a single port.

FIGURE 10.6 Port numbers.

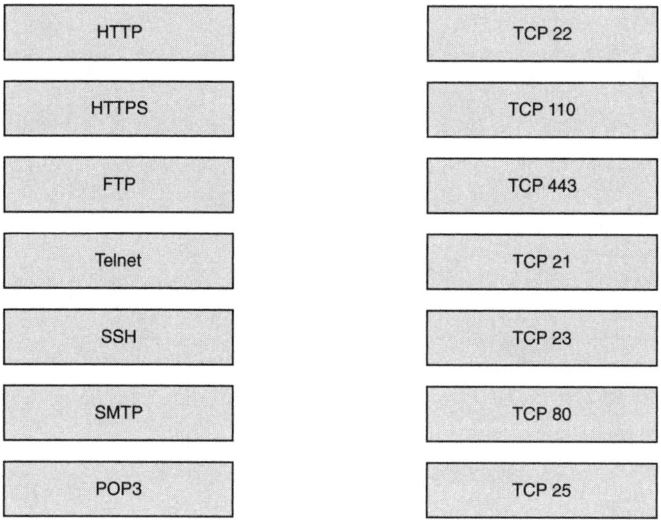

HTTP	TCP 22
HTTPS	TCP 110
FTP	TCP 443
Telnet	TCP 21
SSH	TCP 23
SMTP	TCP 80
POP3	TCP 25

Quick Check

Quick Answer: **230**
Detailed Answer: **234**

17. Based on your organization's security policy, you must create an access list that allows the Accounting VLAN (shown in Figure 10.7) to access the corporate database server. All other users should not have access to this database server, but should not be restricted from reaching other servers. Which of the following configurations accomplish this objective? (Choose two.)

FIGURE 10.7 Network diagram.

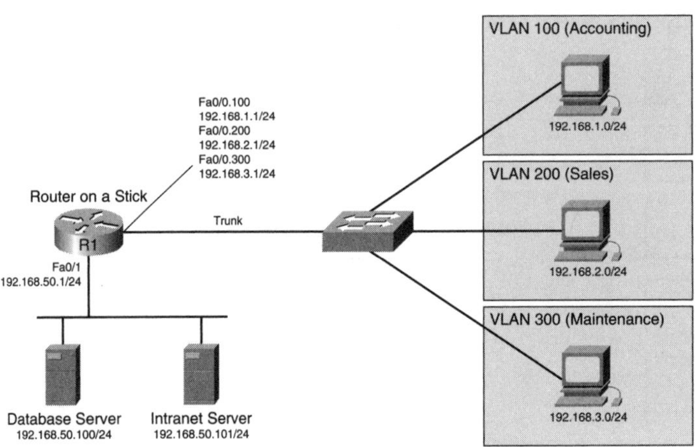

❍ **A.**

```
ip access-list extended RESTRICT_DB
 deny ip 192.168.0.0 0.0.0.255 host 192.168.50.100
 permit ip any any
interface fastethernet 0/0.200
 ip access-group RESTRICT_DB in
interface fastethernet 0/0.300
 ip access-group RESTRICT_DB in
```

❍ **B.**

```
ip access-list extended RESTRICT_DB
 deny ip 192.168.2.0 0.0.0.255 host 192.168.50.100
 deny ip 192.168.3.0 0.0.0.255 host 192.168.50.100
 permit ip any any
interface fastethernet 0/0.100
 ip access-group RESTRICT_DB in
interface fastethernet 0/0.200
 ip access-group RESTRICT_DB in
interface fastethernet 0/0.300
 ip access-group RESTRICT_DB in
```

Quick Check

❍ **C.**

```
ip access-list extended RESTRICT_DB
 permit ip host 192.168.50.100 192.168.1.0 0.0.0.255
 deny ip host 192.168.50.100 any
 permit ip any any
interface fastethernet 0/1
 ip access-group RESTRICT_DB out
```

❍ **D.**

```
ip access-list extended RESTRICT_DB
 permit ip 192.168.1.0 0.0.0.255 host 192.168.50.100
 deny ip any host 192.168.50.100
 permit ip any any
interface fastethernet 0/1
 ip access-group RESTRICT_DB out
```

18. You are configuring a small, nonprofit office to use a Cisco router to connect to the Internet. The onsite network administrator wants to publish an internal email server, two internal web servers, and an internal FTP server to the Internet so that outside users can access them. Because of the limited budget, the company wants to use the lowest-cost solution available. What is necessary for this configuration?

Quick Answer: **230**
Detailed Answer: **234**

❍ **A.** You need a public Internet IP address for each internal server. These addresses can be mapped using Static NAT features.

❍ **B.** You need a single public Internet IP address for this configuration and use NAT Overload to share it among all four internal servers.

❍ **C.** You need a single public Internet IP address for this configuration and use Static NAT to map specific ports to all four internal servers.

❍ **D.** You need two public Internet IP addresses to accommodate the internal web servers. The FTP and email server can be mapped to individual ports on either of the addresses.

Quick Check

Quick Answer: **230**
Detailed Answer: **235**

19. The company shown in Figure 10.8 has a large number of users that require Internet access. Because of the large number of users, it will be necessary to configure a pool of addresses for NAT Overload.

FIGURE 10.8 Network diagram.

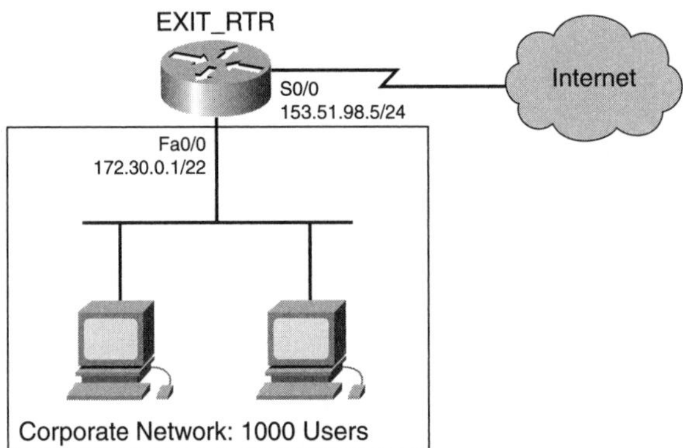

Create a NAT configuration that meets the following requirements:

- No previous NAT configuration exists on the router.
- Uses an outside pool of addresses named "NAT_OUTSIDE" that uses the range 200.5.9.50 to 200.5.9.55 with a 255.255.255.224 subnet mask.
- Uses NAT Overload such that the 172.30.0.0/22 subnet is translated; identify these addresses using access list 60.

Write the syntax to create and apply the NAT configuration on the following lines; some key configuration prompts and starting syntax have been filled in:

EXIT_RTR(config)#**interface serial 0/0**

EXIT_RTR(config-if)#________________________________

EXIT_RTR(config)#**interface fa0/0**

EXIT_RTR(config-if)#________________________________

EXIT_RTR(config)#**access-list 60** ________________________

EXIT_RTR(config)#**ip nat pool** ________________________

EXIT_RTR(config)#**ip nat inside source** ____________________

Quick Check

20. Which of the following commands can you use to verify the current IP addresses that are being processed by the NAT Overload process on your router?

Quick Answer: **230**
Detailed Answer: **235**

- ❍ **A. show ip nat translations**
- ❍ **B. show ip nat process**
- ❍ **C. show ip nat statistics**
- ❍ **D. debug ip nat process**

Use the following output to answer the next two questions:

```
NAT_Router#show ip nat translations

Pro Inside global         Inside local        Outside local     Outside global
tcp 172.15.233.209:12811 192.168.1.89:11012 192.169.53.112:23 192.169.53.112:23
```

21. Based on the output, what address is the internal host attempting to access on the Internet, and how does the Internet host see the internal host?

Quick Answer: **230**
Detailed Answer: **235**

- ❍ **A.** Internet host: 172.15.223.209; Seen as: 192.168.1.89
- ❍ **B.** Internet host: 172.15.223.209; Seen as: 192.169.53.112
- ❍ **C.** Internet host: 192.169.53.112; Seen as: 172.15.233.209
- ❍ **D.** Internet host: 192.169.53.112; Seen as: 192.168.1.89
- ❍ **E.** Internet host: 192.168.1.89; Seen as: 192.169.53.112
- ❍ **F.** Internet host: 172.15.223.209; Seen as: 192.169.53.112

22. Based on the output, what is the source and destination port used when the NAT_Router communicates with the Internet host?

Quick Answer: **230**
Detailed Answer: **235**

- ❍ **A.** Source port: 23, Destination port: 11012
- ❍ **B.** Source port: 11012, Destination port: 23
- ❍ **C.** Source port: 23, Destination port: 12811
- ❍ **D.** Source port: 12811, Destination port: 23
- ❍ **E.** Source port: 12811, Destination port: 11012
- ❍ **F.** Source port: 11012, Destination port: 12811

Quick Check

23. While investigating some complaints about connectivity to a specific Internet server, you verify your NAT process:

Quick Answer: **230**
Detailed Answer: **235**

```
R1#show ip nat statistics
Total active translations: 1138 (15 static, 1132 dynamic; 1 extended)
Outside interfaces:
  Ethernet0/1
Inside interfaces:
  Ethernet0/0
Hits: 3129721  Misses: 15911
Expired translations: 22109
Dynamic mappings: 1132
-- Inside Source
[Id: 3] access-list NAT_ADDRESSES interface Ethernet0/1 refcount 0
```

According to this output, there have been 15911 misses. What does this mean?

- ❍ **A.** 15911 packets did not match the access list defining the internal NAT addresses and were not translated.
- ❍ **B.** 15911 packets did not have an existing NAT translation in the table, causing the router to create a new NAT translation.
- ❍ **C.** 15911 packets were translated to the Internet but did not reach a valid Internet host, causing the translation to immediately expire.
- ❍ **D.** 15911 Internet hosts attempted to access the internal network, but were denied by the NAT process.

24. You have just finished implementing NAT for an organization. While testing the NAT process, you find that pings originating from an internal host do not receive replies from an Internet web server. Pings to the Internet host from the NAT router are successful. What are likely causes for this problem? (Choose two.)

Quick Answer: **230**
Detailed Answer: **236**

- ❍ **A.** The IP address of the internal host does not match the access list applied to the NAT process.
- ❍ **B.** The default route on the NAT router is incorrectly configured.
- ❍ **C.** The Internet server does not allow ICMP echo requests.
- ❍ **D.** The **ip nat inside** or **ip nat outside** command has not been correctly configured on the NAT router.
- ❍ **E.** NAT only supports TCP- and UDP-based traffic. ICMP traffic will not be translated by NAT.

Quick Check

Quick Answer: **230**
Detailed Answer: **236**

25. You are managing the network shown in Figure 10.9. Users connected to the LAN behind the Batman router should not be able to telnet to the host on the LAN behind the Robin router. However, further testing reveals that Telnet connections from the users on the Batman LAN are successful to the host (172.16.5.100) behind the Robin router. Based on the shown configuration, what is the most likely cause of the problem?

```
Robin#show access-lists 195
Extended IP access list 195
    10 deny tcp host 172.16.20.1 any eq telnet
    20 deny tcp 192.168.1.0 0.0.0.255 any eq smtp
    30 permit ip any any
Robin#show run interface serial 2/0
Building configuration...

Current configuration : 149 bytes
!
interface Serial2/0
 ip address 172.16.20.2 255.255.255.0
 ip access-group 195 in
 ip nat inside
end
```

FIGURE 10.9 Network diagram.

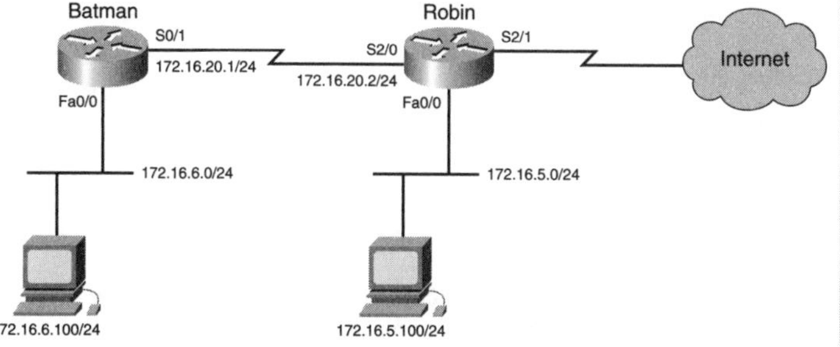

- ❍ **A.** The access list 195 is applied in the wrong direction.
- ❍ **B.** The access list 195 is applied to the wrong interface.
- ❍ **C.** The access list 195 is blocking the incorrect source address.
- ❍ **D.** The access list 195 is blocking the incorrect destination address.

Quick Check

Use the following output to answer the next three questions:

```
Canary#show access-list 130
Extended IP access list 130
    10 permit tcp 172.30.100.64 0.0.0.31 any
    20 permit ip host 172.30.100.180 192.168.1.0 0.0.0.255
    30 permit udp any any
    40 deny icmp 172.30.100.64 0.0.0.31 any
    50 permit icmp any any
```

26. A host with the IP address 172.30.100.90 attempts to access a web server (192.168.1.50) using HTTP. Assuming that access list 130 matched this traffic, which sequence number would be applied?

Quick Answer: **230**
Detailed Answer: **236**

- ❍ **A.** Sequence 10
- ❍ **B.** Sequence 20
- ❍ **C.** Sequence 30
- ❍ **D.** Sequence 40
- ❍ **E.** Sequence 50
- ❍ **F.** Final sequence (implicit deny)

27. A host with the IP address 172.30.100.100 attempts to ping the IP address 192.168.1.50. Assuming that access list 130 matched this traffic, which sequence number would be applied?

Quick Answer: **230**
Detailed Answer: **236**

- ❍ **A.** Sequence 10
- ❍ **B.** Sequence 20
- ❍ **C.** Sequence 30
- ❍ **D.** Sequence 40
- ❍ **E.** Sequence 50
- ❍ **F.** Final sequence (implicit deny)

28. A host with the IP address 192.168.1.82 attempts to access the IP address 172.30.100.180 using FTP. Assuming that access list 130 matched this traffic, which sequence number would be applied?

Quick Answer: **230**
Detailed Answer: **236**

- ❍ **A.** Sequence 10
- ❍ **B.** Sequence 20
- ❍ **C.** Sequence 30
- ❍ **D.** Sequence 40
- ❍ **E.** Sequence 50
- ❍ **F.** Final sequence (implicit deny)

Quick Check

29. Which of the following two commands can be used to apply an access list to some component of a router? (Choose two.)

Quick Answer: **230**
Detailed Answer: **236**

- ❍ **A. access-group**
- ❍ **B. access-class**
- ❍ **C. access-list**
- ❍ **D. ip access-group**
- ❍ **E. ip access-class**
- ❍ **F. ip access-list**

30. What is the complete command to create an access list with the following criteria:

Quick Answer: **230**
Detailed Answer: **236**

- ▶ Source IP address is 192.168.1.4 – 192.168.1.7.
- ▶ Destination IP address is 192.168.1.128 – 192.168.1.255.
- ▶ Destination port is TCP 443.
- ▶ ACL number is 155.
- ▶ This traffic is allowed.

- ❍ **A. ip access-list permit 155 tcp 192.168.1.4 0.0.0.255 192.168.1.128 0.0.0.255 eq 443**
- ❍ **B. ip access-list 155 permit tcp 192.168.1.4 0.0.0.31 192.168.1.128 0.0.0.255 eq 443**
- ❍ **C. access-list 155 permit tcp 192.168.1.4 0.0.0.3 192.168.1.128 0.0.0.127 eq 443**
- ❍ **D. access-list 155 permit tcp hosts 192.168.1.4 192.168.1.7 hosts 192.168.1.128 192.168.1.255 eq 443**
- ❍ **E. access-list 155 permit tcp 192.168.1.4 0.0.0.31 eq 443 192.168.1.128 0.0.0.255**

Quick Check Answer Key

1. F
2. A
3. B
4. E
5. B, D
6. B, E
7. B
8. C
9. B
10. See detailed answer
11. D
12. A, D
13. B
14. C
15. A
16. See detailed answer
17. B, D
18. D
19. See detailed answer
20. A
21. C
22. D
23. B
24. A, D
25. C
26. A
27. E
28. F
29. B, D
30. C

Answers and Explanations

1. **F.** Based on the options given, the access list should be applied to R2, S0/1 interface in the outbound direction. This would allow the access list to identify both HostA and HostB as they tried to access the server. Answers A, D, E, H, and I would never work because the access list is placed in the wrong direction; HostA and HostB would never access the interfaces in that direction. Answers B and C are incorrect because this location would only catch HostA; HostB would pass unfiltered. Answers G and J would accomplish the objective (preventing HostA and HostB from accessing ServerA); however, the hosts would cross more network links than was necessary before access is revoked, making these not the most efficient placements.

2. **A.** The Standard access list range is from 1–99. Answer B is incorrect because Extended access lists used the range 100–199. Answers C and E are incorrect because these are not valid access list types. Answer D is incorrect because Dynamic access lists are another form of Extended access lists (they use the same number range).

3. **B.** When a router blocks access to an IP address due to an assigned access list, it will return ICMP Destination Unreachable messages to the sender. These appear in ping results as the "U" character. Answers A, D, and E are incorrect because any of these issues would result in a failed ping response (.....) message. Answer C is incorrect because an improperly load balanced connection will return consistent success/failure results, such as .!.!..

4. **E.** HostA will be able to send data to ServerA unhindered. However, when ServerA sends return traffic, it will be blocked by access list 5 on the Jerusalem router. Access list 5 permits only HostA's IP address. If you are not HostA, you will be denied by the implicit deny at the bottom of all access lists. Answer A is incorrect because ServerA is stopped from returning traffic. Answers B, C, and D are incorrect because HostA and ServerA can pass through the identified interfaces just fine.

5. **B, D.** Anytime you have a wildcard mask of all 255s (255.255.255.255), everything in the IP address field is ignored. In this case, answers B and D have this wildcard mask. Answers A and C are incorrect because a wildcard mask of all 0s (0.0.0.0) provides a specific match. In these two answers, specifically the IP address 0.0.0.0 and 255.255.255.255 would be permitted.

6. **B, E.** The wildcard mask used in access list 1 is unconventional: **access-list 1 permit 10.53.210.5 255.255.0.0**. This will match any IP address that ends with the digits "210.5". The 10.53 digits at the start of the IP address are ignored. Answers A, C, and D are incorrect because the last two octets of the IP addresses are not 210.5.

7. **B.** The **ip nat** syntax can be cryptic because the Cisco router gives you plenty of flexibility with the form and directions of NAT translation. In this case, you are looking to create a static NAT translation to allow TCP port 80 (HTTP) to pass through the Cisco router to the internal web server. There are two ways to accomplish this: You can create a static NAT translation from the inside perspective or from the outside perspective. In this question, the only correct answer is the translation performed from the inside: **ip nat inside source static tcp 172.16.55.10 80 interface fastEthernet 0/1 80**. If you were to perform the static NAT translation from the outside perspective, you would not be given the option to choose to translate from an interface (FastEthernet 0/1, in this case). All other answers result in an invalid syntax message.

8. **C.** The correct configuration with comments is as follows:

```
interface fastethernet 0/0
 ip nat inside  !labels this as the interface connecting to the inside of the network
interface serial 0/0
 ip nat outside !labels this as the interface connecting to the outside of the network
ip access-list standard INSIDE_ADDRESSES !Creates a named standard access list
 permit 192.168.254.0 0.0.0.255 !Identifies addresses to be translated by NAT
ip nat inside source static 192.168.254.32 210.51.95.56 !Creates a static NAT mapping
➥for the FTP server
ip nat inside source list INSIDE_ADDRESSES interface serial 0/0 overload !Enables NAT
➥Overload for the small office clients
```

A named access list is not mandatory for this configuration, but it sure is nice to have a named identifier rather than just an access list number. Answer A is incorrect because the NAT Overload configuration requires you to identify internal addresses using an access list. Answer B is incorrect for two reasons: First, it is not necessary to assign the FTP server's public IP address to the interface. The router will respond because of the static NAT command even if the IP address is not directly assigned to an interface. Second, the NAT Overload configuration requires you to identify internal addresses using an access list. Answer D is incorrect because the static NAT mapping cannot use a secondary address assigned to an interface.

9. **B.** An easily overlooked command, **ip nat inside**, is missing from the FastEthernet 0/0 interface of the router. Answer A is incorrect because static routes can point to the next-hop IP address or the exit interface. Answer C is incorrect because these features can be combined. Answer D is incorrect because NAT Overload can work with static or dynamically assigned addresses.

10. Just as on the exam, some of your access list requirements may be deceiving. In this example, you can create an access list with only one line that solves the problem. Solution:

```
Router(config)#access-list 1 permit 10.1.5.0 0.0.0.255
Router(config)#line vty 0 4
Router(config-line)#access-class 1 in
```

11. **D.** Access list 150 is denying based on the source port rather than the destination. The correct implementation should be

```
access-list 150 permit tcp 192.168.1.0 0.0.0.255 any 80
access-list 150 permit tcp 192.168.1.0 0.0.0.255 any 443
```

Answer A is incorrect because HTTP and HTTPS both use the TCP protocol. Answer B is incorrect because the NAT Overload configuration is fine. Answer C is incorrect because the access list is applied in the right direction on the right interface (it could also be applied to the Fa0/0 interface in the inbound direction).

12. **A, D.** Extended access lists should go near the source of the traffic, and standard access lists should go close to the destination. Answer B is incorrect because extended access lists close to the destination cause routers to process more packets than necessary. Answer C is incorrect because standard access lists close to the source may drop too much traffic and prohibit network communications.

13. **B.** Based on the output of **show ip interface**, you can see that the inbound access list is set to 131. This is the access list that will filter the incoming Internet traffic. Answer A is incorrect because access list 130 filters the traffic moving from the internal network to the Internet on the S0/0 interface. Answer C is incorrect because access list 180 filters the traffic moving from the internal network to the Internet on the Fa0/0 interface.

14. **C.** Reflexive access lists inspect inside-to-outside requests and dynamically allow responses to those requests from the outside network. Answer A is incorrect because extended access lists allow basic source and destination filtering. Answers B and E are incorrect because there are no expanded or inspection access lists. Answer D is incorrect because dynamic access lists require a user to authenticate, and then provide temporary resource access to that user.

15. **A.** The **show access-list** command allows you to see the access lists on your router and the number of packets that have matched each of the entries. Answer B is incorrect because the **show interface** command does not display any access list information. Answer C is incorrect because the **show ip interface** command will show what access lists are applied, but no more detail about them. Answer D is incorrect because the **show running-config** command displays the access list entries and the interfaces that are using them, but does not display packet hits. Answer E is incorrect because the **show interface access-list** command does not exist.

16.

FIGURE 10.10 Port numbers.

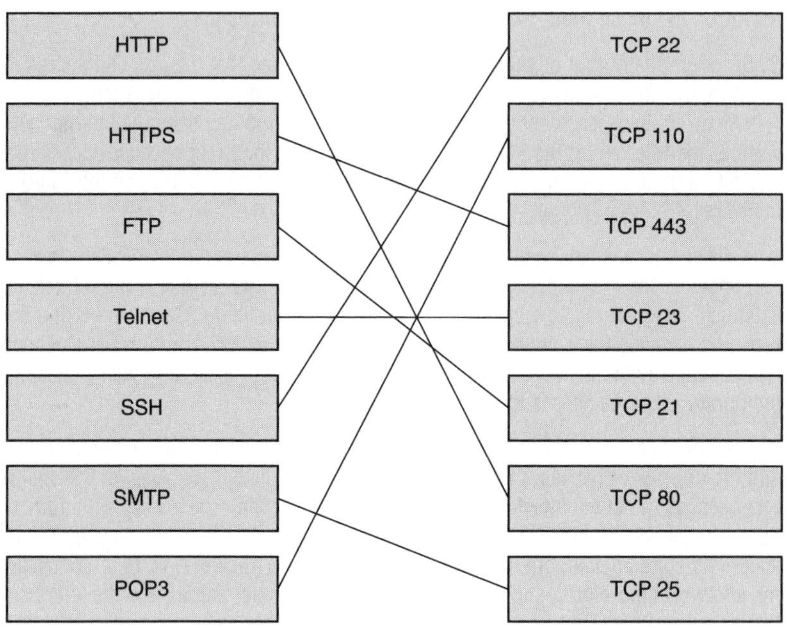

17. B, D. The two access lists that accomplish the objective perform similar functions on different interfaces. Answer B denies the 192.168.2.0/24 and 192.168.3.0/24 subnets from accessing the database server as they come in the routed interface on R1. This access is applied unnecessarily on the Fa0/0.100, but because the Accounting VLAN has IP addresses from the 192.168.1.0/24 subnet, they do not match either of the deny statements. Answer D permits only the Accounting VLAN to access the database server as they leave the Fa0/1 interface. All other VLANs are then denied from accessing the server. Answer A is incorrect because the deny statement only matches the 192.168.0.0/24 subnet, which no VLAN shown is using. Answer C is incorrect because the source and destination IP addresses are flip-flopped in the access list.

18. D. NAT can accomplish some pretty amazing feats; however, sharing an IP address for two servers that use the same port number is not one of them. In this case, you need two public Internet addresses to allow both internal web servers to be accessed on TCP port 80. The other servers can use port 21 (FTP) and port 25 (SMTP) on either of the public Internet IP addresses. Answer A could be used to solve this problem, but it is not the best solution because it is more costly to deploy than answer D. Answer B is incorrect because NAT Overload allows the servers to share only a single IP address when accessing the Internet, not when the requests originate *from* the Internet. Answer C is incorrect because you can map only TCP port 80 on the single IP address to one of the internal web servers. The other cannot be accessed from the Internet.

19. The following configuration will complete the NAT Overload requirements:

```
EXIT_RTR(config)#interface serial 0/0
EXIT_RTR(config-if)#ip nat outside
EXIT_RTR(config)#interface fa0/0
EXIT_RTR(config-if)#ip nat inside
EXIT_RTR(config)#access-list 60 permit 172.30.0.0 0.0.3.255
EXIT_RTR(config)#ip nat pool NAT_OUTSIDE 200.5.9.50 200.5.9.55 netmask
➥255.255.255.224
EXIT_RTR(config)#ip nat inside source list 60 pool NAT_OUTSIDE overload
```

20. **A.** The **show ip nat translations** command will allow you to see the current translated IP addresses in table format. Answers B and D are incorrect because these commands do not exist. Answer C is incorrect because the **show ip nat statistics** command shows only the number of translations the router has processed and some basic configuration items.

21. **C.** Based on this translation table, you can determine the outside host to be 192.169.53.112 (shown in the table as the Outside Local and Outside Global address). The Inside Local address represents the original address of the client *before NAT translation*, which is 192.168.1.89. The Inside Global address represents the address of the client *after NAT translation*, which is 172.15.233.209. Answers A, B, D, E, and F use the wrong IP address for one of these definitions.

22. **D.** Because the Outside Local and Outside Global represent the external, destination address of the Internet host, the port number attached to these addresses represents the destination port; in this case, that port is 23 (Telnet). Because the Inside Local address represents the internal (privately addressed) client, the port number attached to it represents the source port used between the internal client and the NAT router. The Inside Global address represents the source port used between the NAT router and the Internet host; in this case, that port is 12811. The source ports used in the Inside Local and Inside Global addresses are usually the same. However, the source port may differ in a busy network where many NAT translations are occurring. Answers A, B, C, E, and F use the wrong port for one or both of the entries.

23. **B.** The number of hits and misses logged in the **show ip nat statistics** command shows the number of times a packet passed through the router where a NAT translation already existed in the NAT translation table (logged as a hit) and the number of times a packet passed through the router where a NAT translation did not exist causing the router to create a new entry in the NAT translation table (logged as a miss). If the NAT translation table is cleared (through the **clear ip nat translation *** command) in a busy network you will see the number of "misses" suddenly increment as new NAT translations are created. In the big network picture, seeing the number of hits and misses increment indicates the NAT process is working. Answer A is incorrect because addresses not matching the access list applied to NAT will not cause the hits or misses counter to increment. Answers C and D are incorrect because misses indicate an initial, successful NAT translation rather than an expiring or denied translation.

24. **A, D.** The ability to ping the Internet host from the NAT router verifies that the Internet routing is working successfully without the NAT process (because traffic originating from the NAT router passes directly to the ISP without NAT). This immediately rules out answers B and C. This makes answers A and D the most likely causes of the connectivity issue. Answer E is incorrect because NAT does support ICMP traffic.

25. **C.** Access list 195 denies the host 172.16.20.1 from using the Telnet protocol to access any destination. In this case, the requests are not coming from a source IP address of 172.16.20.1 (the serial interface of the Batman router), but rather, the source IP addresses of hosts on the LAN interface of the Batman router (172.16.6.0/24). The objective can be accomplished by changing the access list 195 entry to read as follows:

```
access-list 195 deny tcp 172.16.6.0 0.0.0.255 any eq 23
```

Based on this, answers A, B, and D do not apply.

26. **A.** Sequence number 10 of the access list matches the IP address range 172.30.100.64–172.30.100.95. Because the source IP address (172.30.100.90) falls within this range and the device is using HTTP (a TCP-based protocol), sequence number 10 matches. The access list permits the traffic and then stops processing. Answers B through E are incorrect because the access list never reaches these statements.

27. **E.** The ping command uses the ICMP protocol. This immediately rules out sequence 10 and 30 (answers A and C). Because the source IP address is not 172.30.100.180, sequence 20 (answer B) does not match, and it does not fall in the proper range for sequence 40 (answer D) to match. In this case, sequence 50, which permits all ICMP traffic from any source to any destination matches the request.

28. **F.** Because the traffic comes from a source IP address of 192.168.1.82 and uses the TCP protocol, none of the shown sequence numbers (answers A–E) match. In this case, the traffic hits the implicit deny statement at the bottom of the access list and is dropped.

29. **B, D.** You can use the **access-class** command to apply an access list to line ports (such as VTY ports) of your router. The **ip access-group** command is used to apply an access list to an interface. Answers C and F are incorrect because the **access-list** and **ip access-list** commands are used to create an access list rather than apply it. Answers A and E are incorrect because the initial **ip** syntax is incorrectly applied.

30. **C.** This access list is formatted perfectly. Answer A is incorrect because the permit statement and access list number are flip-flopped, and incorrect wildcard masks are used. Answer B is incorrect because incorrect wildcard masks are used. Answer D is incorrect because there is no "hosts" keyword for access lists. The "host" keyword will allow you to specify a host. Answer E is incorrect because the wildcard masks are incorrect, and the TCP port 443 is in the wrong location (it would be considered the source port).

CHAPTER ELEVEN

Frame Relay, PPP, and VPN Connectivity

This chapter covers the following ICND2 objectives that fall under the content areas, **Implement and verify WAN links:**

- ▶ Configure and verify Frame Relay on Cisco routers.
- ▶ Troubleshoot WAN implementation issues.
- ▶ Describe VPN technology (including importance, benefits, role, impact, and components).
- ▶ Configure and verify PPP connection between Cisco routers.

Quick Check

1. Using the locations identified in Figure 11.1, select three places where LMI signaling would be used. (Choose three.)

Quick Answer: 251
Detailed Answer: 252

FIGURE 11.1 Network diagram.

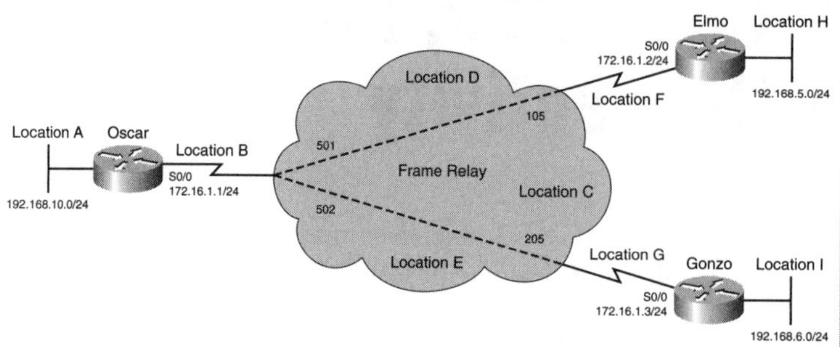

- ❍ **A.** Location A
- ❍ **B.** Location B
- ❍ **C.** Location C
- ❍ **D.** Location D
- ❍ **E.** Location E
- ❍ **F.** Location F
- ❍ **G.** Location G
- ❍ **H.** Location H
- ❍ **I.** Location I

2. The nonbroadcast multiaccess nature of Frame Relay causes issues with what routing loop preventative mechanism?

Quick Answer: 251
Detailed Answer: 252

- ❍ **A.** Route poisoning
- ❍ **B.** Hold-down timers
- ❍ **C.** Triggered updates
- ❍ **D.** Split-horizon

3. Which of the following commands configures a static map of the remote IP address 172.16.12.2 to the DLCI of 100?

Quick Answer: 251
Detailed Answer: 252

- ❍ **A. frame relay map dlci 100 ip 172.16.12.2**
- ❍ **B. frame relay rarp ip 172.16.12.2 100**
- ❍ **C. frame relay lmi dlci 172.16.12.2 100**
- ❍ **D. frame relay map ip 172.16.12.2 100**

Quick Check

4. You are troubleshooting your Frame Relay connections. After you type in the **show frame-relay pvc** command, one of your PVCs shows up as DELETED. What causes this message?

   Quick Answer: **251**
   Detailed Answer: **252**

   ❍ **A.** Your router is incorrectly configured. You need to add the right DLCI information, and the circuit should come up.

   ❍ **B.** The remote router is incorrectly configured.

   ❍ **C.** You are physically disconnected from the service provider.

   ❍ **D.** You need to switch from a multipoint configuration to a point-to-point configuration and create a subinterface for each PVC you plan on using.

5. You type the following configuration into a router. When you execute the **show ip route** command, however, you do not notice any new routes. What is wrong with the configuration?

   Quick Answer: **251**
   Detailed Answer: **252**

```
router rip
 network 10.0.0.0
 network 172.19.0.0
 version 2
interface serial 0/0
 ip address 10.0.0.1 255.0.0.0
 frame-relay map ip 10.0.0.2 100
 frame-relay interface-dlci 100
 no frame-relay inverse-arp
interface ethernet 0/0
 ip address 172.19.0.0 255.255.0.0
```

   ❍ **A.** The **frame-relay map** command is missing the **broadcast** keyword.

   ❍ **B.** RIP should be running version 1, not version 2.

   ❍ **C.** Inverse ARP should be enabled.

   ❍ **D.** RIP is not activated on the interfaces.

   ❍ **E.** RIP is not able to operate over a Frame Relay network.

Quick Check

Use Figure 11.2 to answer the following two questions.

FIGURE 11.2 Network diagram.

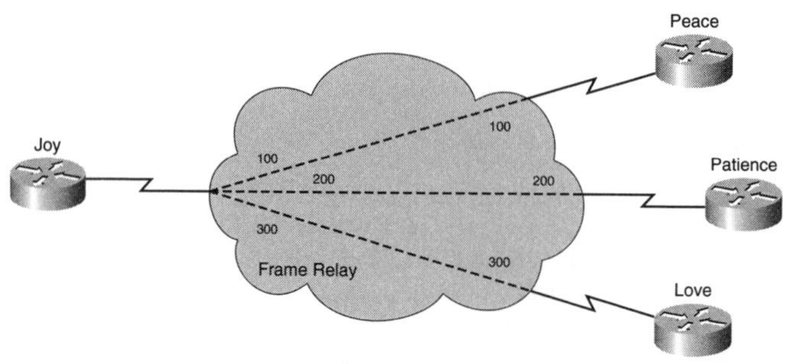

6. You are designing a subnetting scheme for the network shown in Figure 11.2. What is the fewest number of subnets you can use on the Frame Relay network?

   ❍ **A.** 1

   ❍ **B.** 2

   ❍ **C.** 3

   ❍ **D.** 4

Quick Answer: **251**
Detailed Answer: **252**

7. Based on the DLCI configuration shown in Figure 11.2, what issues might you encounter assuming Frame Relay map statements have been correctly configured?

   ❍ **A.** The Peace, Patience, and Love routers will be able to reach the Joy router, but not each other.

   ❍ **B.** The routers will not be able to communicate due to a DLCI duplication issue.

   ❍ **C.** The routers will experience one-way communication.

   ❍ **D.** There are no DLCI issues in this Frame Relay design.

Quick Answer: **251**
Detailed Answer: **252**

8. Which of the following are valid LMI signaling types? (Choose three.)

   ❍ **A.** Cisco

   ❍ **B.** ANSI

   ❍ **C.** ITU-T

   ❍ **D.** Q.933a

   ❍ **E.** IEEE

Quick Answer: **251**
Detailed Answer: **253**

Quick Check

9. If you are unable to support Inverse ARP to map DLCIs to network layer addresses, what method do you need to use?

Quick Answer: **251**
Detailed Answer: **253**

- ❍ **A.** Static routes
- ❍ **B.** Static maps
- ❍ **C.** DHCP
- ❍ **D.** LMI mapping

10. While troubleshooting your Frame Relay connection, you execute the following command:

Quick Answer: **251**
Detailed Answer: **253**

```
Router#show frame-relay map
Serial1/2 (up): ip 172.16.1.4 dlci 401(0x191,0x6410), dynamic,
       broadcast,, status defined, active
Serial1/2 (up): ip 172.16.1.5 dlci 501(0x1F5,0x7C50), dynamic,
       broadcast,, status defined, active
Serial1/2 (up): ip 172.16.1.2 dlci 301(0x12D,0x48D0), dynamic,
       broadcast,, status defined, inactive
```

What is a likely reason DLCI 301 is marked as inactive?

- ❍ **A.** The service provider does not have a mapping for DLCI 301.
- ❍ **B.** The remote router DLCI 301 reaches is currently powered off.
- ❍ **C.** The LMI signaling between you and the service provider is incorrect.
- ❍ **D.** The remote IP address is in a different subnet than the local router.

Quick Check

11. FDI Coffee, Inc., is bringing up a new serial connection between the HQ office and a remote location. The remote office router is a non-Cisco router. How should you configure the HQ router serial interface to make the connection?

Quick Answer: **251**
Detailed Answer: **253**

❍ **A.**

```
HQ(config)#interface serial 2/1
HQ(config-if)#ip address 192.168.1.1 255.255.255.252
HQ(config-if)#no shutdown
```

❍ **B.**

```
HQ(config)#interface serial 2/1
HQ(config-if)#ip address 192.168.1.1 255.255.255.252
HQ(config-if)#encapsulation frame-relay
HQ(config-if)#no shutdown
```

❍ **C.**

```
HQ(config)#interface serial 2/1
HQ(config-if)#ip address 192.168.1.1 255.255.255.252
HQ(config-if)#encapsulation ietf
HQ(config-if)#no shutdown
```

❍ **D.**

```
HQ(config)#interface serial 2/1
HQ(config-if)#ip address 192.168.1.1 255.255.255.252
HQ(config-if)#encapsulation ppp
HQ(config-if)#no shutdown
```

12. How should a router experiencing split-horizon issues while connected to a Frame Relay WAN connection be configured to resolve these issues?

Quick Answer: **251**
Detailed Answer: **253**

❍ **A.** Configure multiple subinterfaces that use the same IP subnet.

❍ **B.** Configure a separate subinterface for each Frame Relay PVC; assign only one DLCI per subinterface.

❍ **C.** Convert all Frame Relay links into point-to-point leased line connections.

❍ **D.** Configure a single subinterface that handles multiple PVCs connecting to remote routers.

Quick Check

13. Your corporate router is connected to a Frame Relay service provider using a serial DTE cable. How does the serial interface receive the clock rate?

Quick Answer: **251**
Detailed Answer: **253**

❍ **A.** The clock is supplied by the remote router.

❍ **B.** The clock is entered through a manual **clock rate** command.

❍ **C.** The clock is supplied by the CSU/DSU.

❍ **D.** The clock is entered from privileged mode.

14. Which PPP subprotocol negotiates features and options for a WAN connection?

Quick Answer: **251**
Detailed Answer: **253**

❍ **A.** HDLC

❍ **B.** TCP

❍ **C.** LAPB

❍ **D.** NCP

❍ **E.** LCP

Quick Check

15. While doing an audit of your corporate routers, you execute the following command:

Quick Answer: **251**
Detailed Answer: **254**

```
R1#show interfaces serial 0/0
Serial0/0 is up, line protocol is up
  Hardware is PQUICC with 56k 4-wire CSU/DSU
  Internet address is 192.168.50.23/24
  MTU 1500 bytes, BW 56 Kbit, DLY 20000 usec,
     reliability 255/255, txload 1/255, rxload 1/255
  Encapsulation HDLC, loopback not set
```

Draw lines in Figure 11.3 to match the output with the respective OSI layer. Note: Not all output will be used.

FIGURE 11.3 Matching OSI layers.

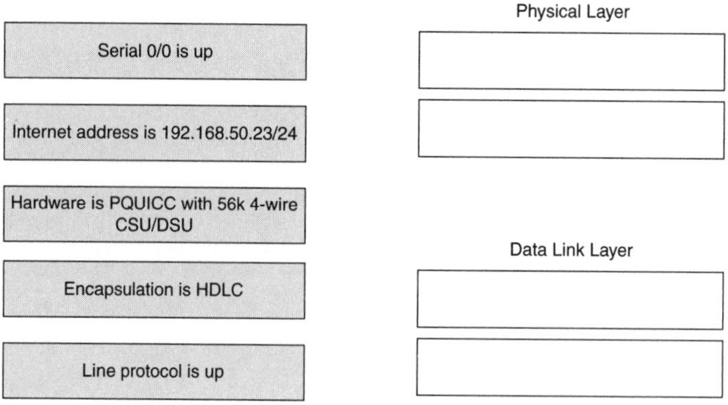

Output		Layer
Serial 0/0 is up		**Physical Layer**
Internet address is 192.168.50.23/24		
Hardware is PQUICC with 56k 4-wire CSU/DSU		
Encapsulation is HDLC		**Data Link Layer**
Line protocol is up		

16. Your organization is considering converting its connections to PPP encapsulation. What will the organization gain by using PPP? (Choose three.)

Quick Answer: **251**
Detailed Answer: **254**

- ❍ **A.** Multiple VLANs on a single interface
- ❍ **B.** Authentication
- ❍ **C.** Isolation of users
- ❍ **D.** Compression
- ❍ **E.** Multilink capability
- ❍ **F.** Broadcast control

Quick Check

17. You are putting together a proposal to convert many of your organization's WAN connections to VPN connections. Which of the following are valid benefits to using VPN connections over leased-line connections? (Choose three.)

Quick Answer: 251
Detailed Answer: 254

- ❍ **A.** Improved performance
- ❍ **B.** Lower cost
- ❍ **C.** Scalability
- ❍ **D.** Improved quality of service
- ❍ **E.** Support for home users

18. Sally needs to connect the corporate network through a VPN connection. She opens a web browser and accesses the corporate VPN logon page. After entering her credentials over a secured connection, a small VPN client downloads to her PC and connects her to the corporate network. What type of VPN connection did Sally establish?

Quick Answer: 251
Detailed Answer: 254

- ❍ **A.** Site-to-site VPN
- ❍ **B.** Clientless VPN
- ❍ **C.** SSL VPN
- ❍ **D.** Microsoft VPN
- ❍ **E.** DMVPN

19. What type of VPN connections are represented in Figure 11.4? (Choose two.) Note: The Cisco VPN client is installed on all shown PCs.

Quick Answer: 251
Detailed Answer: 254

FIGURE 11.4 Network diagram.

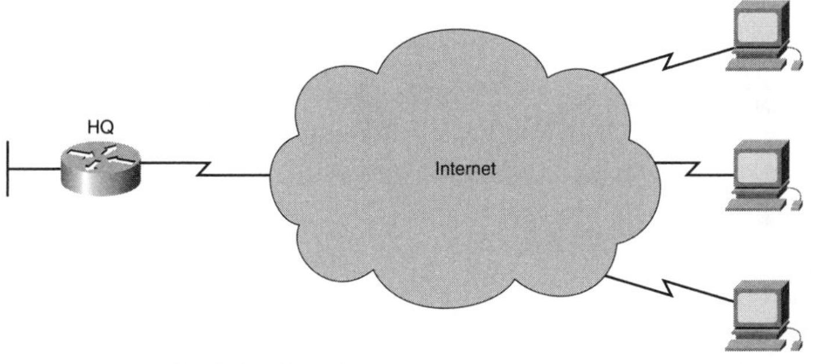

- ❍ **A.** IPSec-based
- ❍ **B.** Remote Access
- ❍ **C.** WebVPN
- ❍ **D.** Unsecured
- ❍ **E.** Diffie-Hellman

Quick Check

20. Which of the following components of the IPSec framework are used to ensure data is not spoofed or changed when it is sent over a secure network connection? (Choose two.)

Quick Answer: **251**
Detailed Answer: **255**

- ❍ **A.** DES
- ❍ **B.** 3DES
- ❍ **C.** AES
- ❍ **D.** MD5
- ❍ **E.** SHA-1
- ❍ **F.** DH

21. You enter the command **frame-relay map ip 192.168.1.5 683 broadcast** into your router. Which of the following statements is true regarding this command?

Quick Answer: **251**
Detailed Answer: **255**

- ❍ **A.** 192.168.1.5 is assigned to one of the serial ports on this router.
- ❍ **B.** This command is required for all Frame Relay connections.
- ❍ **C.** The remote DLCI of the connection is 683.
- ❍ **D.** The **broadcast** option allows the RIP routing protocol to function over the Frame Relay network.

Use the network diagram shown in Figure 11.5 and shown configurations to answer the following three questions:

FIGURE 11.5 Network diagram.

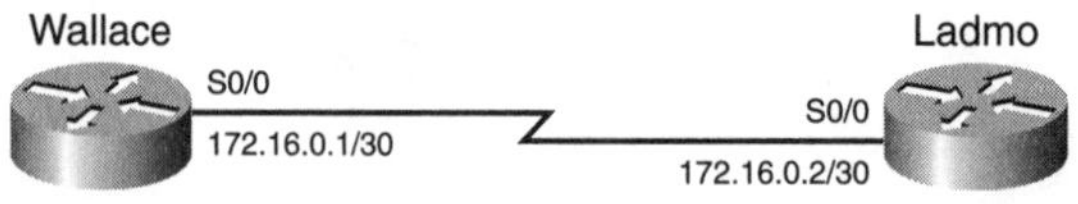

Configuration 1:

```
Router(config)#hostname Wallace
Wallace(config)#username Ladmo password $ecr3t
Wallace(config)#interface s0/0
Wallace(config-if)#ip address 172.16.0.1 255.255.255.252
Wallace(config-if)#encapsulation ppp
Wallace(config-if)#ppp authentication pap chap
Wallace(config-if)#no shut
```

Quick Check

Configuration 2:

```
Router(config)#hostname Ladmo
Ladmo(config)#username Wallace password $uper$secr3t
Ladmo(config)#interface s0/0
Ladmo(config-if)#ip address 172.16.0.2 255.255.255.252
Ladmo(config-if)#encapsulation ppp
Ladmo(config-if)#ppp authentication chap pap
Ladmo(config-if)#no shut
```

22. The Ladmo router is the first to initiate PPP signaling to the Wallace router. What type of authentication will be used for the connection?

Quick Answer: **251**
Detailed Answer: **255**

- ❍ **A.** PPP-based
- ❍ **B.** PAP
- ❍ **C.** CHAP
- ❍ **D.** The routers will experience an authentication mismatch.

23. After the WAN link is initialized, the administrator at the Wallace site reports that the connection seems to be flapping. You verify and find that the Ladmo router is experiencing a similar symptom. What is the most likely cause of the problem?

Quick Answer: **251**
Detailed Answer: **255**

- ❍ **A.** The connection needs to be converted to HDLC because only Cisco routers are used.
- ❍ **B.** The Wallace router has the wrong PPP authentication configured.
- ❍ **C.** The commands **username Wallace** and **username Ladmo** need to have the same password.
- ❍ **D.** The routers have been addressed using invalid IP addresses.

24. Which of the following **debug** commands would expose the cause of the problem?

Quick Answer: **251**
Detailed Answer: **255**

- ❍ **A.** **debug ppp**
- ❍ **B.** **debug ppp authentication**
- ❍ **C.** **debug ppp negotiation**
- ❍ **D.** **debug interface serial 0/0**

Quick Check

Use the network diagram shown in Figure 11.6 and shown configurations to answer the following four questions:

FIGURE 11.6 Network diagram.

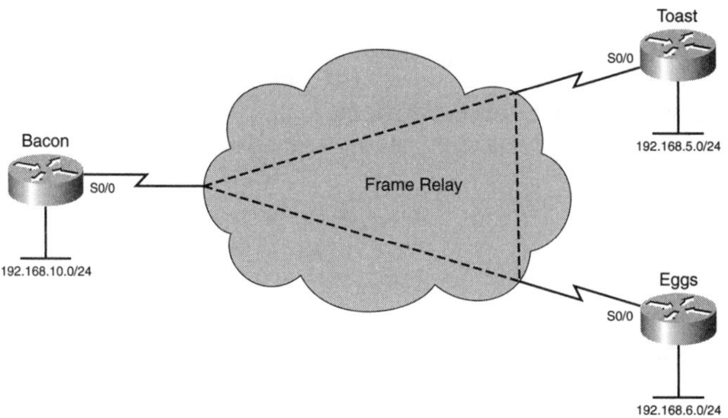

Configuration 1:

```
Bacon(config)#router rip
Bacon(config-router)#network 172.30.0.0
Bacon(config-router)#version 2
Bacon(config-router)#interface serial 0/0
Bacon(config-if)#no ip address
Bacon(config-if)#encapsulation frame-relay
Bacon(config-if)#interface serial 0/0.501 point-to-point
Bacon(config-subif)#ip address 172.30.1.1 255.255.255.252
Bacon(config-subif)#frame-relay interface-dlci 501
Bacon(config-subif)#interface serial 0/0.502 point-to-point
Bacon(config-subif)#ip address 172.30.1.5 255.255.255.252
Bacon(config-subif)#frame-relay interface-dlci 502
```

Configuration 2:

```
Toast(config)#router rip
Toast(config-router)#network 172.30.0.0
Toast(config-router)#version 2
Toast(config-router)#interface serial 0/0
Toast(config-if)#no ip address
Toast(config-if)#encapsulation frame-relay
Toast(config-if)#interface serial 0/0.105 point-to-point
Toast(config-subif)#ip address 172.30.1.2 255.255.255.252
Toast(config-subif)#frame-relay interface-dlci 105
Toast(config-subif)#interface serial 0/0.609 point-to-point
Toast(config-subif)#ip address 172.30.1.9 255.255.255.252
Toast(config-subif)#frame-relay interface-dlci 609
```

Quick Check

Configuration 3:

```
Eggs(config)#router rip
Eggs(config-router)#network 172.30.0.0
Eggs(config-router)#version 2
Eggs(config-router)#interface serial 0/0
Eggs(config-if)#no ip address
Eggs(config-if)#encapsulation frame-relay
Eggs(config-if)#interface serial 0/0.205 point-to-point
Eggs(config-subif)#ip address 172.30.1.6 255.255.255.252
Eggs(config-subif)#frame-relay interface-dlci 205
Eggs(config-subif)#interface serial 0/0.906 point-to-point
Eggs(config-subif)#ip address 172.30.1.10 255.255.255.252
Eggs(config-subif)#frame-relay interface-dlci 906
```

25. Which of the following Frame Relay topologies is shown in Figure 11.6?

Quick Answer: **251**
Detailed Answer: **255**

- ❍ **A.** Hub and Spoke
- ❍ **B.** Partial Mesh
- ❍ **C.** Full Mesh
- ❍ **D.** Site-to-Site
- ❍ **E.** Remote Access

26. Based on the configuration, this network has chosen to run the RIPv2 routing protocol. What issues will this cause in the network?

Quick Answer: **251**
Detailed Answer: **256**

- ❍ **A.** The RIPv2 protocol will not cause any problems in the shown network.
- ❍ **B.** The auto-summarization features of RIPv2 will cause unreachable WAN connections.
- ❍ **C.** The split-horizon features of RIPv2 will prevent some networks from being advertised.
- ❍ **D.** The multicast features of RIPv2 will not be supported on this network.

27. Assuming all subnets are configured correctly in the shown configuration, what DLCI will the Toast router use when communicating with the Eggs router?

Quick Answer: **251**
Detailed Answer: **256**

- ❍ **A.** DLCI 609
- ❍ **B.** DLCI 906
- ❍ **C.** DLCI 501
- ❍ **D.** DLCI 105

Quick Check

28. A network administrator has added the command **network 192.168.10.0** to the RIP routing process on the Bacon router. How will this network be seen by the Toast and Eggs routers?

Quick Answer: **251**
Detailed Answer: **256**

- ❍ **A.** 192.0.0.0/8
- ❍ **B.** 192.168.0.0/16
- ❍ **C.** 192.168.10.0/24
- ❍ **D.** The network will not be received due to split-horizon.

29. The administrator of your Canada office is having issues with a newly installed Frame Relay circuit. Based on the following output, what is the most likely cause of the problem?

Quick Answer: **251**
Detailed Answer: **256**

```
Router#show frame-relay lmi
LMI Statistics for interface Serial1/2 (Frame Relay DTE)
➥LMI TYPE = CISCO
 Invalid Unnumbered info 0        Invalid Prot Disc 0
 Invalid dummy Call Ref 0        Invalid Msg Type 0
 Invalid Status Message 0        Invalid Lock Shift 0
 Invalid Information ID 0        Invalid Report IE Len 0
 Invalid Report Request 0        Invalid Keep IE Len 0
 Num Status Enq. Sent 159        Num Status msgs Rcvd 158
 Num Update Status Rcvd 0        Num Status Timeouts 1
```

- ❍ **A.** The router has an LMI-mismatch.
- ❍ **B.** The cable is backward on the connection; on a Frame Relay circuit, the DCE end of the cable should connect to the local router.
- ❍ **C.** The line protocol on the circuit is down.
- ❍ **D.** The Layer 2 communication is fine; it may be an IP addressing issue.

30. You have crafted a remote access VPN proposal to management to allow employees to continue work from home, which is beneficial for the corporation and detrimental to the employee's family life. Management has expressed interest in this proposal, but wants to make sure the strongest possible encryption is used. What type of encryption will you recommend?

Quick Answer: **251**
Detailed Answer: **256**

- ❍ **A.** WPA2
- ❍ **B.** DES
- ❍ **C.** 3DES
- ❍ **D.** AES

Quick Check Answer Key

1. B, F, G
2. D
3. D
4. A
5. A
6. A
7. D
8. A, B, D
9. B
10. B
11. D
12. B
13. C
14. E
15. See detailed answer
16. B, D, E
17. B, C, E
18. C
19. A, B
20. D, E
21. D
22. C
23. C
24. B
25. C
26. A
27. A
28. C
29. D
30. D

Answers and Explanations

1. **B, F, G.** The Local Management Interface (LMI) signaling occurs between your router and the local service provider connection. It is used to transmit circuit status information (such as DLCI numbers, packets received, bytes sent, and so on) between you and the service provider. All other answers do not apply.

2. **D.** Split-horizon prevents routing updates (broadcasts) from going back out the interface they came in on. If you have multiple virtual circuits coming in on a physical interface, this causes issues. Answer A is incorrect, as route poisoning still functions. Answer B is incorrect, as hold-down timers do not affect Frame Relay. Answer C is incorrect, as triggered updates still occur.

3. **D.** The Cisco IOS command is **frame relay map [protocol] [network address] [dlci number] [broadcasts allowed or not (optional)]**. Answer A is incorrect, as you do not specify the DLCI before the IP address. Answer B is incorrect, as RARP is not involved. Answer C is incorrect, as the LMI is not involved in the **frame relay map** command.

4. **A.** Three primary PVC states indicate the status of the line. ACTIVE means there are no problems. Answer B is incorrect, as INACTIVE means that there is a problem with the remote router; DELETED means that there is a problem with your local router. Typically, this is caused by using the incorrect DLCI information. Answer D is eliminated because multipoint and point-to-point designs use DLCI information in the same way. If the DLCI shows up as DELETED under a multipoint configuration, it shows up as DELETED under a point-to-point configuration. Finally, if you are physically disconnected from the service provider, you do not see DLCI information (because LMI is used to send the DLCI status to your router); thus, answer C is incorrect as well.

5. **A.** Without the **broadcast** keyword, broadcast and multicast-based routing updates are not sent across the link. Answer B is incorrect because the RIP version is irrelevant to getting RIP working across Frame Relay. Answer C is incorrect because Inverse ARP has nothing to do with getting your routing updates across a Frame Relay network. Answer D is incorrect because RIP is activated on the interfaces. When you enter the network statements under the RIP configuration mode, it automatically enables RIP on the interfaces where those networks reside. Finally, answer E is incorrect because RIP does function over Frame Relay if the **broadcast** keyword is used properly.

6. **A.** By configuring the routers using a multipoint Frame Relay design, you can get by using only a single subnet. Although multipoint is the less preferred Frame Relay design, it does have the advantage of using fewer IP subnets. All other answers do not apply.

7. **D.** DLCI numbers are locally significant. This means that the numbers are only required to be unique at each single location. Frame Relay service providers often use a DLCI configuration like that shown in Figure 11.2. Answer A is incorrect. As long as you configure your Frame Relay map statements correctly (in a multipoint environment) or use your routing protocol correctly (in a point-to-point environment), this configuration will work just fine. Answer B is incorrect because the DLCIs are unique at each location. Answer C is incorrect because the routers shown can communicate two ways by using the locally assigned DLCI.

8. **A, B, D.** The three standards of LMI are Cisco, ANSI, and Q.933a. These standards can be auto-detected by most modern router implementations when linked up to the service provider. Answers C and E are incorrect because the ITU-T and IEEE are standards organizations who produce telecommunication and networking standards.

9. **B.** Static map statements need to be entered if Inverse ARP is not supported or is not working correctly. Answer A is incorrect, as static routes do not give you correct DLCI-to-Layer 3 address mappings. Answer C is incorrect, as DHCP assigns IP addresses to host interfaces. Answer D is incorrect, as there is no such thing as LMI mapping. LMI does assist in the Inverse ARP process, however.

10. **B.** A DLCI marked with an inactive status means the remote end of the connection is either misconfigured or disconnected. In this case, the router was powered off. Answer A is incorrect because the service provider not having a mapping for DLCI 301 would return a status of "deleted." Answer C is incorrect because an LMI mismatch would result in no DLCIs being displayed. Answer D is incorrect because an IP addressing issue would result in the DLCI being active, but the communication not working successfully.

11. **D.** PPP encapsulation is an industry standard protocol typically used on leased line WAN links. Answer A is incorrect because the default encapsulation on a serial interface of a Cisco router is Cisco HDLC, which is Cisco proprietary. Answer B is incorrect because you cannot use Frame Relay encapsulation unless you are connected to a Frame Relay network, which was not mentioned in the question. Even if you were connecting to a Frame Relay network, you would need to use IETF Frame Relay encapsulation to connect to a non-Cisco router. Answer C is incorrect because IETF is a standards organization rather than a WAN encapsulation.

12. **B.** Frame Relay multipoint configurations are famous for split-horizon issues with distance vector routing protocols. To solve these issues you should convert the router's multipoint configuration into a point-to-point subinterface configuration. Answer A is incorrect because multiple subinterfaces cannot be assigned to the same subnet. Answer C is incorrect because you can solve the split-horizon problem without moving off Frame Relay technology. Answer D is incorrect because multiple PVCs under a single interface is what causes the split-horizon issue in the first place.

13. **C.** The CSU/DSU connects to the DCE end of the cable and provides clocking to the router. Answer A is incorrect because the remote router gets the clock rate from its own CSU/DSU. Answer B is incorrect because the **clock rate** command is only applicable in lab environments. Answer D is incorrect because the clock entered in privileged mode only affects the time of day on the router not the speed of the serial interfaces.

14. **E.** The Link Control Protocol is responsible for negotiating compression, authentication, multilink, and callback features for the PPP connection. Answer A is incorrect because HDLC is a separate Layer 2 protocol. Answer B is incorrect because TCP is part of the TCP/IP suite, not PPP. Answer C is incorrect because LAPB is an old X.25 protocol standard. Answer D is incorrect because the Network Control Protocol (NCP) is responsible for allowing multiple Layer 3 protocols to work over the PPP WAN connection.

15.

FIGURE 11.7 Matching OSI layers.

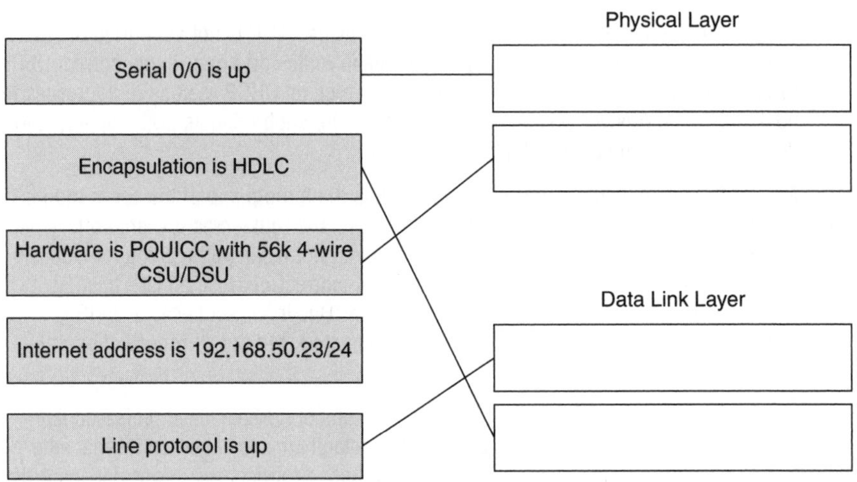

16. **B, D, E.** PPP is the alternative protocol to HDLC for use on point-to-point WAN links. It supports four features over HDLC: authentication, compression, callback, and multilink. Answers A, C, and F are incorrect because these relate to VLANs and VLAN trunking technology.

17. **B, C, E.** VPN connections only require a corporate Internet connection, which is significantly cheaper than leased line connections. The single Internet connection can act as a VPN connection to many remote sites and remote access home users, making VPN connections far more scalable than leased line WAN links. Answers A and D are incorrect because VPN connections traverse the Internet, which has no guarantee on quality of service and performance.

18. **C.** SSL VPN connections are often called WebVPN connections because they are accessed through an Internet web browser. The VPN connection can use a thin-client (which downloads after the user authenticates) or be clientless (where the user accesses resources through a web page only). Answer A is incorrect because site-to-site VPNs are established between offices. Answer B is incorrect because clientless VPNs would not have a small VPN client download as the question stated. Answer D is incorrect because Microsoft VPN connections use PPTP or L2TP technology in a built-in client rather than a web page. Answer E is incorrect because Dynamic Multipoint VPN (DMVPN) connections are purely a routing function to enhance existing site-to-site VPNs.

19. **A, B.** Figure 11.4 shows a Remote Access VPN, where remote clients connect directly to the VPN server using a software-based client. In this case, the question stated that the Cisco VPN client was used, which uses IPSec-based security. Answer C is incorrect because a WebVPN would not require a Cisco VPN client to be installed on the PC. Answer D is incorrect because Remote Access VPNs are very secure. Answer E is incorrect because Diffie-Hellman is a key exchange algorithm rather than a VPN.

20. **D, E.** MD5 and SHA-1 are two hashing algorithms that authenticate data (verify the sender) and ensure that the data does not change from one end of the VPN connection to the other. MD5 is the older and weaker (128-bit) algorithm, which is typically used with older encryption protocols (such as DES and 3DES). SHA-1 is the newer and stronger (160-bit) algorithm, which is typically used with the newer encryption protocols (such as AES). Answers A, B, and C are incorrect because these represent encryption protocols. Answer F is incorrect because DH represents a key exchange algorithm.

21. **D.** The **broadcast** keyword allows the router to send broadcast traffic, such as RIP updates, over the Frame Relay PVC. By default, they are disallowed by the router. Answer A is incorrect because 192.168.1.5 represents the remote IP address in the **frame-relay map** command. Answer B is incorrect because this command is only necessary on multipoint Frame Relay circuits. Answer C is incorrect because 683 represents the local DLCI in the **frame-relay map** command.

22. **C.** The command **ppp authentication chap pap** means that the router will first attempt to authenticate using CHAP and then fail over to PAP if CHAP is not supported. Because the Ladmo router initiated the PPP connection, it will attempt to use CHAP authentication, which the Wallace router supports. Answer A is incorrect because PPP does not have a "PPP-based authentication" method. Answer B is incorrect because the Wallace router still supports CHAP and PAP; it just prefers the PAP protocol. If the Wallace router were to initiate the PPP connection, the first attempt would use PAP. Answer D is incorrect because the routers both support the same authentication protocols; they just have different authentication preferences.

23. **C.** When using CHAP authentication, the passwords *must* be the same between the two endpoints. Answer A is incorrect because a conversion to HDLC is not necessary if the PPP authentication issue is fixed. Answer B is incorrect because (as discussed in question 22) both Wallace and Ladmo support the same authentication protocols. Answer D is incorrect because the router IP addressing is accurate and in the same subnet.

24. **B.** Performing a **debug ppp authentication** would expose that CHAP authentication was failing between the Wallace and Ladmo routers. Answer A is incorrect because there is no base **debug ppp** command; it requires at least one more argument. Answer C is incorrect because the **debug ppp negotiation** command shows general PPP messages as the link is established. Answer D is incorrect because there is no **debug interface** command.

25. **C.** This is considered a Full Mesh Frame Relay topology because every location has a direct PVC to every other location. This is the best, but most expensive, method you can use to build a Frame Relay network. Answer A is incorrect because Hub and Spoke topologies consist of a central location with direct PVCs to multiple remote locations. Answer B is incorrect because a Partial Mesh topology has some sites with more PVCs than others. Answers D and E are incorrect because Site-to-Site and Remote Access are VPN types rather than Frame Relay topologies.

26. **A.** The RIPv2 protocol will support this Frame Relay design without any problems. Answer B is incorrect because the auto-summarization features will only take effect if the 172.30.0.0/16 networks are advertised in a non-172.30.0.0/16 address space, which is not shown in this diagram. Answer C is incorrect because split-horizon only causes issues in a multipoint configuration. Because this is a point-to-point configuration, these problems should not exist. Answer D is incorrect because the multicast features of RIPv2 only cause issues in a multipoint configuration where the **frame-relay map** statements do not have the **broadcast** keyword on the end of them.

27. **A.** The Toast router will use DLCI 609 when communicating with the Eggs router. Based on the subnets, the Toast subinterface Serial0/0.609 is used when communicating to the Eggs subinterface Serial0/0.906. Because the local DLCI number is used to reach a remote site, DLCI 609 is identified. Answer B is incorrect because DLCI 906 is used when the Eggs router attempts to reach the Toast router. Answer C is incorrect because DLCI 501 is used when the Bacon router attempts to reach the Toast router. Answer D is incorrect because DLCI 105 is used when the Toast router attempts to reach the Bacon router.

28. **C.** While auto-summarization features are still running in the RIPv2 routing process, the 192.168.10.0/24 network is still a Class C network, which has a default mask of 255.255.255.0 (/24). The Toast and Eggs routers will receive the advertisement like this. This immediately makes answers A and B incorrect. Answer D is incorrect because split-horizon only causes issues in a multipoint Frame Relay configuration.

29. **D.** Based on the close proximity of the “Num Status Enq. Sent” and the “Num Status msgs Rcvd,” the LMI signaling seems to be working just fine. This makes answers A and C incorrect (because the LMI would not function if the line protocol was down). Answer B is incorrect because routers connecting to a Frame Relay service provider still connect to the DTE end of the cable. The problems being experienced in Canada are most likely related to a Layer 3 or higher-related issue.

30. **D.** AES is currently the strongest, mainstream encryption supported by VPN connections. Answer A is incorrect because WPA2 is a security scheme designed for wireless networks. Answers B and C are incorrect because DES and 3DES are older, weaker algorithms.

APPENDIX

What's on the CD-ROM

The CD-ROM features an innovative practice test engine powered by MeasureUp™, giving you yet another effective tool to assess your readiness for the exam.

Multiple Test Modes

MeasureUp practice tests can be used in Study, Certification, or Custom Mode.

Study Mode

Tests administered in Study Mode allow you to request the correct answer(s) and explanation to each question during the test. These tests are not timed. You can modify the testing environment during the test by selecting the Options button.

You can also specify the objectives or missed questions you want to include in your test, the timer length, and other test properties. You can also modify the testing environment during the test by selecting the Options button.

In Study Mode, you receive automatic feedback on all correct and incorrect answers. The detailed answer explanations are a superb learning tool in their own right.

Certification Mode

Tests administered in Certification Mode closely simulate the actual testing environment you will encounter when taking a licensure exam and are timed. These tests do not allow you to request the answer(s) and/or explanation to each question until after the exam.

Custom Mode

Custom Mode allows you to specify your preferred testing environment. Use this mode to specify the categories you want to include in your test, timer length, number of questions, and other test properties. You can modify the testing environment during the test by selecting the Options button.

Attention to Exam Objectives

MeasureUp practice tests are designed to appropriately balance the questions over each technical area covered by a specific exam. All concepts from the actual exam are covered thoroughly to ensure that you're prepared for the exam.

Installing the CD

System Requirements:

- Windows 95, 98, ME, NT4, 2000, or XP
- 7MB disk space for testing engine
- An average of 1MB disk space for each individual test
- Control Panel Regional Settings must be set to English (United States)
- PC only

To install the CD-ROM, follow these instructions:

1. Close all applications before beginning this installation.
2. Insert the CD into your CD-ROM drive. If the setup starts automatically, go to step 6. If the setup does not start automatically, continue with step 3.
3. From the Start menu, select **Run**.
4. Click **Browse** to locate the MeasureUp CD. In the Browse dialog box, from the Look In drop-down list, select the CD-ROM drive.
5. In the Browse dialog box, double-click on **Setup.exe**. In the Run dialog box, click **OK** to begin the installation.
6. On the Welcome screen, click **MeasureUp Practice Questions** to begin installation.
7. Follow the Certification Prep Wizard by clicking **Next**.

8. To agree to the Software License Agreement, click **Yes**.
9. On the Choose Destination Location screen, click **Next** to install the software to C:\Program Files\Certification Preparation. If you cannot locate MeasureUp Practice Tests on the Start menu, see the section titled "Creating a Shortcut to the MeasureUp Practice Tests" later in this appendix.
10. On the Setup Type screen, select **Typical Setup**. Click **Next** to continue.
11. In the Select Program Folder screen, you can name the program folder where your tests will be located. To select the default, simply click **Next** and the installation continues.
12. After the installation is complete, verify that **Yes, I Want to Restart My Computer Now** is selected. If you select **No, I Will Restart My Computer Later**, you cannot use the program until you restart your computer.
13. Click **Finish**.
14. After restarting your computer, choose **Start > Programs > Certification Preparation > Certification Preparation > MeasureUp Practice Tests**.
15. On the MeasureUp Welcome screen, click **Create User Profile**.
16. In the User Profile dialog box, complete the mandatory fields and click **Create Profile**.
17. Select the practice test you want to access and click **Start Test**.

Creating a Shortcut to the MeasureUp Practice Tests

To create a shortcut to the MeasureUp Practice Tests, follow these steps:

1. Right-click on your desktop.
2. From the shortcut menu, select **New > Shortcut**.
3. Browse to C:\Program Files\MeasureUp Practice Tests and select the **MeasureUpCertification.exe** or **Localware.exe** file.
4. Click **OK**.

5. Click **Next**.
6. Rename the shortcut MeasureUp.
7. Click **Finish**.

After you complete step 7, use the MeasureUp shortcut on your desktop to access the MeasureUp products you ordered.

Technical Support

If you encounter problems with the MeasureUp test engine on the CD-ROM, please contact MeasureUp at (800) 649-1687 or email support@measureup.com. Support hours of operation are 7:30 a.m. to 4:30 p.m. EST. In addition, you can find Frequently Asked Questions (FAQ) in the Support area at www.measureup.com. If you want to purchase additional MeasureUp products, call (678) 356-5050 or (800) 649-1687, or visit www.measureup.com.

Notes

Notes

Notes

Notes

Notes

Notes

Notes

Notes

Notes

Notes

Notes

Notes

Notes

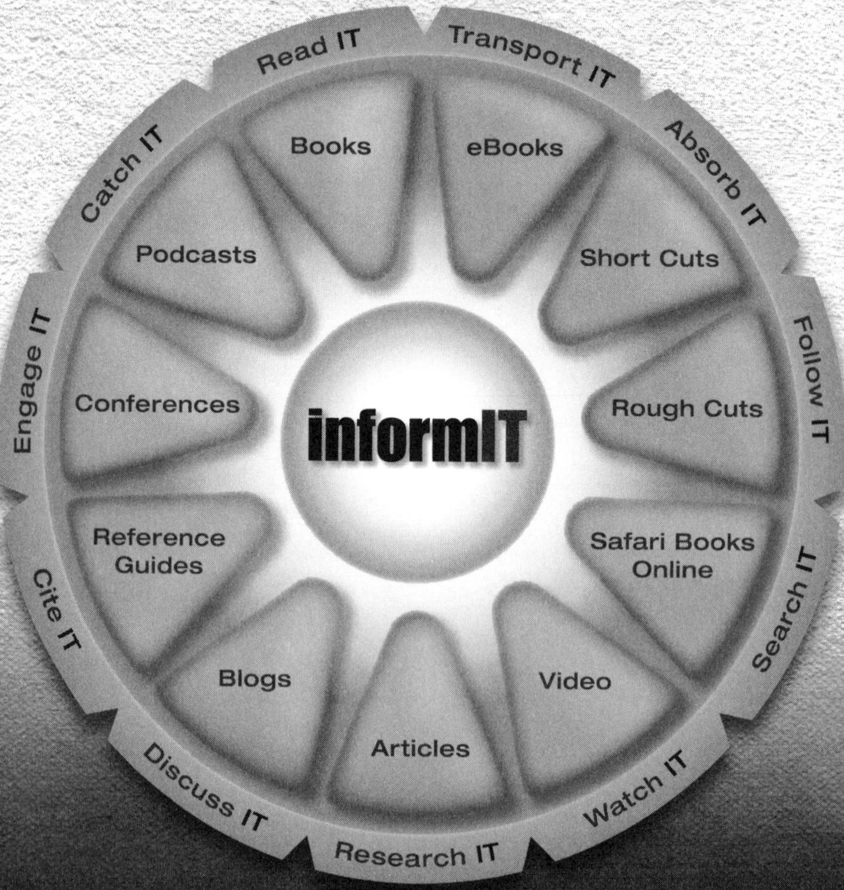

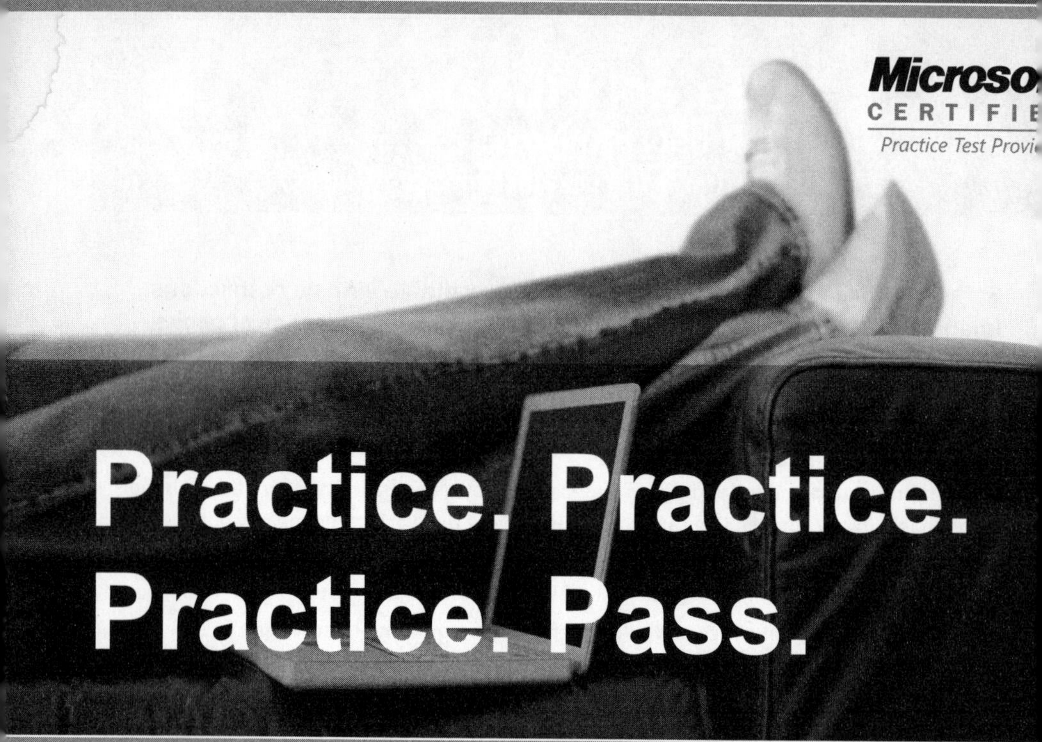
Practice. Practice.
Practice. Pass.